KU-505-839

Developing software with UML

The Addison-Wesley Object Technology Series

Grady Booch, Ivar Jacobson, and James Rumbaugh, Series Editors

For more information check out the series web site [http://www.aw.com/cseng/otseries/].

Arlow/Neustadt, *UML and the Unified Process*

Armour/Miller, *Advanced Use Case Modeling, Volume 1*

Atkinson, *Component Based Product Line Engineering with UML*

Binder, *Testing Object-Oriented Systems: Models, Patterns, and Tools*

Blakely, *CORBA Security: An Introduction to Safe Computing with Objects*

Booch, *Object Solutions: Managing the Object-Oriented Project*

Booch, *Object-Oriented Analysis and Design with Applications, Second Edition*

Booch/Rumbaugh/Jacobson, *The Unified Modeling Language User Guide*

Box, *Essential COM*

Box/Brown/Ewald/Sells, *Effective COM: 50 Ways to Improve Your COM and MTS-based Applications*

Cockburn, *Surviving Object-Oriented Projects: A Manager's Guide*

Collins, *Designing Object-Oriented User Interfaces*

Conallen, *Building Web Applications with UML*

D'Souza/Wills, *Objects, Components, and Frameworks with UML-The Catalysis Approach*

Douglass, *Doing Hard Time: Developing Real-Time Systems with UML: Objects, Frameworks, and Patterns*

Douglass, *Real-Time UML, Second edition: Developing Efficient Objects for Embedded Systems*

Fontura/Pree/Rumpe, *The UML Profile for Framework Architectures*

Fowler, *Analysis Patterns: Reusable Object Models*

Fowler/Beck/Brant/Opdyke/Roberts, *Refactoring: Improving the Design of Existing Code*

Fowler/Scott, *UML Distilled. Second Edition: A Brief Guide to the Standard Object Modeling Language*

Gomaa, *Designing Concurrent, Distributed, and Real-Time Applications with UML*

Gorton, *Enterprise Transaction Processing Systems: Putting the CORBA OTS, Encina++ and Orbix OTM to Work*

Heinckiens, *Building Scalable Database Applications: Object-Oriented Design, Architectures, and Implementations*

Hofmeister/Nord/Dilip, *Applied Software Architecture*

Jacobson/Booch/Rumbaugh, *The Unified Software Development Process*

Jacobson/Christerson/Jonsson/Overgaard, *Object-Oriented Software Engineering: A Use Case Driven Approach*

Jacobson/Ericsson/Jacobson, *The Object Advantage: Business Process Reengineering with Object Technology*

Jacobson/Griss/Jonsson, *Software Reuse: Architecture, Process and Organization for Business Success*

Jordan, *C++ Object Databases: Programming with the ODMG Standard*

Kruchten, *The Rational Unified Process, An Introduction, Second Edition*

Lau, *The Art of Objects: Object-Oriented Design and Architecture*

Leffingwell/Widrig, *Managing Software Requirements: A Unified Approach*

Marshall, *Enterprise Modeling with UML: Designing Successful Software through Business Analysis*

Mowbray/Ruh, *Inside CORBA: Distributed Object Standards and Applications*

Oestereich, *Developing Software with UML: Object-Oriented Analysis and Design in Practice*

Page-Jones, *Fundamentals of Object-Oriented Design in UML*

Pohl, *Object-Oriented Programming Using C++, Second Edition*

Pooley/Stevens, *Using UML: Software Engineering with Objects and Components*

Quatrani, *Visual Modeling with Rational Rose 2000 and UML*

Rector/Sells, *ATL Internals*

Reed, *Developing Applications with Visual Basic and UML*

Rosenberg/Scott, *Use Case Driven Object Modeling with UML: A Practical Approach*

Royce, *Software Project Management: A Unified Framework*

Ruh/Herron/Klinker, *IIOP Complete: Understanding CORBA and Middleware Interoperability*

Rumbaugh/Jacobson/Booch, *The Unified Modeling Language Reference Manual*

Schneider/Winters, *Applying Use Cases: A Practical Guide*

Shan/Earle, *Enterprise Computing with Objects: From Client/Server Environments to the Internet*

Warmer/Kleppe, *The Object Constraint Language: Precise Modeling with UML*

White, *Software Configuration Management Strategies and Rational ClearCase: A Practical Introduction*

Whitehead, *Component-based Development: Principles and Planning for Business Systems*

Component Software Series

Clements Szyperski, Series Editor

Allen, *Realizing eBusiness with Components*

Cheesman/Daniel, *UML Components: A Simple Process for Specifying Component-Based Software*

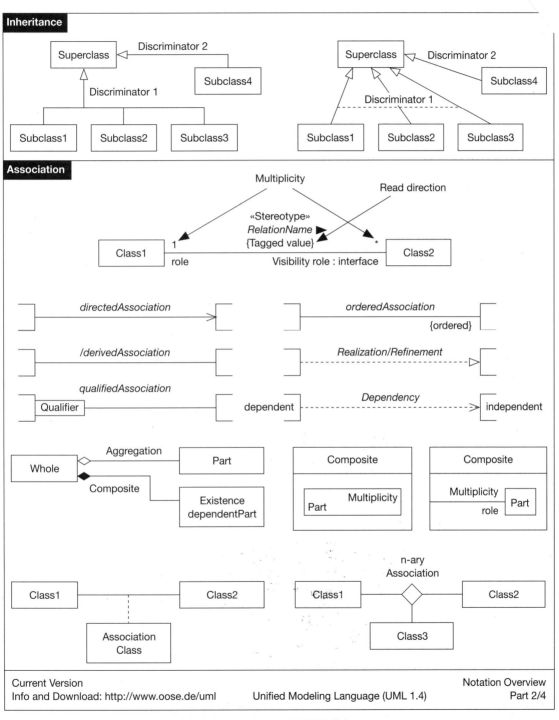

Inheritance

Superclass ◁ — Discriminator 2 — Subclass4

Superclass △ — Discriminator 1

Subclass1 Subclass2 Subclass3

Superclass ◁ — Discriminator 2 — Subclass4

Discriminator 1

Subclass1 Subclass2 Subclass3

Association

Multiplicity

Read direction

«Stereotype»
RelationName ▶
{Tagged value}

Class1 1 ◀——————————— * Class2

role

Visibility role : interface

directedAssociation →

orderedAssociation
{ordered}

/derivedAssociation

Realization/Refinement ⊳

Qualifier — *qualifiedAssociation*

dependent ----*Dependency*---▷ independent

Whole ◇ — Aggregation — Part

Whole ◆ — Composite — Existence dependentPart

Composite
Part   Multiplicity

Composite
Multiplicity
role   Part

Class1 ———————— Class2
        ¦
   Association
   Class

n-ary
Association

Class1 ——◇—— Class2

Class3

LIVERPOOL JMU LIBRARY

3 1111 01084 4916

LIVERPOOL
JOHN MOORES UNIVERSITY
AVRIL ROBARTS LRC
TEL. 0151 231 4022

BERND OESTEREICH

Developing software with UML

Object-oriented analysis and design in practice

Second edition

Addison-Wesley

An imprint of **Pearson Education**

London • Boston • Indianapolis • New York • Mexico City • Toronto
Sydney • Tokyo • Singapore • Hong Kong • Cape Town • New Delhi
Madrid • Paris • Amsterdam • Munich • Milan • Stockholm

PEARSON EDUCATION LIMITED

Head Office:
Edinburgh Gate
Harlow CM20 2JE
Tel: +44 (0)1279 623623
Fax: +44 (0)1279 431059

London Office:
128 Long Acre
London WC2E 9AN
Tel: +44 (0)20 7447 2000
Fax: +44 (0)20 7447 2170

Website: www.it-minds.com
www.awprofessional.com

Originally published as *Objektorientierte Softwareentwicklung mit der UML, 5. Auflage*
© R. Oldenbourg Verlag 2001

All rights reserved.

English edition © Pearson Education Ltd 2002
Authorised translation from German language edition published by Oldenbourg
Wissenschaftsverlag GmbH

The right of Bernd Oestereich to be identified as the Author of this Work has been asserted by him
in accordance with the Copyright, Designs and Patents Act 1988.

ISBN 0-201-75603-X

British Library Cataloguing in Publication Data
A CIP catalogue record for this book can be obtained from the British Library.

Library of Congress Cataloging-in-Publication Data

Oestereich, Bernd.
  [Objektorientierte Softwareentwicklung mit der UML. English]
  Developing software with UML : object-orientated analysis and design in practice /
Bernd Oestereich.-- 2nd ed.
    p. cm.
  Includes bibliographical references and index.
  ISBN 0-201-75603-X (alk. paper)
   1. Object-orientated methods (Computer science) 2. UML Computer science) 3.
Computer software--Development. I. Title

QA76.9.O63 O3713 2002
005.1'17--dc21

                                                                                      2002018543

All rights reserved; no part of this publication may be reproduced, stored in a retrieval system,
or transmitted in any form or by any means, electronic, mechanical, photocopying, recording,
or otherwise without either the prior written permission of the Publishers or a licence
permitting restricted copying in the United Kingdom issued by the Copyright Licensing Agency
Ltd, 90 Tottenham Court Road, London W1T 4LP.

This book may not be lent, resold, hired out or otherwise disposed of by way of trade in any
form of binding or cover other than that in which it is published, without the prior consent of
the Publishers.

10 9 8 7 6 5 4 3 2

Illustrations by Stephan Westphal.
Designed by Claire Brodmann Book Designs, Lichfield, Staffs.
Typeset by Pantek Arts Ltd, Maidstone, Kent.
Printed and bound in Great Britain by Biddles Ltd of Guildford and King's Lynn.

The Publishers' policy is to use paper manufactured from sustainable forests.

Language is the dream we make from the world.
Schuldt

Contents

Preface   ix

1 Introduction   1

1.1 Object-oriented Software Development   2
1.2 History of Object-orientation   3
1.3 OOAD in Practice   8
1.4 Holistic Approach   11

2 Object-orientation for Beginners   17

2.1 Object-orientation for Beginners   18
2.2 Classes, Objects, Instances   19
2.3 Attributes, Operations, Constraints, Relationships   20
2.4 Object Identity   22
2.5 Responsibilities   24
2.6 Taxonomy and Inheritance   25
2.7 Abstract Classes   34
2.8 Associations   35
2.9 Aggregations   35
2.10 Message Exchange   39
2.11 Collections   42
2.12 Polymorphism   44
2.13 Persistence   47
2.14 Classification of Classes   50
2.15 Design Patterns   56
2.16 Components   58

3 Analysis   63

3.1 Introduction   64
3.2 Developing the System Idea and Objective   64
3.3 Identifying Stakeholders   65
3.4 Identifying Business Processes   68
3.5 Identifying Stakeholders' Interests   70
3.6 Identifying Business Use Cases   72

3.7	Describing the Essence of Use Cases	76
3.8	Identifying System Use Cases	82
3.9	Collecting and Studying Materials	87
3.10	Describing the Requirements	89
3.11	Identifying Business Classes	92
3.12	Creating a Technical Dictionary	94
3.13	Developing a Use Case Process Model	99
3.14	Describing the System Interface	104
3.15	Explorative Interface Prototyping	108

4 Design — 113

4.1	Defining the Application Architecture	114
4.2	Identifying Domain Components	118
4.3	Developing Component-specific Class Models	120
4.4	(Further) Developing State Models	123
4.5	Identifying and, if Necessary, Restructuring Component Dependencies	125
4.6	Designing Component Interfaces	127
4.7	Developing Collaboration Models	129
4.8	Developing Process-oriented Component Tests	132
4.9	Developing Class Tests	135
4.10	Defining Attributes	138
4.11	Specifying Dialogs	142
4.12	Discussion of Design	145

5 UML Fundamentals — 157

5.1	Introduction	158
5.2	Types of Diagrams	160
5.3	Use Case Diagrams	161
5.4	Class Diagrams (Basic Elements)	172
5.5	Class Diagrams (Relational Elements)	219
5.6	Behavioral Diagrams	250
5.7	Implementation Diagrams	272

Appendices	275
Appendix A Glossary	277
Appendix B References	289
Index	293

Preface

To which class of reader do you belong?

- You leave unimportant details to others because you have enough to do. You do not intend to carry out object-oriented analysis or implementation yourself, but you are interested in modern technology and are potentially involved in decision-making on its practical employment.

- You know how software is developed because of your many years of practical experience. From your point of view, object-orientation has reached a degree of maturity, so you feel that you should devote more time to this subject. You would like to have a practice-oriented introduction.

- Object-orientation (OO) is an established technique in your repertoire. You have been interested in this subject for some time and probably have experience with implementation of object-oriented programs. Your interests lean towards analysis and design, and the latest developments in the area of object-oriented methodology and notation.

- You are interested in software development and have gathered some experience in the field. You have a basic knowledge of the concepts of object-oriented methodology, but feel you need a comprehensive and systematic introduction to the subject.

Dear reader

Starting point
Do you still have time to dedicate yourself to several hundreds of pages of technical papers? Do you still read a book from cover to cover? As someone who has suffered enough from the burden of heavy books, I have tried to provide you with a not too bulky, practice-oriented, and easily readable book.

Structure
The book has a modular structure – the individual sections are didactically self-supporting and linked to each other by cross-references (direct page

Ways of reading
specifications). Thus, you have the option of reading from beginning to end, crosswise or hopping from point to point. A streamlined way of familiarizing yourself with the subject is to read through the chapters *Analysis* and *Design* and to follow the cross-references where needed, to look up and delve deeper into individual subjects in the Fundamentals section.

This book provides you with a digest presentation, but with all-important information on the Unified Modeling Language (UML 1.4), whose notation and semantics are the current standard in object-oriented modeling. Despite this, the present book is above all an introduction to object-oriented analysis and object-oriented design. Presentation of the UML fundamentals takes place in the context of general problems and discussions about object-oriented software development. To further ease entry into the subject, the UML metamodel is not included in the discussion. Special elements, and elements less relevant in practice, are marked as "UML advanced" and, where necessary, critically presented.

The use case-driven, architecture-centered, and evolutionary development method underpinning this book is centered on the development of socially embedded corporate information systems, but it is also well suited for technical and other application domains.

Acknowledgments

For their help with this book, I would like to thank all my friends and colleagues, in particular the people listed on the imprint. Furthermore, I would like to thank the readers of the previous editions and the participants in my seminars for their suggestions and critical remarks.

Bernd Oestereich

We are grateful to the following for permission to reproduced copyright material:

Extract from *Abziehbilder, heimgeholt.* Essay 27, reprinted with permission, © by Literaturverlag Droschl, Graz-Wien 1995 (Kelly, R., Roubaud, J. and Schuldt, 1995); Extract Means of abstraction by Nicolai Josuttis, reprinted with permission of the author;

The methodology presented in Chapters 3 and 4 has been developed and is used with the kind permission of oose.de GmbH; Section 5.4.6 is based on formulations made available by and reprinted with permission of Christine Rupp, Sophist Group.

In some instances we have been unable to trace the owners of copyright material, and we would appreciate any information that would enable us to do so.

chapter **1**

Introduction

This chapter explains the special features of object-oriented software development, its history, and the differences from older methods.

Object-oriented Software Development 2
History of Object-orientation 3
OOAD in Practice 8
Holistic Approach 11

1.1 Object-oriented Software Development

Synopsis

■ What are the benefits of object-oriented software development?

Using a bulldozer for potting flowers is as misplaced as using a teaspoon to dig out an excavation for a high-rise building. What matters are the right tools and the right methods.

Demands are rising

Software development is becoming more and more complex – but also more fascinating. Software systems are among the most complex systems created by man. Sophisticated software development never gets boring – it requires creativity, precision, the ability to learn, and the willingness to analyze and structure new facts intelligently, efficient inbound and outbound communication (within the development team as well as with clients and users), knowledge of and experience with procedures, methods, techniques and tools, clever handling of open questions, ideas which are not fully developed, and so on.

High-quality software development is becoming more and more expensive. The change from alphanumeric interfaces to event-driven graphical user interfaces (GUIs), the introduction of multi-layer client–server architectures, distributed databases, the Internet, and so on caused a considerable increase in complexity.

Implementation of such software in C++ or similar programming languages is a very labor-intensive enterprise. Visual and 4GL development tools, in contrast, bring quick success – but for this very reason lead to skipping the planning and conception stage and use the FBTT (From Brain to Terminal) method instead. Regardless of the way it is realized, each implementation of an application should, however, be preceded by a planning phase, and this is precisely the central point of this book: analysis and design of modern software.

Technical Complexity

Conceptional stability vs. evolution

Software is never completely finished. There is always something to be modified or improved. And even if changes are not mandatorily required, they often remain desirable – until the program is taken off the market. Too many modifications and extensions obviously cause the program to deviate more and more from the original concept. This danger is particularly relevant when the program is successful and is therefore continuously being improved.

For these reasons, it is sensible to look for adequate methods that allow complexity to be mastered, or at least delay the process of decay and help to maintain quality and reliability of the software despite structural disintegration and evolution.

A new way of thinking

The history of software development is a continuous increase in abstraction, from bit patterns via macro instructions, procedures, and abstract data types to objects, frames, design patterns, and business objects. The significantly stronger abstraction of object-orientation not only improves and further develops the classical methods but generates a new way of thinking.

Similarities and relationships can always be found, but simplistic statements such as "messages are only procedure calls" or "object-orientation – just an old concept with a new label" misunderstand the essence of object-orientation.

Social Complexity

Communication is the central point

The widespread opinion that software development is mainly a technical task turns out to be only one side of the truth when we take a closer look at the development process. Today, software development is also a complex social process. The decisive reasons for this lie in the fact that software development is very much a person-related process in which psychological and epistemological knowledge together with communication skills play a major role. Many software systems are embedded in a social environment, that is, in an organization involving people – these are the systems (as opposed to technical or other systems) which this book is dedicated to.

Experts in the application area and experts in the development team share the same problem: the more specialized you are, the more difficult you are to understand. Correct mutual understanding, however, is the cornerstone of successful cooperation. During the course of a project, models are created of the application world and the software to be developed – most of these to be found in the minds of the people involved. Documentation produced in such a project is at most the tip of an iceberg. Since much more stays in the minds of the developers than will ever appear in the documentation, a consensus about the whole context is indispensable.

Communication – the exchange of the models, the knowledge and the experience present in people's minds – is thus a central issue. Since software, more than other technical systems, is intertwined with human abstractions, with all its complexity, inaccuracies and peculiarities, it resembles human organizational structures far more than typically technical ones.

1.2 History of Object-orientation

Synopsis

- How did the UML come about?
- What is the historical context of object-orientation and its analysis and design methods?

In the beginning, there was Smalltalk

The object-orientation concept dates back more than 30 years, and the development of object-oriented programming languages is almost as old. There have always been publications on object-oriented programming, but the first books on object-oriented analysis design methods started to appear only at the beginning of the 1990s.

These include publications by Booch, Coad and Yourdon, Rumbaugh *et al.*, Wirfs-Brock and Johnson, Shlaer and Mellor, Martin and Odell, Henderson-Sellers, and Firesmith. An important push was given in particular by Goldberg and Rubin, as well as Jacobson. Many methods are specialized and restricted to specific application areas.

In the early 1990s, the methods of Grady Booch and James Rumbaugh became by far the most popular. The Rumbaugh method was more structure-oriented, while Booch covered the commercial and technical areas, including also time-critical applications, which were reasonably covered. In 1995, Booch and Rumbaugh began to combine their methods, first in the form of a common notation, to create the *Unified Method* (UM). This was soon renamed the *Unified Modeling Language* (UML), which was in fact a more appropriate name, as it was essentially a question of standardizing the graphical representation and semantics of the modeling elements, rather than describing a particular method. *Modeling language* is basically a more stylish way of saying *notation*.

Shortly afterwards, Ivar Jacobson joined in, integrating his so-called *use cases*. Henceforth, the three called themselves "Amigos." Since the methods of Booch, Rumbaugh, and Jacobson were already very popular and held a large market share, their combination into the UML formed a quasi-standard. Finally, in 1997, UML Version 1.1 was submitted to the Object Management Group (OMG) for standardization, and accepted. Versions 1.2, 1.3, and 1.4 include a few corrections. Version 2.0 is underway at the OMG. You can find the latest information on this at http://www.omg.org/uml/. (See Fig. 1.2.)

See UML introduction ⇨158.

UML is primarily a description of a unified notation and semantics together with the definition of a metamodel. The description of a development method is not directly part of it – it was only supplied at the beginning of 1999 with the publication of Jacobson's *The Unified Software Development Process*, the so-called *Unified Process* (UP).

Notation and methodology

UP, OEP processes ⇨7.

In this book, the analysis and design chapters describe a procedure based on a special concrete expression of the Unified Process which has proved successful in practice. This book focuses on commercial, socially embedded information systems such as those encountered in service or commercial enterprises. For more technically oriented systems, such as embedded and real-time systems, adjustments may be needed.

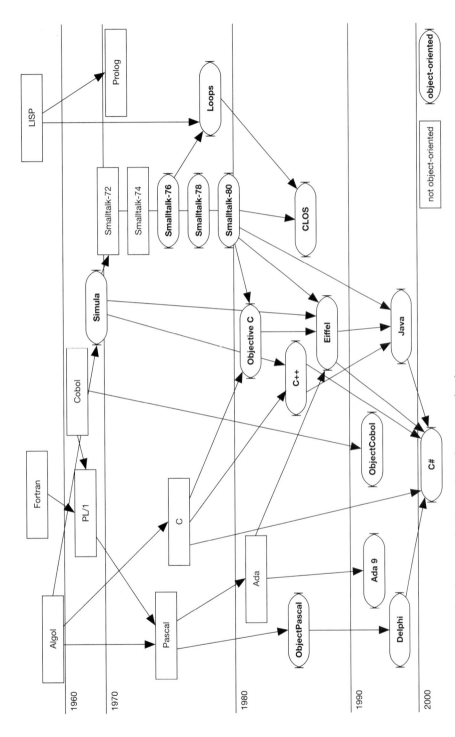

Figure 1.1 Historical development of object-oriented programming languages

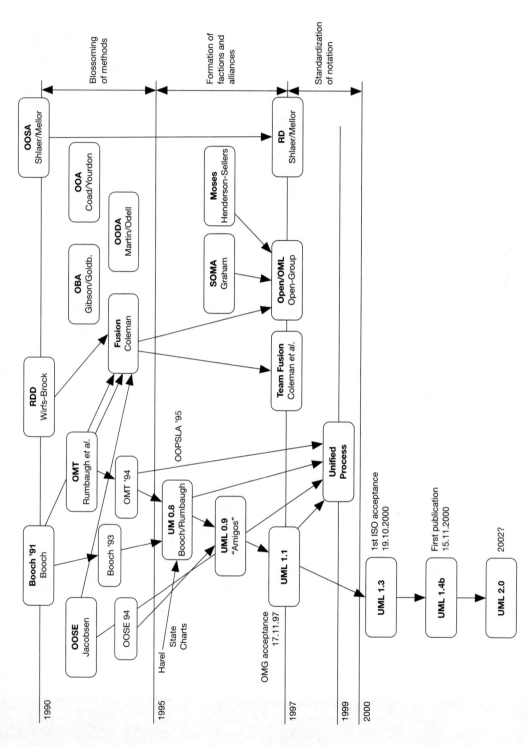

Figure 1.2 Historical development of object-oriented methods and the UML

UML is multi-facetted and also integrates interesting ideas and concepts from other authors. Thus, besides the ideas of Booch, Rumbaugh, and Jacobson, you will find those of Harel (state diagrams).

Thanks to the "Amigos," different notations have widely converged. On the other hand, independently of the notation, different methodological approaches exist which differ in distinct ways from each other, such as the method of Shlaer and Mellor and the Open Process (with OML – Open Modeling Language – as its modeling language). More than 30 active supporters belong to the OPEN consortium, including, among others, Brian Henderson-Sellers, Ian Graham, and Donald Firesmith.[1]

The Unified Modeling Language is a modeling language, and as such predestined for translation into programming languages, that is, for code generation. On the one hand, its high expressiveness puts high demands on CASE tools and makes reverse engineering more difficult; on the other hand, it offers extensive modeling capabilities. Currently available tools are far from being able to use UML to its full potential. (See also http://www.oose.de/uml)

Overwhelming Variety of Choices?

The fundamental concepts of object-oriented software development methodology are mature and established in practice. However, UML in particular offers a notable wealth of detail and is therefore to be used with caution.

The various possibilities of description may be perceived as quite oppressing; a deeper understanding of UML constructs in all their variety requires some effort. As a first approach, one should therefore restrict oneself to the basic elements. Potentially, semantic gaps may remain in the modeling, but in practice, work at this level may be sufficient. Besides, there are lots of places where no systematics at all are applied.

Moreover, some methodological concepts are relevant only in special or highly detailed circumstances. Here, the choice of elements to be employed is guided by the kind of application (information system, technical system, real-time application, and others) and the depth of detail required. Details such as visibility marks, sophisticated stereotype, and so on lead not only to better security and higher quality results but also to higher development efforts and costs. The advantage of the UML compared to other methods is that it takes longer to reach notational or semantic limits, owing to the availability of a wide palette of alternatives of which, however, only the relevant and necessary ones should be applied.

Stereotypes ⇨ 209

---

[1] Graham, 1997b.

1.3   OOAD in Practice

Synopsis

- ■ UML and the methods based on it cannot be applied blindly.

Introduction of object-orientation

If you wish to establish an object-oriented methodology in your company, you may have decided to employ the UML, to use a particular CASE tool, and to follow a particular development process, e.g. Unified Process.

These decisions may be all well and good, but they do not solve all the problems of software development. On the contrary, they will create some new problems for you. The UML is powerful and detailed and probably contains a large number of elements that you (and many others) do not need. In addition, the interplay between UML, tool, and method/process is not obvious, but must first be tested and established in your projects.

For this reason it is sensible first to analyze what the typical problems and boundary conditions are, and which approaches might be appropriate in dealing with them. It only leads to confusion if your development people are methodologically trained but are unable to apply their knowledge in practice because parts of the methodology are not relevant, elementary problems are not sufficiently covered or are not supported by the tools used. Try to work out a simple methodology, omitting all superfluous concepts, and then introduce it systematically. This book will support you in that by not introducing you straightaway to UML details that in all probability you will not need. It is surely more helpful for you when you are introducing an object-oriented methodology to concentrate first on a core area, to become successful with this and then to expand the notation, methodology, and process in a well-defined manner.

The individual concepts of the UML, the methodology presented here, and the related procedures may be considered proven and reliable. However, their application is certainly no easier than that of the old methods

Do not apply a method blindly

Dependencies and relationships between class, activity, collaboration, sequence, and state diagrams can become totally confusing to the eye. Therefore, completeness and consistency of model can be reasonably guaranteed only by appropriate software. Manual modeling is out of the question. Nevertheless, tools will never be able to make up for the technical and methodological errors of their users – one more reason not to employ all the available possibilities of the method and the tools blindly, but to make an educated selection of those which appear useful and necessary for the task.

Experience vs. Method Observance

You may use a newspaper not only for reading but also for swatting annoying insects. In a similar way, software development methods and tools may be employed for various purposes.

Many people still consider the software business to be the incarnation of progress itself, but for experienced users, it does not really have a serious reputation. There are still too many annoying problems, and users are becoming more and more demanding. You will probably find no other branch of engineering involving a higher proportion of amateurishness than software development.

For the purpose of achieving good programs, it is also sensible to consider the opposite when presenting a method: errors and flaws that may derive from unsystematic development.

Collapsing constructions

If you have ever brought forward (or at least had a chance to observe) the development of a major software project mainly by intuition – that is, without conscious application of a development strategy – you will have noticed how problems become increasingly complex during the course of program development and how more and more sub- and side-problems arise, which continue to intertwine with each other. The results bear a certain similarity to the constructions of ambitious Gothic cathedrals which from time to time collapsed before they were finished (except that in those days, the decisive mechanical and physical laws were not yet known). Some typical problems and errors in software development are:

- Coding is started far too early.
- Coding is started too late.

Do-it-yourself approach

- The procedure is ill-planned and lacking a model of how to proceed.
- The model of how to proceed is excessively precise, paralyzing, bureaucratic, and too far removed from practice.
- Intermediate and final results are not (or only insufficiently) verified and validated.
- The application architecture was not planned clearly enough or its development got out of hand.
- The development is driven by a naïve understanding of object-orientation.
- The development is driven by an understanding of object-orientation which is too academic to be used in practice.
- Behind an "object-oriented" disguise, the spirit of procedural software development is still lurking (particularly when hybrid languages such as C++ are employed).
- Guidelines for analysis, design, and implementation are lacking, are not employed, or are too far removed from reality.
- The documentation of results and design decisions leads a marginal existence in suspended animation.
- Requirements are not ascertained systematically.

The complexity of software is often denied, but sometimes trifling errors or lapses in precision, which in isolation are relatively insignificant, accumulated are sufficient to cause unnecessary and tiresome problems.

Basically, the full extent of requirements is underestimated. Delivery dates cannot be kept, the implementation (even without considering the test phase which is practically eliminated) gives in to the pressures of time, and important activities and results are neglected or get lost. If, on top of all this, some elementary system parts are not properly designed or not well thought out, growing complexity leads to persistent or even irreparable problems.

The application of a well-proven procedure helps to avoid such problems.

When applying a method, it is important not to forget the wealth of experience of the developers involved, which allows these people to produce good programs even without the explicit application of a method. Employing methods is not the point of the exercise; the overall purpose is always to be successful. In principle, practical experience is simply the unconscious application of well-proven techniques. The decisive factor is that the quality of the outcome does not happen at random, but systematically.

Methods are not ends in themselves

The important issue is the realization of the ideas that underlie the methods. Rules are "nothing but generalized prescriptions of behavior that tell us what we should do in order to be able to do what we want to do."[2] Adherence

---

[2] Lübber, 1987, p. 118.

to specific conventions that guide us toward more successful actions, however, also opens up new freedoms and mastery (due to the self-assurance gained).

Good people achieve good results even with poor tools and under difficult conditions. Yet strict adherence to a method alone does not lead to success either. Despite new and advanced methods for better mastering of complexity and problems innate to the development process, demands on the qualifications of developers do not diminish but continue to increase. This applies in particular to object-oriented methodology, since it was designed to be used in complex projects.

1.4 Holistic Approach

Synopsis

- The object-oriented way of thinking.

UML and the methods based on it cannot be applied blindly. Humans have difficulties in thinking in systems and networks; thinking in terms of individual causal chains seems to come more naturally.[3]

The old structured software development methods help us get to grips with complexity but reach their limits too quickly: with the traditional separation between data view and functional view, description and implementation of complex software can no longer be mastered or only at a high cost.

SA

Factual descriptions by means of *Structured Analysis* (SA) and *Entity-Relationship Modeling* (ERM) represent different views which complement each other only when applied to areas with little overlap.

ERM

SD

The incommensurability and difficulty in integrating the approaches at a higher level is even more pronounced between Structured Analysis and *Structured Design* (SD). Through various methodological improvements and integration efforts, the structured methods have achieved a notable degree of performance.[4] Nevertheless, the structural deficits remain obvious. Object-oriented software engineering reflects the existing and proven concepts, but is much more powerful.

In system theory, reality is perceived as a network: the individual facts and phenomena are no longer reduced to their elements but are seen as an integrated whole, where the links and interdependencies between the components are an essential part of the entirety (holistic thinking).

Object-oriented software development not only describes data and functions; their interconnection and their relationship with the surrounding world, that is, with other data and functional units, can be defined in a

---

[3] See Dörner, 1989.
[4] See Raasch, 1993.

differentiated way. These definitions of mutual relationships and dependencies are always present in the object-oriented model wherever they are needed (from analysis to coding) and are assigned the corresponding responsibilities. This facilitates work and allows programmers to cope with a higher degree of complexity.

The essential differences between structured and object-oriented methods are:

Differences from older procedures

- *Holistic objects to work on.* The class concept is used to work with units of data and operations, instead of a separation between data and operations.
- *Better possibilities of abstraction.* More than their structured counterparts, object-oriented methods shift the focus of modeling from the solution area towards the problem area.
- *Methodological uniformity.* The results of an activity *i* in the object-oriented development process can easily be taken over into activity *i+1* and vice versa: all phases of software development operate with the same concepts (classes, objects, relationships, and so on). There is no rupture between different model representations.
- *Evolutionary development.* A complex system is not built in one go. All complex systems in nature have developed step by step, each intermediate step had to stabilize first and prove its functional and survival capabilities. In the course of time, this has led to the development of the complicated system called a *human being*. With object-oriented software development methods, the evolutionary principle can be transferred to software development.

→ Human-oriented

In a certain sense, object-orientation is also a *Weltanschauung* (view of the world, in the literal sense of the word). In contrast to conventional software development methods, object-oriented methods are based on a paradigm[5] that places the human being more at the center. This means that the current technocentric view is replaced with an anthropocentric one.[6]

Traditional software development methods have copied their deductive procedure from empirical sciences, which makes their action oriented towards goals separated from the objective world.[7] Objectivity, however, comes into being only because "a community of subjects capable of language and action considers it as one and the same world. A necessary condition for this is that communicatively acting subjects agree with each other on what occurs in the world or what is to be done in it."[8]

Deductive separation is replaced with consensual communication. Traditional development methods fail when faced with more demanding tasks because in their deductivism they have not considered the limitations of human communication possibilities – which does not necessarily mean that OO methodology cannot fail as well. Object-oriented procedures, however, are open for the consciousness of a communicative rationality and thus lead to a different view of the world.

[5] From the Greek *paradeigma* = model, pattern.
[6] See Quibeldey–Cirkel, 1994.
[7] See Habermas, 1987, *"cognitive-instrumental rationality."*
[8] Valk, 1987 and Habermas, 1987, vol. 1, p. 32.

The transition from older, more technocentric methods to more holistic, object-oriented procedures can be viewed as a paradigm shift.[9] Transitions of this kind take place (according to Molzberger, 1984) through three reaction patterns:

- *Emotional rejection*. Despite their contradictions, old convictions continue to be adhered to.

- *Unreflected euphoria*. Deficits in the old approach have been recognized, but the new ideas have not yet been questioned.

- *Déjà-vu experience*. The new paradigm looks so self-evident that one wonders why it has appeared only now, or one even doubts that it is new.

Evolution

The last point about evolutionary development seems to be fairly uncommon in the application development of many enterprises. On the contrary, the argument that everything will have to be redone from scratch is used to create barriers for switching to object-oriented techniques.

VW Beetle with trunk

In other areas – think of the automotive industry – mixed procedures are traditionally practiced: after a given phase of further development and improvement of existing models, entirely new models are developed periodically. The VW Beetle was given up in spite of its success because the cost of producing the body was no longer competitive. It needed twice the number of welding points than the bodies of big American cars, namely around 6,000.[10] Moreover, because of the position of the engine, no trunk could be integrated into the design.

The analysis of Bittner *et al.* (1995) shows that, as actually practiced, software development is far more "evolutionary" than envisaged officially or in procedural models.

In software development, many people share the opinion that permanent further development and enhancement of existing programs is economical and thus is the only practicable road. This is, however, a false conclusion if the whole life cycle of the product is taken into account. A small change can affect the entire system. Thus, if stability is crucial, caution requires an analysis of the entire system before the change can be made.[11] What we need is a middle course.

[9] In a paradigm shift one *model* replaces another one in the same context, and they mutually exclude each other.
[10] See Railton.
[11] Valk, 1987.

Coherent Model Representation

One way of clarifying methodological uniformity is to compare the beginning and end of the development process. At the beginning, we may find, for example, the following developer–user dialog:

Developer: *What is important for you?*
User: *The customer.*
Developer: *What is a customer, which features are relevant for you?*
User: *A customer has a name, an address, and a solvency which we check.*

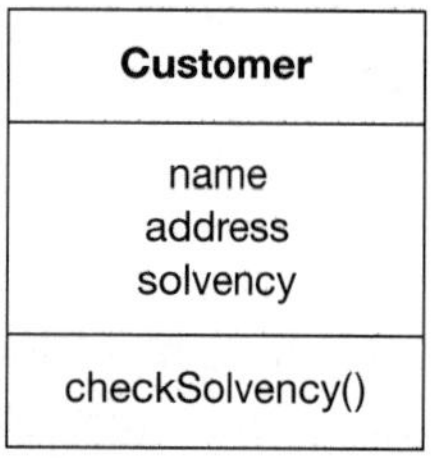

Customer
name
address
solvency
checkSolvency()

Figure 1.3 Class in UML

At the end of the process we find a class which, coded in (simplified) Java, looks as follows:

```
class Customer
{
    String      name;
    Address     address;
    Solvency    solvency;
    public void checkSolvency()
    {
        ...
    }
}
```

The holistic and human-oriented approach, pursued from the very beginning by the leading pioneers of object-orientation (at Xerox PARC), becomes clearly visible at many points:

- The class concept facilitates development of software units that do not serve a specific application but a specific concept or a specific idea of reality and as such can operate in different contexts and therefore in different applications.

- The world of object-oriented software development is full of images: terms such as inheritance, message exchange, the tool-material image, and so on are part of the metaphorics (or vividness) and indicate the basic ontological principles.

- The symbols of the graphical user interface, such as trash can, printer, magnifying glass, folder, brush, scissors, and so forth, allow users visual and intuitive action.

- Object-oriented graphical user interfaces help achieve uniform screen organization and coherent operating standards; they induce application developers to adopt these standards and imitate their look and feel.

The structured methods (SA, SD, ERM, and so on) build on similar principles for coping with complexity as the object-oriented ones, but they are methodologically not as uniformly applicable and capable of integration; and in systemic, networked thinking, object-oriented methods go a step further. Object-orientation is the current answer to the increased complexity of software development.

→ Means of abstraction *Nicolai Josuttis*

Programming is the process of representing facts in a computer. Describing these facts requires abstraction. Items which are irrelevant for the problem are omitted. Otherwise, you would always arrive at bits and quarks.

The faculty of describing things in a sensible way by means of abstraction is also used in everyday life. We normally use two kinds of abstraction:

Part/whole relationship (*has-a* relationship)

The part/whole relationship combines several parts into one object. An object consists of parts. Example:

A car *consists of* engine, body, seats, steering wheel, tires, and so on.

You say "Look at that car down there" instead of "Look at that engine with a body, a steering wheel, and four tires down there."

For this purpose, programming languages have structures (records).

Generic relationship (*is-a* relationship)

The generic relationship combines several kinds or variations of objects under one term. An object *is a* particular variation. Example:

A convertible *is a* car; a car *is a* vehicle.

You say "There are three cars down there" instead of "There are a convertible, a sedan, and a station wagon down there."

This means of abstraction is not supported in non-object-oriented programming languages.

The following points summarize the most important advantages of the object-oriented approach.

Advantages of object-orientation

- Owing to the evolutionary process, new requirements can also be added at later stages of the development process and integrated relatively easily.

- It is possible to deal with more demanding and more complex areas of application.

- Communication between software developers and experts in the application area is improved through the anthropomorphic metaphors.

- Coherent modeling favors the quality of results. The individual development steps remain fairly consistent with each other.

- Concepts uniformly applicable in all development steps facilitate development and improve documentation.

- The holistic view in modeling does better justice to structures, relationships, and dependences in the real world.

- Seen over the whole of their lifetime, object-oriented models are more stable and thus easier to modify. Even essential global system changes are mostly obtained by limited local changes.

- Object-oriented abstractions allow increased reusability of work outcomes.

- Object-oriented software development is more fun.

Nevertheless, object-orientation is not a panacea, and we do not want to be too euphoric: even this approach will not necessarily prevent you from getting lousy results.

📖 Suggested Reading

1. Fayad, M., Laitinen M. (1998) *Transition to Object-Oriented Software Development*, John Wiley & Sons.
2. Larman, C. (1997) *Applying UML and Patterns, An Introduction to Object-Oriented Analysis and Design*, Prentice Hall.
3. Goldberg, A., Rubin, K. (1995) *Succeeding with Objects, Decision Frameworks for Project Management*, Addison-Wesley.
4. Constantine, L., Lockwood, L. (1999) *Software for Use, A Practical Guide to the Models and Methods of Usage-Centered Design*, Addison-Wesley.
5. Habermas, J. (1987) *Theorie des kommunikativen Handelns,* Suhrkamp.
6. Heisenberg, W. (1989) *Ordnung der Wirklichkeit* (1942), Piper.
7. Miller, G. (1975) The Magical Number Seven, Plus Minus Two: Some Limits on Our Capacity for Processing Information. *In The Psychological Review*, vol. 63. Also: *The Magical Number Seven after Fifteen Years*, Wiley.
8. Booch, G., Rumbaugh, J. Jacobson, I. (1998) *The Unified Modeling Language User Guide*, Addison-Wesley.
9. Rumbaugh, J., Jacobson, I., Booch, G. (1999) *The Unified Modeling Language Reference Manual*, Addison-Wesley.
10. Jacobson, I., Booch, G., Rumbaugh, J., (1999) *The Unified Software Development Process*, Addison-Wesley.
11. Graham, I., Henderson-Sellers, B., Younessi, H. (1997) *The OPEN Process Specification*, Addison-Wesley (ACM Press).
12. Coleman, D., Arnold, P., Bodorff, S., Dollin, C., Gilchrist, H. (1993) *Object Oriented Development: The Fusion Method*, Prentice Hall.

chapter **2**

Object-orientation for Beginners

This chapter provides an easy introduction to the concepts of object-orientation.

Object-orientation for Beginners 18

Classes, Objects, Instances 19

Attributes, Operations, Constraints, Relationships 20

Object Identity 22

Responsibilities 24

Taxonomy and Inheritance 25

Abstract Classes 34

Associations 35

Aggregations 35

Message Exchange 39

Collections 42

Polymorphism 44

Persistence 47

Classification of Classes 50

Design Patterns 56

Components 58

LIVERPOOL JOHN MOORES UNIVERSITY
LEARNING SERVICES

2.1 Object-orientation for Beginners

Synopsis

■ Why do beginners often have fewer problems with object-orientation?
■ What is the basic concept of object-orientation?

Novice programmers have fewer problems

Explaining the basics of object-orientation needs only a few examples. Even complete newcomers get rapidly acquainted with the subject, probably even more easily than experienced computer buffs. While professionals are reluctant to abandon their beloved data, function, and process models and always try to fit the new ideas somewhere into their set thinking patterns, computer rookies can light-heartedly get acquainted with object-orientation as an easily accessible approach.

Reducing complexity by means of abstract models

Object-orientation is so called because this method sees things that are part of the real world as objects. A phone is an object in the same way as a bicycle, a human being, or an insurance policy are objects. And these objects are in turn composed of other objects, such as screws, wheels, nose and ears, annual tariffs, and so on. Real-world objects can obviously have a fairly complex structure and cause us some cognitive problems. A complex object, such as a human being, can be perceived only in a simplified way. Obvious external features such as arms, nose and ears can be recognized immediately if we neglect detailed components such as blood corpuscles or nerve synapses.

Playing model railroad

In everyday life, we simplify objects in our thinking – we work with models, as children do. As a boy, I used to play railroads with my father. Not with a real railroad; engine, wagons and crossings were scaled-down representations of reality: we had a model railroad. Software development does essentially the same: objects occurring in reality are reduced to a few features that are relevant in the current situation. Instead of real objects, we work with symbols. Properties and composition of objects correspond only roughly to reality; the model selects only those aspects that are useful for carrying out a specific task. (See Fig. 2.1.)

Thus, besides their names, in a staff accounting system, employees are reduced to social security numbers, together with allowances and so on, while the internal phone book will show their position, department, and extension.

LIVERPOOL JOHN MOORES UNIVERSITY
LEARNING SERVICES

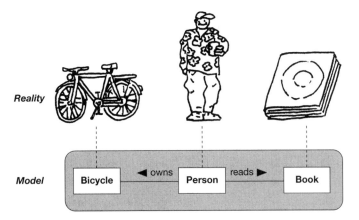

Figure 2.1 Complex realities are made more manageable by abstract models

2.2 Classes, Objects, Instances

Synopsis

■ *The object/class principle*. A class describes the structure and behavior of a set of similar objects. An object is an instance which is present at runtime and allocates memory for its instance variables, and which behaves according to the protocol of its class.

Class = building plan of similar objects

One cow makes moo – many cows make moolah. This phrase, based on an old German farmer's saying, has been taken into account in object-orientation. Objects occurring in the real world are thus not only restricted to their most important, mode-relevant properties, but similar objects are also grouped together.

The objects to be considered in the model are not conceived merely as individual entities. For similar objects, an assembly plan is created, which in object-orientation is called a *class*. This class is then used to create the concrete objects.

The three cows Uma, Molly, and Patty (Fig. 2.2) originate from the prototype class *cow*. The class *cow* itself does not exist as an independent object (although there are exceptions, e.g. in Smalltalk – *see* Wallrabe, 1997).

In this book, classes and objects are represented following the notation of the UML, that is, as rectangles. To differentiate between classes and objects, the names of objects are underlined (Fig. 2.3).

Classes ⇨172
Objects ⇨181

If we want to represent the object–class relationship (instance relationship), we draw a dashed arrow between an object and its class in the direction of the class (Fig. 2.4).

Instance
Object

In the case of Uma Udder, this would be read as "Uma Udder is an instance of the class cow" (Fig. 2.5).

Figure 2.2 Objects from left to right: Uma Udder, Molly Milk and Patty Pasture

Figure 2.3 Notation of class and object

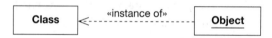

Figure 2.4 Notation of instance relationship

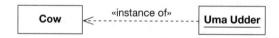

Figure 2.5 Example of an instance relationship

2.3 Attributes, Operations, Constraints, Relationships

Synopsis

- *The encapsulation principle*. Classes combine attributes and operations into a single unit. Attributes are only accessible indirectly via the operations of the class.

In the context of classes and objects, we have also talked about their *properties*. What exactly do we mean by this? What are the significant properties of a class? The following aspects must be considered:

Properties of classes
and objects
⇨183

- *Attributes*: the structure of the objects: their components and the information or data contained therein.

⇨186
see Glossary ⇨282, 283

- *Operations*: describe the behavior of the objects. Commonly, the term *operations* is used. However, sometimes the words *services* or *methods* or, erroneously, *procedure* or *function* are used.

⇨197

- *Constraints*: the conditions, requirements, and rules that objects must satisfy.

- *Relationships*: that a class has to other classes (inheritance relationships, associations, and the like).

Example

A circle which we want to represent on a screen, for example, has the following properties, amongst others:

- *Attributes*: its radius and its position on the screen (x, y).

- *Operations*: the possibility of displaying, removing, repositioning, and resizing it.

How are constraints represented in program code? ⇨22

- *Constraints*: the radius must not be negative and not equal to zero (radius > 0).

- *Relationships*: in this simple example the circle has no relationships.

Operations may or may not have *parameters*. For example, when a new radius is set, the parameter *newRadius* is passed. Parameters are attached to the name of the operation enclosed in parentheses. Also, operations without parameters are followed by a pair of parentheses. This serves to differentiate them from attributes. Constraints are enclosed in braces (Fig. 2.6). Constraints and the possible relationships between classes will be described in further detail later.

{ordered} ⇨ 232
⇨197

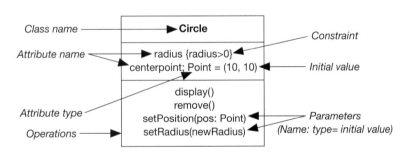

Figure 2.6 Notation elements for classes

Objects: sample attribute values

On the one hand, during analysis and design, classes are modeled, that is, their properties and relationships are considered; on the other hand, use case and sequence diagrams and others are used to represent the interaction between the classes and simulate selected processes. Instead of classes, these diagrams use objects (Fig. 2.7). These are represented in a similar way to classes (in contrast to the class name, the object name is underlined), with the possibility of introducing sample values for the attributes.

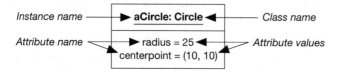

Figure 2.7 Notation elements for objects

Thus, classes and objects are units composed of attributes, operations, and constraints. The corresponding code in (simplified) Java, for example, looks like this:

```java
class Circle
  {
    int radius;
    Point centerpoint;
    public void setRadius(int newRadius)
    {
      if (newRadius > 0)  // constraint
      {
        radius = newRadius;
        ...
      }
    }
    public void setPosition(Point pos)
    { ... }
    public void display();
    { ... }
    public void remove();
    { ... }
  }
```

This example shows only the principle; the actual implementation of the individual operations has been omitted for the sake of simplicity.

2.4 Object Identity

Synopsis

■ *The object identity principle.* Each object is by definition to be uniquely differentiated from all other objects, independent of its concrete attribute values.

Identity is a property that differentiates an object from all other objects. This term is often confused with addressability, equality of attributes, or a unique name. Particularly in relational databases, names or similar things

Equality
vs. identity

are used as keys. Usually, these keys are then also employed to create relationships between objects or entities.

However, such names are only partly suited to identify an object, because the identity of an object (for example a car) usually does not depend on its attributes (for example the number plate). Names may change; different objects may have the same name. Sometimes, unique names are available (for example a social security number) but must not be used (for example for reasons of protection of personal data). To avoid these problems from the very start, artificially generated keys are used which have no substantial reference to the properties of the objects and keep their value unchanged forever. Examples of this are unique time stamps or counters (ID numbers).

Persistence ⇨47

Inheritance ⇨220

Object-oriented database systems and Corba[1] and EJB[2] implementations include their own mechanisms for this purpose, thus guaranteeing the identity of the objects. Objects that are active in a program are usually uniquely identified by their memory address, that is, by a pointer. Object-oriented databases are often based on system-generated ID numbers and corresponding pointers. Figure 2.8 shows three objects: two of these have identical attribute values; as objects however, they are not identical.

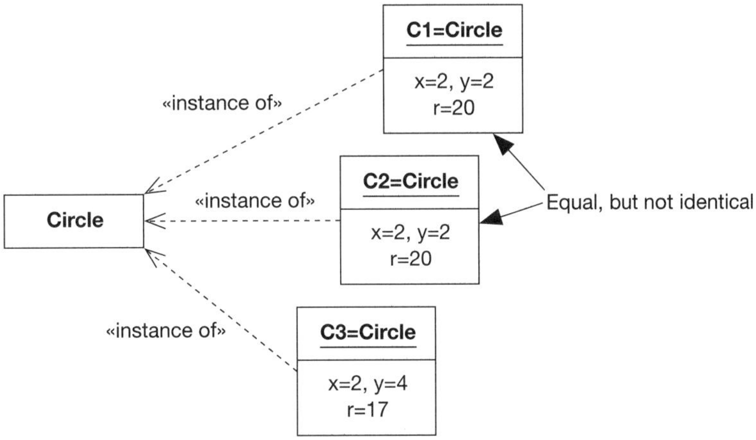

Figure 2.8   **Equality and identity of objects**

---

[1] The Common Object Request Broker Architecture is an architecture for cross-compatibility in heterogeneous systems, i.e. independent from programming languages, operating systems, and computers.

[2] Enterprise Java Beans is a Java-based component architecture.

2.5 Responsibilities

Synopsis

■ *The coherence principle*. Each class should be responsible for precisely one (logical) aspect of the total system. The properties located in this area of responsibility should be grouped into a single class and not divided over various classes. Moreover, a class should not contain properties that do not belong to its area of responsibility.

Divide a problem up and you're halfway to solving it. An important principle in object-oriented software development is the clear demarcation and definition of responsibilities. Each responsibility is assigned to a single class. Each class is responsible for one aspect of the total system.

The various responsibilities are obviously not distributed between the classes in an arbitrary or random fashion but in accordance with certain principles. In this respect the coherence principle is important; this states that related responsibilities should not be divided but concentrated in one class. A class consists of attributes, operations, constraints, and relationships. The coherence principle demands that all the properties of a class should form a logical connection. If, for example, you wish to create a class *Customer*, you first determine its responsibility: for what items is this class going to be responsible?

You should therefore determine the responsibilities first of all. If the responsibilities do not belong together logically, divide them into different classes. For a customer administration system, for example, you might have the responsibilities or classes outlined in Fig. 2.9.

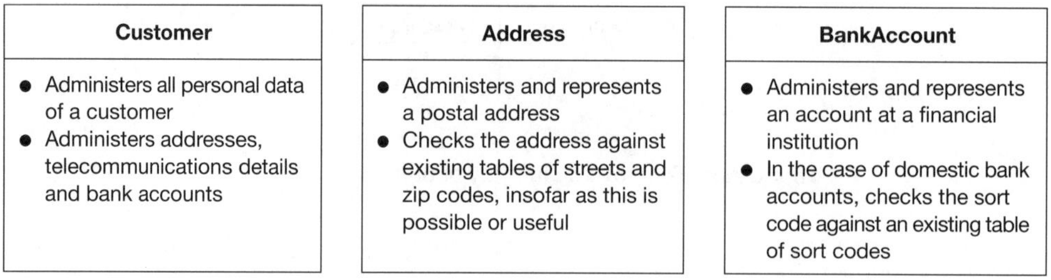

Customer	**Address**	**BankAccount**
● Administers all personal data of a customer ● Administers addresses, telecommunications details and bank accounts	● Administers and represents a postal address ● Checks the address against existing tables of streets and zip codes, insofar as this is possible or useful	● Administers and represents an account at a financial institution ● In the case of domestic bank accounts, checks the sort code against an existing table of sort codes

Figure 2.9 Notation of responsibilities

Try to formulate the responsibilities as succinctly as possible, i.e. keep them general. Thus, do not write "is responsible for managing the customer's first name, last name, date of birth, and sex" but "is responsible for managing all the customer's personal details." Even if the responsibility is expressed in a very general manner, it is usually possible to decide unambiguously whether a property belongs to this class. If, for example, you were to assign the property "Academic title" to a class other than Customer, it would be an infringement of the coherence principle, since an academic title is a component of the name and is therefore a personal detail.

2.6 Taxonomy and Inheritance

Synopsis

- *The inheritance principle or the generalization/specialization principle.* Classes may represent specializations of other classes, i.e. classes can be arranged hierarchically and assume ("inherit") the properties of the classes above them; if required, they can specialize ("overwrite") them, but not eliminate them.
- *The substitution principle.* Objects of subclasses can always be used instead of objects of their superclass(es).
- *A warning on inheritance.* Avoid inheritance if there are alternatives.
- Classes can be divided into subclasses using a discriminator.

Entomology, the science that deals with insects, has a much longer tradition than computer science. It has been practicing for many decades a method which in information science is considered as new (without justification, if one considers mathematical roots or Chomsky's theory of formal languages). Entomologists classify insects present in the whole world using a system called *taxonomy*. Insects are ordered by families and classes. Below the superior group of insects, we find subgroups such as *flying insects* and *primitive insects (without wings)*. These groups are further subdivided into *insects with one pair of wings, insects with two pairs of wings*, and so on.

Inheritance = Reusing properties

The important factor of this hierarchy (*see* Fig. 2.10) is that all insects of a class have identical properties and that derived subclasses represent a specialization. Subclasses derived from a class automatically have all properties of the superior class. Thus, properties are inherited. This principle is the corner stone of reusability in object-orientation.

In this way, we can not only classify insects, we can also hierarchically structure objects and concepts used in the area of software development.

Since this representation reminds us of a family tree and properties are indeed passed from one class down to the next, we also talk about inheritance and hierarchy of inheritance. The class that bestows its properties is called the superclass or base class, while the class that inherits something is called the subclass. The inheritance relation is represented by an arrow, with the subclass always pointing to the superclass. Arrows can also be bundled, as shown in Fig. 2.11.

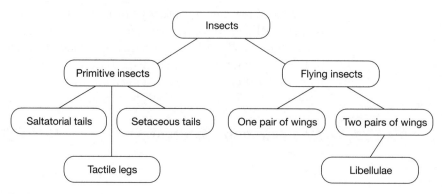

Figure 2.10 Taxonomy

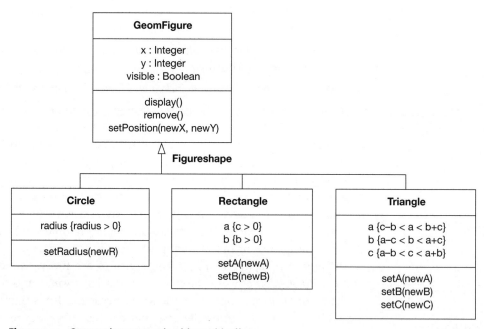

Figure 2.11 Structuring properties hierarchically

Generalization
Specialization
Inheritance ⇨220

Substitution
principle

Discriminator

This principle is usually called generalization or specialization (Fig. 2.12). The class *GeomFigure* is a generalization of *Circle*, and *Circle* is a specialization of *GeomFigure*, depending on the point of view. This is a case of *is-a* semantics: a circle is a geometric figure. Objects of derived classes can always be employed instead of objects of their base class(es) (substitution principle). (Instead of generalization and specialization we should really be talking about *concretization*, but unfortunately this term is not very widespread.)

Superclasses and subclasses are frequently differentiated by means of a distinctive feature, the so-called *discriminator*. In the example above, we differentiate by figure shape.

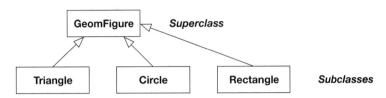

Figure 2.12 Generalization/specialization

Multiple inheritance
⇨ 224

The above illustration showing the hierarchy of geometric objects is an example of so-called simple inheritance. Besides this form of inheritance, we also experience multiple inheritance, in which a class can have more than one superclass.

Problems with
inheritance ⇨ 31

There are various alternatives to inheritance – for example delegation, aggregation, generic programming (e.g. parameterized classes and C++ templates, etc.), generic design (e.g. CASE tool macros and scripts), which can sometimes be more advantageous or even unavoidable, so you should not employ inheritance naïvely. The possibilities and the usefulness of inheritance are often overestimated. One should therefore heed the warning: avoid inheritance if there are alternatives.

2.6.1 Structuring of Properties

Synopsis

Differential
programming

■ Generalization/specialization makes differential designing and programming possible.

■ The concept of generalization/specialization can be illustrated directly in object-oriented programming languages.

■ *The object–responsibility principle*. Each object – and that object alone – is responsible for its own properties.

Differential programming is a politically correct name for object-oriented legacy hunting. In the generalization or specialization process of classes, a subclass inherits the properties of its superclass, but it must also assume its responsibilities and tasks, at least in principle. Particular features may be specialized, i.e. further developed, and new features may be added. Existing properties, however, should be neither suppressed nor restricted.

Structuring by semantic
aspects

But how are properties arranged inside an inheritance hierarchy? Fundamentally, properties are situated precisely in those classes where, according to the responsibility assigned to them, they are effectively a property of the class. Conversely, classes contain precisely those properties for which they are responsible.

This means that properties are not distributed simply according to opti-mization and non-redundancy criteria, and that they are not placed in a superclass for the sole purpose that subclasses can make practical use of them. Class hierarchies are not designed with such goals in mind. Instead, one should attempt to assign a responsibility to each class and to allocate to it all the properties that belong to this area of responsibility. A responsibil-ity should not be divided between different classes.

The class diagram in Fig. 2.11 shows an example of generalization and specialization of geometric figures. It is assumed that all figures can be dis-played on a screen, and that they can be removed and repositioned. Since these properties are to apply to all figures, the corresponding properties should already be situated in the *GeomFigure* class, together with the attrib-utes for screen position and visibility status. The *visible* attribute indicates whether the figure is currently being displayed. The *x* and *y* coordinates specify the center point of the figure.

Further properties cannot be generalized; thus the model looks as shown in Fig. 2.11. The *GeomFigure* class includes the attributes *x*, *y*, and *vis-ible*, together with the operations *display()*, *remove()*, and *setPosition()*. In the derived classes *Circle*, *Rectangle*, and *Triangle*, the sides (*a, b, c*) or the radius are defined, together with constraints on these attributes and operations for modifying the attributes.

The corresponding Java program code for the class model looks as fol-lows (simplified and only for the classes *GeomFigure* and *Rectangle*):

```
class GeomFigure
{
  int x, y;
  boolean visible;

  public abstract void display();
  public abstract void remove();
  public void setPosition(int x, y)
  {
    if (visible)
    {
      remove();
      this.x = x;
      this.y = y;
      display();
    } else
    {
      x = this.x = x;
      y = this.y = y;
    };
  }
}
...
class Rectangle extends GeomFigure
{
  int a, b;  // sides
  public void setA(int a)
  {
    if (a > 0) { this.a = a; };
  }
  public void setB(int newB)
  {
    if (b > 0) { this.b = b; };
  }
}
```

All geometric figures have one thing in common: they have a position (x, y of the figure's center point), they can be displayed, removed, and repositioned. Displaying and removing are common properties of all geometric figures, but they must be implemented individually. A circle is drawn in a different way from a triangle. In the superclass *GeomFigure*, the operations *display()* and *remove()* must therefore be abstract operations. Only inside the classes *Circle*, *Triangle*, and so on do they become concrete operations (see the following sample code).

Abstract operations
⇨186

The *setPosition()* operation too is a common property and therefore situated in the *GeomFigure* class. However, it need not be an abstract operation, because it can be concretely implemented by means of the properties *x*, *y*, *display()*, and *remove()* already present in the *GeomFigure* class, as shown in the next piece of sample code.

Special
properties

Constraints ⇨197

Individual properties in the example are, amongst others, the *radius* of the circle, the *a* and *b* sides of the rectangle, and the *a*, *b*, and *c* sides of the triangle. In addition, special constraints can be formulated for the sides and the radius. Thus, for example, the value of the *radius* attribute in the *Circle* class must be neither negative nor zero.

Since they use individual properties of the figures, the operations *setRadius(r)*, *setA(a)*, and *setB(b)* are not general properties of the *GeomFigure* class but special properties of the subclasses. Things would have been different if we had defined an operation *resize(byFactor)* – this would have been a common abstract property of all geometric figures.

```
class GeomFigure extends Object
{
  int x, y;
  boolean visible;

  public abstract void display();
  public abstract void remove();
  public void setPosition(int x, y)
  {
    if (visible)
    {
      remove();
      this.x = x;
      this.y = y;
      display();
    } else
    {
      this.x = x;
      this.y = y;
    }
  }
}
class Rectangle extends GeomFigure
{
  int a, b;
```

```
public void display()
{ ... }
public void remove()
{ ... }
public void setA(int a)
{
   if (a > 0) { this.a = a; };
}
public void setB(int b)
{
   if (b > 0) { this.b = b; };
}
}
```

2.6.2 Inheritance: Restrictions and Problems

Synopsis

- Inheritance is easy, but it does have its pitfalls.

- *The constraint–responsibility principle.* A subclass should not include any constraints on the properties of a superclass.

In Fig. 2.13 the *Square* class is modeled as a subclass of *Rectangle*, because it is a special form of rectangle. The *Square* class is a specialization of the *Rectangle* class; the sides a and b must be equal, which is formulated as a constraint. Thus, objects of the *Square* class have a redundant attribute (the b side), because the specification of one side would be sufficient. However, we usually put up with this redundancy because it corresponds to our normal view of the world that a square is a special form of rectangle.

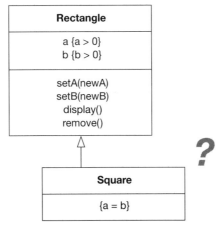

Figure 2.13 Square *is a* rectangle

Pathological
discriminator

The redundancy-free alternative would consist of realizing the rectangle as a specialization of the square: first, we would create a class with a side a, then derive a subclass with a second side b. This would be optimal with regard to memory requirements, but we could no longer specify a reasonable discriminator.

Substitution principle
⇨25

A further argument speaks against the rectangle as a specialization of the square: take two variables s and r, which are of the types *Square* and *Rectangle* respectively. Now you could assign the variable s a rectangle, because according to the class hierarchy, a rectangle is compatible with a square – this possibility can, however, hardly be intended.

```
class Rectangle extends Square { ... }
Rectangle r;
Square s;

...

s = r;   // assignment allowed because type
         // compatible, but not sensible
```

A problem of the variation shown in the class diagram (*Square* is a subclass of *Rectangle*) is constituted by the fact that *Square* contains a constraint on attributes of the superclass. In the present example, reduced to the essential as it is, the consequences are clearly visible and not very critical. Generally, however, use of such constraints is strongly discouraged, because subclasses that define constraints on attributes of superclasses cannot force all operations of the superclasses to observe them. They have no possibility of knowing the constraint because inheritance is a one-way process in the direction of the subclasses. Moreover, the properties constrained in one class (*Square*) would be (at least partially) implemented in another class (*Rectangle*).

Constraint-responsibility
principle

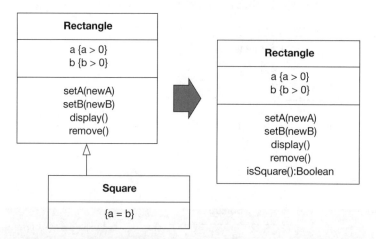

Figure 2.14 Square rectangles

After all, objects of the *Rectangle* class can well be squares or become squares if by chance their sides are equal. This is probably an adequate solution and thus the end of the discussion of this design problem: the *Square* class is not modeled at all (*see* Fig. 2.14); instead, the following operation is envisaged for the *Rectangle* class:

```
public boolean isSquare() {
    return (a == b)
}
```

This discussion shows that generalization and specialization are not solely motivated by optimization and elimination of redundancy, but also by the adopted semantics – and that this too is not always easy.

→ Delegation

Delegation is a mechanism in which an object does not interpret a message completely on its own but forwards the message to another object. Thus it can also be used as an alternative to inheritance.

The figure below shows the class A which provides the interfaces *A1* and *A2*, in the first case directly via multiple inheritance, in the second case indirectly via a delegation mechanism to be implemented.

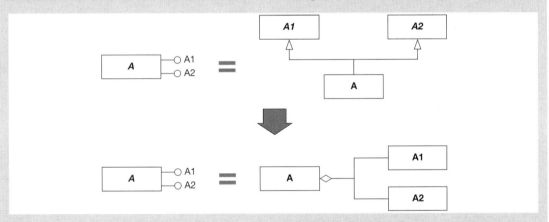

Delegation allows objects to use existing properties of other classes or to provide additional properties. In other words, a class can extend (propagate) its properties by delegation. The effects of inheritance can, for example, be emulated with the means of aggregation, which makes delegation a valid mechanism for prevention of multiple inheritance. Properties which in an inheritance relation would have to be located in the superclass are evacuated into a separate class which can then be incorporated again via an aggregation relation.

In Smalltalk, delegation can very easily and globally be achieved by overwriting the method *doesNotUnderstand:*, while in C++ and Java the implementation effort is substantial (*see* Gamma, 1996, p. 22, p. 367).

An argument against global delegation is that it may have difficulty in controlling side effects and causes runtime losses. It is in any case more advantageous to model delegation and to use code generation to implement it as direct delegation only.

▶

2.7 Abstract Classes

Synopsis

■ *The principle of abstract classes.* Classes of which no concrete instances can be created, i.e. of which there will never be any objects, are called *abstract classes*.

Basics ⇨178

Tagged values ⇨207

In our example, there will be objects of the classes *Circle, Rectangle,* and *Triangle,* but none of the *GeomFigure* class because *GeomFigure* is merely an abstraction. It is only included in the model to sensibly abstract the (common) properties of the other classes. Abstract classes are marked by the property value *{abstract}* below the class name or by the class name set in italics (Fig. 2.15).

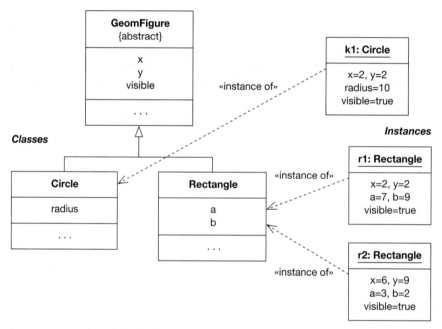

Figure 2.15   Abstact classes have no instances

This does not mean that there can only be objects of the most specialized class in the hierarchy. To illustrate this, the class hierarchy has been extended by a *Square* class (which, as discussed in the previous section, can be problematic). The figure also shows that an object always includes the attributes of its own class and all its superclasses.

2.8   Associations

Synopsis

■ An association is a relationship between different objects of one or more classes.

A simple example of an association is the relationship between a window and a set of geometric figures (Fig. 2.16).

Basics ⇨225

Figure 2.16   Example of an association

Difference relation / association ⇨237f.

In the simplest case, an association is represented by a single line between two classes. Usually, however, associations are shown in as much detail as possible. Then, the association receives a name and a numerical specification (*multiplicity indication*) of how many objects on one side of the association are connected with how many objects on the other side. Furthermore, the role names are added, which describe the meaning of the classes involved or their objects in more detail (for example, *employee, employer – see* Fig. 2.17). An association without any indication of direction is always a bidirectional association.

Multiplicity, cardinality ⇨225

Figure 2.17   Role names in association

2.9   Aggregations

Synopsis

■ An aggregation is a special form of association.

■ An aggregation is a placebo.

Basics ⇨241

Has relationship
Whole-part hierarchy

A particular variation of association is aggregation. This is again a relationship between two classes, but with the peculiarity that the classes relate to each other as a whole relates to its parts.

Aggregation is the composition of an object out of a set of parts. A car, for example, is an aggregation of tires, engine, steering wheel, brakes, and so on. These parts may in turn be aggregations: a brake consists of disk, pads, hydraulic cylinder, etc. Aggregations are *has relationships*: a car *has* an engine. Instead of aggregation, some people talk about *part-whole hierarchy*. Another example of aggregation is shown in Fig. 2.18.

Figure 2.18 Example of aggregations

Composition ⇨244
(aggregation with existence-dependent parts)

A special form of aggregation is one in which the individual parts depend on the aggregate (the whole) for their existence; such a case is called a *composition* (Fig. 2.19). An example is the relationship between an invoice item and the invoice. An invoice item always belongs to an invoice. If the whole (for example, the invoice) is to be deleted, all existence-dependent parts (for example, the invoice items) are deleted as well. In a normal aggregation, only the object and its relationship with the other object would be deleted.

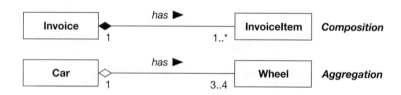

Figure 2.19 Composition and aggregation

An example of a normal aggregation is the relationship "car has wheels:" wheels necessarily belong to a car insofar as this is an aggregation, but they can also be regarded as separate entities that can exist without a car – in contrast to some humans who feel incomplete without a car (so-called pathological reverse composition).

An aggregate may temporarily (mostly at the beginning) also be without parts, that is, a cardinality of 0 is allowed. As a rule, however, the sense of an aggregate is to collect parts, so that cardinalities greater than 1 should really always be allowed.

Propagating operations

An essential property of aggregates is that the whole acts as a proxy for its parts, i.e. takes on operations which are then propagated to the individual parts. In the aggregation "invoice has invoice items" for example, these would be operations such as *computeInvoiceTotal()* and *numberInvoiceItems()*.

In an aggregation, the side of the whole is marked by a lozenge, to identify the relationship as an aggregation. Compositions are marked by solid lozenges and have always a multiplicity of *1* (or *0..1*) on the side of the aggregate, i.e. where the lozenge is located (Fig. 2.20). An individual part (for example an invoice item) whose existence depended on different aggregates would be a contradiction. However, besides that one existence-dependent relationship, an individual part may have any number of normal associations and (non-existence-dependent) aggregations with other classes. Incidentally, existence-dependence can also be generated quite simply by indicating a cardinality of 1 on the side of the aggregate. Then for each part there must be precisely one aggregate object.

Placebo?
see ⇨241

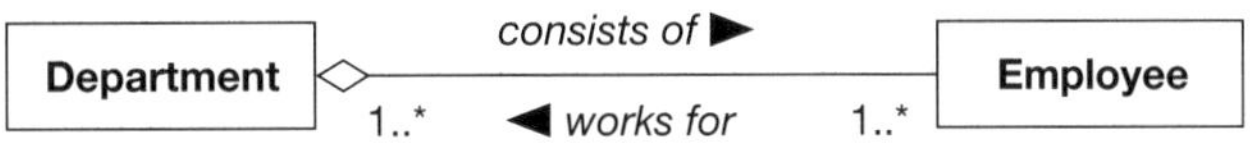

Figure 2.20   Aggregate with a multiplicity of 1..*

Parts of normal aggregations can simultaneously be part of different aggregates which may be instances of different classes or of the same class. The following example shows that one employee can simultaneously work for several departments. Nevertheless, the department is seen as an aggregate because it represents a unit which unites several employees.

The class diagram (Fig. 2.21) contains a further example of a composition, namely a new class *CircSquare* whose objects form an aggregate (here, a graphical overlay) of a square and a circle. As attributes, *CircSquare* therefore only aggregates one circle and one rectangle with equal sides (square). This is a composition because the two partial objects *circle* and *rectangle* that make up a *CircSquare* are existentially related to it. Since a *CircSquare* must know its partial objects, but the latter need not know who aggregates (uses) them, directed relationships are indicated.

Directed
relations⇨237

The code for the CircSquare class looks as follows in (simplified) Java:

```
class CircSquare extends GeomFigure
{
   Circle    c;
   Rectangle r;
```

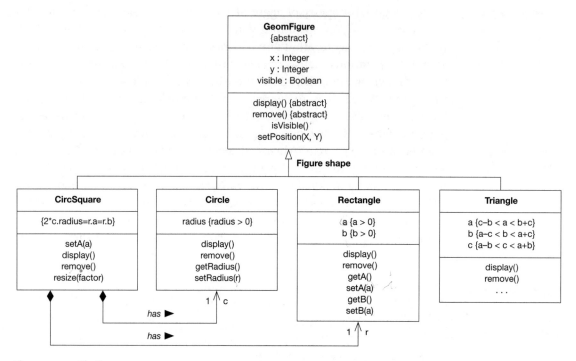

Figure 2.21 CircSquare

```
public void display()
{
  c.display();
  r.display();
}
public void remove()
{
  c.remove();
  r.remove();
}
public void setA(int a)
{
  c.setRadius (a / 2);
  r.setA(a);  // this turns the rectangle
  r.setB(a);  // into a square (a=b)
}
public void resize(float factor)
{
 setA(r.getA() * factor);
}
}
```

2.10 Message Exchange

Synopsis

■ *The message exchange principle.* Objects are independent units that cooperate and interact by means of messages that they send to each other.

Communication between objects is achieved by exchanging messages (Fig. 2.22). These messages lead to the operations, which means that an object understands precisely those messages for which it has operations.

Figure 2.22 Message exchange

A message is represented by means of the name of an operation (with arguments enclosed in parentheses, if required) and an arrow. The arrow indicates the direction of the message.

We return to our example (Fig. 2.21) of geometric figures and look at the class *CircSquare* and its relationships with *Rectangle* and *Circle*. Let us assume that an object of *CircSquare* is sent a *resize()* message. As the following code fragment shows, inside the *resize()* operation, the object sends a message to itself *(setA())*, which in turn generates messages to *Circle* and *Rectangle*. Thus, *CircSquare* delegates the actual task of resizing to its parts.

```
class CircSquare extends GeomFigure
{
  ...

  public void setA(int a)
  {
    c.setRadius (a / 2);
    r.setA(a);
    r.setB(a);
  }
  public void resize(float factor)
  {
    int a;
    a= r.getA();³
    setA(a * factor);
  }
```

---

³ The local variable *a* has been introduced for a better understanding of the following explanations.

Difference
operation/message

Now, one might think that message exchange between objects is no more than a function or procedure call in traditional procedural programming languages. However, this is not exactly the case. The following three arguments hold against it.

● In contrast to conventional programs, operations and data build a unit. An object contains all operations needed for processing its data contents and all of its further behavior. Facts that are related to each other by their contents are concentrated inside the object. In traditional programs, they are strewn all over, or stand unconnected one behind the other. In contrast to a procedural solution, in an object-oriented solution operations or messages can only be accessed via the object:

```
Object message: argument.       "Smalltalk"
object.message(argument);       // C++, Java
```

e.g.:

```
aCircle radius: 17.             "Smalltalk"
aCircle.setRadius(17);          // C++, Java
```

● Moreover, object attributes are usually encapsulated and accessible from outside only via appropriate operations (such as the radius which can only be accessed via the *getRadius()* and *setRadius(newRadius)* operations). In procedural languages, these mechanisms can only be realized with a lot of good will and self-discipline (in this case, *aCircle* is, for example, a pointer to a data structure):

```
setRadius(aCircle, 17);
```

● The most important issue is that a message can only be interpreted by an object if the object possesses a *matching* operation. (In Smalltalk, messages can even be propagated to other objects without any operation at all.) However, in the classes that define an object, this operation can have multiple definitions (for example, the operations *display()* and *remove()*). The operation to be used is decided dynamically. Further explanations can be found in Section 2.12.

Collaboration
diagrams⇨256

Sequence diagrams
⇨261

While the class diagram represents the relationships between the classes in a sort of building plan, collaboration and sequence diagrams are used to show a specific operation or situation. A collaboration or sequence diagram reflects a scenario and shows the individual messages between the objects that are needed to cope with the selected operation. While sequence diagrams emphasize the temporal course of action, collaboration diagrams start from the relational structure of the objects involved. Otherwise, the represented states of affairs are identical.

Figures 2.23 and 2.24 show such a scenario. An object of the *CircSquare* class receives a *resize(factor)* message, which means that the two aggregated individual figures are to be resized by the specified factor (for example 1.5). The *resize(factor)* scenario leads to the message exchange in Fig. 2.24. It is based on the class diagram and the code samples shown on the two preceding pages.

Class diagram ⇨37
Code example ⇨39f.

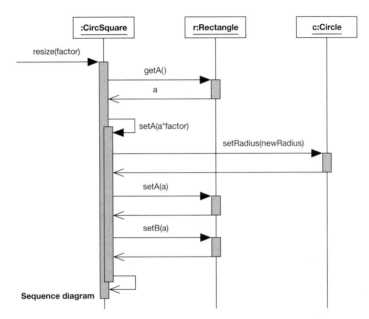

Figure 2.23 Message exchange represented by a sequence diagram

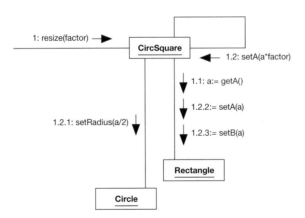

Figure 2.24 Message exchange represented with a collaboration diagram

1.1 The object *CircSquare* sends the rectangle the message *getA()*. The rectangle answers with the value of the current side length, and *CircSquare* stores the answer temporarily in the variable *a*.

1.2 Subsequently, *CircSquare* sends the message *setA(a*factor)* to itself.

1.2.1 Within the *setA(a)* operation, the *CircSquare* object first sends the message *setRadius(a/2)* to the circle.

1.2.2 Subsequently, the rectangle is sent the message *setA(a)*.

1.2.3 Followed by the message *setB(a)*.

Thus, if the initial side length is 12 and the specified factor 1.5, the new radius is 9 and the new side length is 18.

2.11 Collections

Synopsis

■ Collection classes are one of the mainstays of object-oriented software development.

Ordered collection

Container classes

Sequential and associative collections

Collections are classes usually defined in the standard class libraries and have in common that they collect and manage sets of objects. Collections are also called container classes. They have all the operations for adding and removing objects, checking whether a given object is contained in the set, and determining how many objects are currently contained in the set.

A main distinction can be made between sequential collections and associative collections. In sequential collections, objects are collected in a sequential structure; the best known example is the *array*. Associative collections store not only objects but also an additional key for each object through which it can be identified. An example for this is the *dictionary*.

The individual collection classes differ with regard to their sorting possibilities and whether objects may occur more than once, whether objects of different classes may coexist, whether objects may be inserted only at the beginning and the end, whether the number of their elements is variable, whether duplicates may exist, and so on.

Depending on programming language and class library, the class hierarchy of collection classes may vary. The class hierarchy excerpt in Fig. 2.25 is taken from a Smalltalk library. The overview in Fig. 2.26 shows which of these classes are suitable for which purposes.

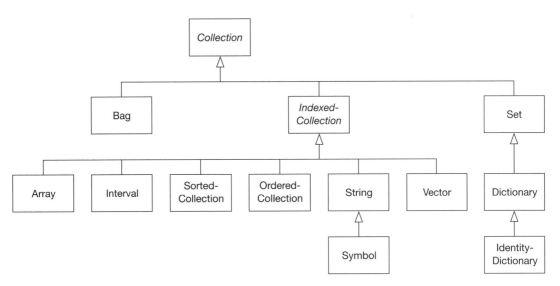

Figure 2.25 Example of a collection class hierarchy

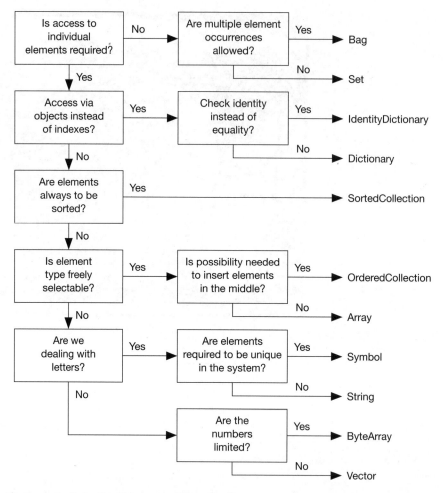

Figure 2.26 Selecting the appropriate collection

2.12 Polymorphism

Synopsis

■ *The polymorphism principle*. Polymorphism means that an operation may behave differently (in different classes). There are two kinds of polymorphism: static (overloading) and dynamic.

This is in reality one of the cornerstones that makes object-orientation so powerful. The inheritance principle together with dynamic typing of some programming languages or the interface concept of Java form the basis for *polymorphism* (Greek for "many forms").

Generic
operators

Static polymorphism is already known from the procedural world, namely in the form of operators such as + or –. These (generic) operators can be applied to both integer and real numbers. Object-oriented programming languages (or hybrid ones such as C++) offer the possibility of using these operators for user-defined data types or classes as well. Precisely speaking, operators are nothing more than operations with special names. Therefore, the same effect can also be achieved for normal operations.

A further aspect of polymorphism consists in interface variations of operations of the same name (here in a C++ sample):

```
class TimeOfDay {
  public:
  void setTime(char[8] time);
  void setTime(int h, int m, int s);
}

...

TimeOfDay aClock;
aClock.setTime(17, 1, 0);
aClock.setTime('11:55:00');
```

In this example, two operations of the same name exist which differ only by their signature, or which, in other words, only need to be supplied with different parameters. Depending on which parameters are specified (hour, minute, and second as individual values or as a character string), one or the other operation is activated. Users of this class behave in the same way. This should, indeed, always be the case – otherwise, if homonymous operations of a class did not have the same effect, they would sooner or later be used in the wrong way.

Late binding

A precondition for **dynamic polymorphism** is so-called *late binding*. From a physical point of view, binding is the point in the life of a program at which the caller of an operation is given the (memory) address of that operation. Usually, this happens when the program is compiled and linked. Most of the traditional programming languages have this form of binding exclusively, which is called *early binding*. Smalltalk exclusively has late binding.

In late binding, the precise memory location of an operation is determined only when the call takes place, i.e. when the corresponding message is sent to the object. Thus the association between message and receiving operation does not occur at compile time but dynamically at runtime of the program. Why all this fuss?

Inheritance ⇨220

Inheritance means that a class inherits all the properties of its superclass. Thus, without having to define its own attributes and operations, it can have inherited ones. It is, however, free to redefine an inherited operation and to overwrite it with the new definition. Which of these operations is to be used at runtime in response to a corresponding message – i.e. which class the called operation comes from – is only decided at runtime.

Example

See Fig. 2.27 for an example where the classes *Circle* and *Rectangle* are both derived from the superclass *GeomFigure*. A feature shared by all geometric figures is that they can be displayed, removed, and repositioned. Therefore the superclass already contains these properties, including the *display()* and *remove()* operations, although these are abstract and can only be filled with contents by the derived classes *Circle* and *Rectangle* because rectangles are displayed (or drawn) differently from circles.

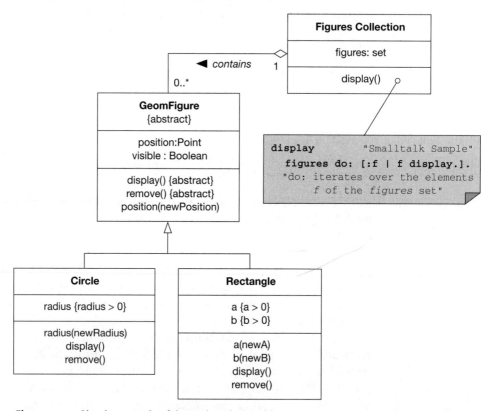

Figure 2.27 **Simple example of dynamic polymorphism**

Collections ⇨42

The figure collection shown in the illustration contains a set of geometric operations, namely circles and rectangles. In a (*do:*) loop, the *display()* operation of the *FigureCollection* class calls the figures one by one and sends them the *display()* message. At this point, it is not known whether the addressed object is a circle or a rectangle.

The object understands the *display()* message in any case because *display()* is a property of the *GeomFigure* class, from which *Circle* and *Rectangle* are derived. Although the *GeomFigure* class cannot know how a circle or a rectangle is displayed, it can nevertheless include this function, albeit with no concrete contents.

At the moment in which the *display()* message encounters an object, it is decided which concrete operation will be used: if the object is a rectangle, the *Rectangle.display()* operation is called. Use is always made of the operation of the most specialized class. Thus, although an operation of the *GeomFigure* class calls operations which it also contains itself, the homonymous operation of another class (namely *Rectangle*) is activated. This is polymorphism (Fig. 2.28).

Circles and rectangles

Figure 2.28   Principle of polymorphism

2.13   Persistence

Synopsis

■ Persistence is the storing of objects on a non-volatile medium.

■ There is no one-to-one mapping to relational databases.

Objects are created at runtime of the application program, and if nothing else is done about them, they are deleted at program termination. If objects are to be kept in existence beyond the runtime of the application, they need to be stored in a non-volatile storage medium, i.e. a database. Thus, persistent objects are long-term storable objects. All other objects are transient objects. Objects that are stored but do not exist in the running program are called *passive objects*, while instances that exist at runtime are called *active objects*.

Persistent objects may contain data exclusively contained in the active object. The data is computed during creation or loading of the object or is added during execution, but is not taken into consideration for later storage. Creation and loading of objects is carried out by special operations.

Persistent objects
⇨47

For storage of persistent objects, object-oriented database systems can be used. The persistent parts are mapped one-to-one in the database. Loading and storing of objects is usually performed autonomously.

Object identity
⇨22

Object-oriented database systems have not yet established themselves in every area of application. With very large data amounts and with sensitive data (think of the millions of records kept by insurance companies and banks), data continues to be stored in well-proven relational databases. Existing databases are also often preferred for reasons of cost.

Application architecture
⇨117

However, as shown in the section on application architecture, an implementation-neutral database connection can be realized. Some object-oriented development environments provide special tools for connection of SQL databases (so-called mapping tools, persistence object managers, persistence frameworks, and so on).

The question remains which database scheme is necessary or sensible in the underlying database when a relational database is to be employed. Three principal alternatives need to be distinguished:

● *All objects are stored in one single table* (Fig. 2.29). A simple solution. The data record length varies depending on the class of the stored object – the database should support this efficiently. With large amounts of data or numerous associations, a noticeable loss of performance may occur.

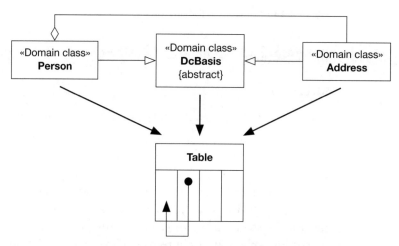

Figure 2.29 All persistent objects are stored in one single table

● *One table is created for each class* (Fig. 2.30). All data records in a table are the same length, but this does not cause specific requirements for the database. Objects of classes which have superclasses (which is mostly the case) need to collect their data from different tables. *Disadvantage of this solution*: in order to load an object, data needs to be picked from a (potentially large) number of tables. To simplify this, appropriate database views can be defined, for example:

```
create view Person
    as select tabPerson.*, tabDcBasis.*,
    from    tabPerson, tabDcBasis,
    where   (tabPerson.ObjId = tabDcBasis.ObjId);
```

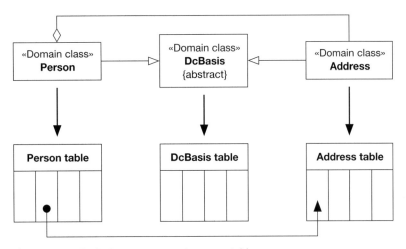

Figure 2.30 Each class corresponds to one table

● *One table is created for each object type* (Fig. 2.31). This means that an object is stored in one data record. One table is created for each concrete class. To load an object, only one single record needs to be read. *Disadvantage*: when reading a set of objects belonging to a common subclass or abstract class, partial sets of different tables need to be assembled. For simplification purposes, appropriate database views can be defined.

```
create view BusinessPartner as
  select * from tabPerson
union
  select * from tabCustomer
union
  select * from tabSupplier;
```

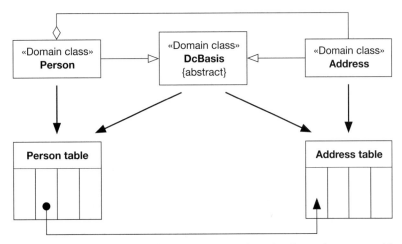

Figure 2.31 There is a table for each concrete class, i.e. for each concrete object type

A further disadvantage: attributes of superclasses are strewn across different tables. A change of an attribute definition in an abstract class (which, as experience shows, happens less frequently than in concrete classes) needs to be redundantly maintained in different tables.

This latter variation is implemented frequently. It represents an acceptable compromise between implementation cost and performance.

Associations and aggregations can also be realized with relational databases, as shown in Fig. 2.32. Relationships between objects are mainly expressed via object IDs. In contrast to the relational model, data contents, i.e. attribute values, are not used for this purpose.

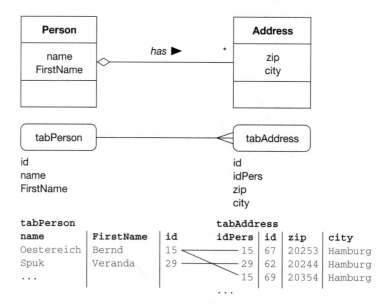

Figure 2.32 Representation of objects in tables

2.14 Classification of Classes

Synopsis

■ Classes are not just classes; it is useful to distinguish various types.

Over the past few years various purposes and connections have been developed for the use of classes. In many cases these are linked to specific design patterns. The boundaries between these various types of classes are not always clear. Table 2.1 gives an overview of the most important class types, which are marked with corresponding stereotypes. For reasons of completeness, the table also includes the abstract class, but it is not marked by a stereotype, since *abstract* really only represents a general property with which other classes such as entity or control classes, etc. can be marked.

Table 2.1 Frequently used class types

Construct	Associations		Operations		Class membership		Usage, modeling
	Attributes	Persistent	Signature	Implementation	Multiplicity	Type	
«type»	yes	–	yes	no	0..*	dynamic	Analysis models, component design, dynamic object roles
«interface»	no	–	yes	no	0..*	fixed	Analysis models, component design, component models, behavior specification
«entity»	yes (usually many)	possible (generally)	yes (usually few or simple)	yes	1	fixed	Component design, data models, structure specification
«control»	possible (usually transient)	possible	yes (often complex, somtimes delegating)	yes	1	fixed	Component design, behavior/process specification
«boundary»	possible	no	yes (predominantly delegating)	possible	1	fixed	Façade specification
{abstract}	yes	–	yes	possible	0	–	Component design, logical abstraction for «entity», «control», and «boundary»
«primitive»	yes	no	yes	yes	1	fixed	Generally no explicit modeling; specific to programming language/architecture
«enumeration»	yes	yes	yes	yes	1	fixed	Generally no explicit modeling; configurable sets of values and "constants"

2.14.1 «entity»

Entity classes usually represent a domain-specific situation or real-world object and:

- generally have a large number of attributes;
- have many primitive operations (*getAttr()*, *setAttr()*, etc.);
- do not have many complex operations;
- often only have a few life cycle states or simple state sequences.

They should always be included in analysis and design models. Examples are classes such as *Contract, Customer, Address*, etc.

2.14.2 «control»

Control classes represent a workflow, control, or calculation process and:

- generally have few or no attributes of their own;
- often only have a short transient lifetime, i.e. they exist only for the time of the process that they control;

- often have access to a set of entity classes, from which they request data or call elementary operations, and to which they write back the results of the process or the calculation, for example;
- have some complex operations;
- sometimes have no states;
- sometimes have very complex state models that describe comprehensive processes.

These classes should also be considered in analysis and design models. Many control classes are not discovered or do not become relevant until the design process.

Farewell to object-orientation?

If we were to look critically at this subdivision into entity and control classes, we might believe that a basic principle of the object-oriented approach is being abandoned. Objects are units that combine and encapsulate data and functionality. It might be thought that this is contradicted by a differentiation into entity and control classes.

In fact, the motivation behind it is quite different. Entity classes may very well contain functionality, i.e. operations, that can be as complex as you like. A decisive aspect, however, is that these operations should always relate to the class's area of responsibility. Occasionally during modeling one might come across processes, sequences or calculations that concern more than one class. In such a situation it is often impossible to include the corresponding operations in any of the available entity classes because they do not cover the appropriate area of responsibility. In such an event, i.e. whenever the content of operations relates to several classes and represents something higher, this is a clear indicator that a control class should be created.

Control classes therefore often contain very few attributes of their own, but gather data from various classes, process it, often with the support of other classes which provide elementary operations for this purpose, and then supply the result(s) back to one or more other classes. Examples of this are calculations of rates and premiums.

2.14.3 «interface»

See also interface classes in UML Fundamentals ⇨192

Interface classes are abstract definitions of purely functional interfaces.

- They do not define any attributes or associations.
- They have no instances.
- They define a set of abstract operations.
- They often define preconditions and postconditions, invariants and possible exceptions for these operations.

- They are an important aid for dividing software development between different teams (design by contract).
- They often have the same names as entity and control classes and are then generally implemented by these classes.

Interface classes should also be included in analysis and design models, unless they have an exclusively technical motivation or can be derived fully automatically.

2.14.4 «boundary» (interface object)

While interface classes represent an abstract definition, interface objects are special concrete objects that supply a special view of a set of other objects.

They represent a compilation of properties of other objects that are frequently required in common or that would otherwise have to be distributed over a large number of individual objects.

Design pattern façade ⇨57

The motivation for this is to shield and hide the structural connections and dependencies of a set of (entity and control) classes with respect to other classes. This allows one to achieve a better separation of the various areas of a large model. In this sense, interface objects specify facades.

Interface objects:

- have attributes that are almost all derived or which may be derived. Insofar as they contain attributes, then they are only for the intermediate storage of entity attributes or control results, e.g. for performance reasons;
- are not persistent;
- do not actually describe any business processes, i.e. they do not contain any domain-specific logic;
- do not actually have any operations of their own but simply delegate operation calls. Sometimes the operations of interface objects represent simple combinations of several external operations. However, this often involves including domain-specific logic and should therefore be avoided. Control classes are more suitable for this purpose;
- do not actually have any states;
- are usually *singletons*, i.e. in contrast to interface classes they are concrete classes for interface objects.

Design pattern singleton ⇨57

An example is *CustomerView* (as a summary of *Customer, Customer.Addresses, Customer.BankDetails*, etc.).

2.14.5 «type»

Types define a set of operations and attributes. Other elements conform to the type if they possess the properties defined by the type. Like interfaces, types are abstract definitions, but they can also contain attributes and relationships (e.g. associations).

Types are used for the abstract specification of structural interfaces.

- They generally define attributes and abstract operations.
- They have associations to other types.
- They often have the same names as entity classes and are then generally implemented by these classes.
- They describe the externally visible structure model of components as part of type models.
- Analysis models often consist predominantly of types.
- They are suitable for describing dynamic object roles.

They should be included in class models. Particularly in the case of component-oriented software development, they should be included in component-specific class models (type models). Examples are *Person*, *PolicyHolder*, *Contributor*, etc.

2.14.6 «primitive»

Primitive classes:

- represent elementary classes of the programming language being used, e.g. *integer*, *string*, etc.;
- represent standard classes of the frameworks being used, e.g. *Collection*, *Hashtable*, etc.;
- represent self-developed domain-specific neutral standard classes, such as *CustomerNo*, *Term*, *Period*, *Money*, etc.;
- are usually not persistent, i.e. they may persist as part of entity classes for example, but they do not possess any autonomous persistence mechanisms;
- possess a small number of attributes, e.g. *Money* has the attributes *amount* and *currency* (see Table 2.2);
- generally possess a few simple operations for reading and writing, e.g. *set(amount, currency)*;
- sometimes possess some simple calculation functions, e.g. *getTermIn Months():Integer* in the class *Period*;

▓ may possibly have operations for converting to other primitives, e.g. *asString():String* in the class *Date*.

Table 2.2 Primitive class

«primitive» Money
amount: Double currency: Currency
convertTo(otherCurrency): Money getAmount(): Double getCurrency(): Currency setAmount(amount: Double) setCurrency(currency: Currency)

Primitive classes appear in the declaration of attributes, but they are not represented as classes in the class model. In the same way, there are usually no associations to or from primitive classes.

2.14.7 «enumeration»

Enumerations are sets of values that can be expressed as lists, e.g. *MaritalStatus* = {*single, married, divorced, widowed*} (*see* Table 2.3) or *Sex* = {*male, female*}. Enumerations:

● are generally configurable, i.e. they are stored in corresponding key tables and can be modified dynamically. Typically, they are modified only rarely;

Primitive classes ⇨54

● are used almost exclusively in the declaration of attributes. These save only the reference to a specific value. In this respect they are treated like primitive classes;

● often have a limited validity in terms of time, i.e. are used historically. For example, the value *East German* in the enumeration *Nationality* would only be used for cases up to 1990;

● generally have a freely configurable sequence of individual values, which is then visible in selection lists, etc. For example, the individual values of the enumeration *MaritalStatus* are not arranged alphabetically, but logically (see above);

● sometimes consist of only a single value that is treated as an enumeration for reasons of simplicity, i.e. they represent a domain-specific constant, for example *AgeOfMajority = 18*.

LIVERPOOL
JOHN MOORES UNIVERSITY
AVRIL ROBARTS LRC
TEL. 0151 231 4022

Table 2.3 Enumeration

«enumeration» MaritalStatus
single married cohabiting divorced widowed
asString(): String

2.14.8 «structure»

Data structures are not generally used within object-oriented (sub)systems but are employed for exchanging data with other systems or subsystems. In order to define such data exchange formats, classes may be used with the stereotype «structure».

type ⇨54

They contain only attribute definitions and no operations. In this respect they are similar to types without operations.

The structure definitions for XML-based data can also be derived from these structure definitions.

2.15 Design Patterns

Synopsis

■ Design patterns are tried and tested ideas for solving recurring design problems.

They are, however, not readily coded solutions, but describe the solution path. Design patterns exist for design problems of all sizes:

● Architecture patterns describe solutions to problems with coarse design, such as the structure of a multi-layer architecture.

Architecture patterns

● (Normal) design patterns describe solutions to problems with fine-grained design; examples follow below. They are independent of a specific programming language or environment.

Idioms

● Idioms (from the Greek for "characteristic, peculiarity") are programming language-specific solution descriptions.

See framework ⇨117

Many of the design patterns known today were originally implemented in Smalltalk, i.e. they were idioms. After undergoing a thorough abstraction process, they have become language-neutral design patterns.

Below we briefly list some design patterns. There is no particular, finished theory behind the concept of design pattern; instead, there are various authors who have systematically collected and published such ideas for solutions. For a detailed discussion of design patterns, we recommend Gamma *et al.*, 1995.

Examples

Adapter. An adapter provides an existing class with a new interface. This can be sensible, for example, if an existing class is to be used but its interface in the existing form does not fit in with the remaining implementation.

Bridge. A bridge separates the interface of a class from its implementation, thus achieving a higher degree of independence from a concrete (for example platform-specific) implementation.

Decorator. The decorator pattern allows the properties of a concrete object to be dynamically changed and extended independently of its class.

Façade. A façade is used to give a set of classes, a subsystem, or a class category a single simple interface that shields it against the complexity of the subsystem classes.

Singleton. A singleton is a class of which globally there is only one instance. While normally you can generate as many instances of a class as you like, singletons contain mechanisms that prevent this.

Memento. The memento pattern shows a simple way to restore previous states of objects, for example for an implementation of undo functions.

Observer. This pattern describes a mechanism that allows all other objects that depend on a given object to be informed about changes in its state (for example changes of attributes).

Visitor. The visitor pattern shows how an iterative operation can be performed on a set of objects without the involved objects having to know who is iterating over them and how.

See design pattern notation ⇨ 219

Composite. The composite pattern (Fig. 2.33) is used to create (assemble) tree-like aggregations which can be used equally as individual objects and as a combination of objects. We will explain this in more detail with the aid of a couple of illustrations.

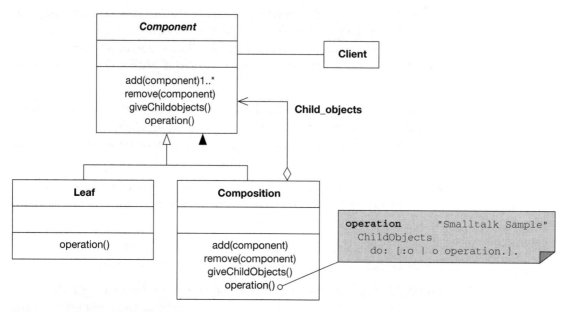

Figure 2.33   Composite design pattern

GeomFigure ⇨28f.

Assuming that *Leaf* was the *GeomFigure* class known from the previous examples (with its subclasses *Circle*, *Triangle*, and *Rectangle*), this structural pattern could be used to build groups of geometric figures (Fig. 2.34).

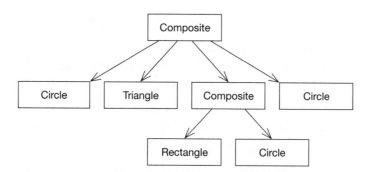

Figure 2.34   Tree-like structure of composite instances

2.16 Components

Synopsis

▪ A distinction should be made between component definitions and component instances.

- In contrast to classes, components should in principle be exchangeable without any further intervention.

- Components communicate as far as possible by standardized, primitive protocols (factory, observer and object interfaces).

Component is a frequently used but not clearly defined term. According to the UML, a component is an executable software module with its own identity and defined interfaces, i.e. it is defined in very general and abstract terms. It might just as well be an SAP system as an MS Word macro. On the other hand, in connection with popular component technologies such as Enterprise Java Beans, the definition is very concrete and technology-specific. In this book the term *component* is defined in accordance with EJB.

First of all, a distinction should be made between component definitions (e.g. "Person") and component instances (e.g. "Gabby Goldsmith") – similar to classes and objects. A component (definition) consists of one or more classes and has defined interfaces. A component instance, like an object, has its own identity. The most important difference between components and classes/objects, however, is that components should be exchangeable. In the same way that on your PC you can, for instance, replace one network card with another without having to make any further modifications to the PC, the idea is that it should also be possible to exchange software components. A component from manufacturer XY could simply be replaced with one from manufacturer Z. In theory at least.

In order to reach this goal, however, various preconditions must be fulfilled:

- The interfaces must be technically compatible (cf. hardware: voltage, clock speed, standardized bus protocol, etc.).

- The interfaces must be compatible on a domain-specific level (cf. hardware: graphics modes on graphics cards, etc.).

- The dependencies between the various components must be kept to a minimum (cf. hardware: no soldering iron necessary, when the graphics card is exchanged the existing mouse and keyboard can still be used, etc.).

This has the following consequences for software components:

- The interfaces of a component should, as far as possible, contain only primitive types (Integer, String, etc.).

- Appropriate domain-specific standards are required for domain-specific compatibility.

- Associations between components should, as far as possible, be replaced by messaging and observation mechanisms.

Object identity ⇨22

Independent of their attribute values, objects have a unique identity (object ID), which associations generally rely upon. In order to minimize the resulting (technical) dependencies between components, relationships can be implemented between component instances, for example, while only the domain-specific key (e.g. customer number) is stored as the reference. This means that a relationship continues to be present on a domain-specific level, but on a technical level a greater degree of independence has been achieved. Communication between the components is, however, not as straightforward as before, since they can no longer be addressed directly but must first be explicitly loaded by means of the domain-specific key.

Observer pattern⇨57

Moreover, the message exchange is implemented – as far as possible – on an anonymous level with the aid of so-called observer mechanisms. This type of communication functions in such a way that one instance sends the others the message *addListener()*, which means something like "please inform me if you have changed." An instance therefore subscribes to modification messages. As soon as the instance in question changes, it sends a message to all subscribers telling them that it has changed. The subscribers can then turn to the modified instance and query the details, e.g. modified data, etc.

This type of communication between components is interesting because it does not imply any significant dependencies. The instances only administer a list of subscribers, but it is completely irrelevant to them who the subscribers are. It is therefore an anonymous type of communication. Only when the subscribing objects require details do domain-specific dependencies arise. In order to keep this to a minimum, i.e. to restrict it to the unavoidable domain-specific level, one should try here (in the so-called object interface) as far as possible to use only primitive types, or structures of primitive types (records, structs, XML data, or similar).

See UML Fundamentals Components ⇨217

Components therefore typically have three different types of interface (Fig. 2.35):

- an interface for generating or loading instances, for example with the aid of a domain-specific key. In EJB this would typically be called *findByKey()*;
- an interface that defines the observation and messaging services;
- a domain-specific interface (object interface).

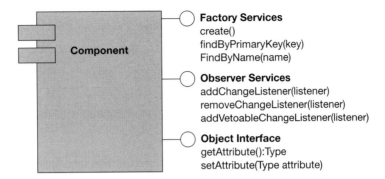

Figure 2.35 Principal interfaces of a component

Suggested Reading

1 Booch, G., Rumbaugh, J., Jacobson, I. (1998) *The Unified Modeling Language User Guide*, Addison-Wesley.

2. Rumbaugh, J., Jacobson, I., Booch, G. (1999) *The Unified Modeling Language Reference Manual*, Addison-Wesley.

3. Jacobson, I., Booch, G., Rumbaugh, J. (1998) *The Unified Software Development Process*, Addison-Wesley.

4. Gamma, E., Helm, R., Johnson, R., Vlissides, J. (1995) *Design Patterns: Elements of Reusable Object-Oriented Software*, Addison-Wesley.

5. Buschmann, F., Meunier, R., Rohnert, H., Sommerlad, P., Stal, M. (1996) *Pattern-Oriented Software Architecture: A System of Patterns*, Wiley.

6. Larman, C. (1997) *Applying UML and Patterns, An Introduction to Object-Oriented Analysis and Design*, Prentice Hall.

chapter 3

Analysis

It is not precision that counts, but the fertility
of the concepts.

Werner Heisenberg

This chapter demonstrares and discusses object-oriented analysis with
the aid of an example, and shows the application of the individual
methodological concepts. Their detailed description in Chapter 5 on UML
Fundamentals is referred to using page cross-references.

Introduction 64

Developing the System Idea and Objective 64

Identifying Stakeholders 65

Identifying Business Processes 68

Identifying Stakeholders' Interests 70

Identifying Business Use Cases 72

Describing the Essence of Use Cases 76

Identifying System Use Cases 82

Collecting and Studying Materials 87

Describing the Requirements 89

Identifying Business Classes 92

Creating a Technical Dictionary 94

Developing a Use Case Process Model 99

Describing the System Interface 104

Explorative Interface Prototyping 108

3.1 Introduction

This chapter illustrates and explains object-oriented analysis with the aid of one coherent example. The UML elements and concepts used in this description are, however, explained only rudimentarily. The emphasis lies on the demonstration of their application. Detailed descriptions of the individual UML concepts can be found in Chapter 5 (⇨161), to which page cross-references are made.

This chapter describes the individual activities of object-oriented analysis in a sequential order. In practice, many of these activities are carried out in parallel, in a different order or even several times over, which cannot be properly represented in a book. Therefore, the order of activities shown here is intended above all to be helpful and instructive, but is not meant to be dogmatic.

3.2 Developing the System Idea and Objective

Synopsis

- Formulate the system idea in writing in around 5–20 sentences.

☑ 3.2.1

☑ 3.2.2

The development of a system begins by identifying the basic objective and "system idea." What is the system intended to achieve? Usually, you start with nothing more than vague ideas and visions, expressions of intent and naive wishes. Formulate the system idea in writing on about half a page – just the act of writing this down sets in motion the process of goal identification and concretization.

The example used in this book is based on the following idea.[1]

System idea

In a car rental company, vehicle reservations, rentals, and billing are to be supported by an information system.

The new system should provide all functions directly related to handling customers. These include customer information, management of core data (addresses, bank details, and so on), reservations, vehicle rental, and customer billing.

Indirect areas and those remote from business partners, such as internal accounting, tariff and product planning, vehicle transfer and disposition, are not part of the system.

---

[1] The example was originally developed for training purposes and does not stem from a real project. Readers who have developed such a system are kindly asked to overlook simplifications and inaccuracies where they occur.

Checklist:

☑ 3.2.1: Does the description of the system idea cover about half a page?

☑ 3.2.2: Does the system idea describe what the system to be developed is intended to achieve?

3.3 Identifying Stakeholders

Stakeholder elicitation

Synopsis

■ Identify the stakeholders.

■ Identify the project contact partners.

■ Divide the contact partners into domain experts, people responsible for the requirements on the system, and people affected by the system.

Identify the stakeholders. Even before determining the requirements on the system to be created, you should first try to find out who might be placing these requirements on the system.

Viewpoint Resolution

In this respect you should try to identify all the involved parties who will be directly or indirectly affected by the system (or project) to be developed or by whom the system (or project) will be affected. These are the people or organizational units which may wish to formulate specific expectations of and requirements on the system to be created. The indirectly affected people are those who will not actually have any direct contact with the system, but who are involved in the commercial area or the business that is to be supported by the system.

Stakeholders might be, for example:

Stakeholders are people who are affected by the system or product.

☑ 3.3.1

- users of the system;
- technical department;
- accounts department;
- clients, financial backers, management, board of directors;
- legislators, standards;
- customers;
- system administrators, service personnel, training personnel, hotline, support;
- system developers, system maintenance personnel;
- buyers of the system;
- marketing, sales;
- project opponents and supporters. (See Fig. 3.1.)

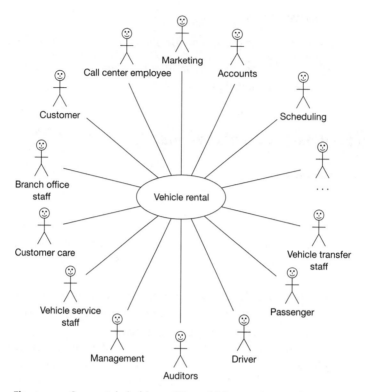

Figure 3.1   Some stakeholders of the vehicle rental example

Some of the stakeholders are known from the start, since they are obvious or have been named as contact partners for the project, often for example the client and the representatives of the technical department. You can discover the other stakeholders by holding conversations and interviews with the stakeholders you already know. General knowledge, common sense, and a little industry knowledge will also help you quickly identify the most important stakeholders.

If you cannot determine all the stakeholders of a system, it becomes more probable that you will also fail to recognize all the requirements on the system, or at least not recognize them early enough. Many errors and defects that occur immediately after the introduction of a system can be traced back to forgotten stakeholders. After the introduction of the system, these stakeholders come into contact with the system in some way, directly or indirectly, and notice that their requirements were either not properly taken into account or were ignored.

Identify the project contact partners. You must first determine the actual contact partners so that the application domain can be analyzed.

Domain experts

When proceeding in the project, it is sensible to differentiate the contact partners in terms of whether they are novice users, expert users, application domain experts, or responsible management staff, and what decision-making power they have with regard to agreeing on the requirements.

☑ 3.3.2

Divide the contact partners into:

- **Domain experts**, i.e. people who are experts in the sphere of application, who can help you to understand the application domain, and who are qualified to answer technical questions. The domain experts are also often, but not always, the subsequent users of the system.

- **People responsible for the requirements on the system**, i.e. people who are authorized to define the requirements on the new system and/or to agree them with you. These people are often not domain experts, but commonly base their decisions on the opinions of domain experts and people affected by the system.

- **People affected by the system**, i.e. people who will be directly concerned by the finished system, e.g. the subsequent users. They are also called (system) actors.

The quality of the analysis results is highly influenced by these contact partners, which is why communication with these people is initially a priority. The users need to support these results; otherwise, the finished application system will have to fight against acceptance problems and resistance.

Discussion with users and domain experts can be carried out independently – this allows for a comparison of the presented and recognized facts. In case of deviations, further data needs to be gathered. If required, all people involved need to meet and discuss the issues, to reach a consensus or clarify the contradictions.

For the example used in this book, the contact partners in Table 3.1, among others, can be identified:

Table 3.1 Contact partners in the example

People affected by the system	Actual contact partners
Call center staff	Mrs. Gladstone Mr. Walters Mrs. Rich
Branch office	Mr. Boon Mr. Naughtie Mr. Lamb
Vehicle service	Mr. Powers
Domain experts	**Actual contact partners**
Reservation	Mrs. Gladstone
Information	Mrs. Gladstone
Branch office	Dr. Newman (branch office manager)
Managers	**Actual contact partners**
Branch office manager	Dr. Newman
Call center manager	Mrs. Rich

Checklist:

☑ 3.3.1: Has a list of actual contact partners been created for each of the stakeholder categories: *users, technical department, client/management/financial backer, legislators/standards, customers, administration/service/training/ hotline, developers, buyers, marketing/sales, project opponents/supporters*?

☑ 3.3.2: Has it been determined whether each contact partner is a domain expert, a person responsible for the requirements on the system, or a person affected by the system?

3.4 Identifying Business Processes

Synopsis

- Identify the business processes that the system is to support or in which it is integrated.

- Visualize the system idea with the aid of a use case diagram.

- Describe, as abstractly as possible, the basic domain-specific actors or the actors involved in the business process.

- Describe the identified business processes in abstract terms, using an activity diagram in each case.

Definition of
business
process ⇨279

A business process is a combination of organizationally potentially distributed, but technically related activities needed to process a commercial event (for example a concrete application form) in a result-oriented fashion. The activities of a business process are usually chronologically and logically related to each other. A commercial event is usually triggered by an event (for example receipt of an application form) and has at least one visible domain-specific result (e.g. a contract).

In contrast to a business process, a use case always describes a chronologically continuous interaction of one or more actors with a system. A business process can therefore consist of a set of use cases.

In which business processes is the system to be integrated, or which business processes must it support? Which actors are involved in it? These questions must now be answered at the most abstract level possible. In many cases the system idea can provide important clues, so that this step can also be seen as a visualization and organization of the system idea.

☑ 3.4.1

Business processes are marked as use cases with the stereotype «workflow» (Fig. 3.2) and are described in more detail with a simple flowchart (UML activity diagram) (or alternatively by an event-controlled process chain (EPC), e.g. with the ARIS toolset).

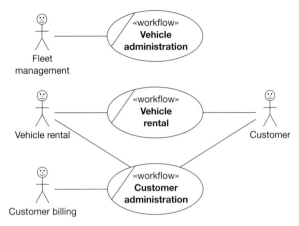

Figure 3.2   Important business processes of the vehicle rental company marked as UML use cases

☑ 3.4.2

UML Fundamentals –
Activity Program ⇨250

At this point the use cases are reduced to the intentions of the external commercial actors and described as abstractly as possible. How the business will actually be handled, e.g. by a call center or over the Internet, is not mentioned at first.

The activity diagram of the *Vehicle Reservation* business process shows the basic time sequence and its subdivision into individual steps (Fig. 3.3). Between these steps there are generally quite large time intervals (for example between the reservation (2) and the handover(3)) or various actors, organizational units, or other systems are involved (for example in billing (6) and making the vehicle ready for rental (7)). The individual steps in the business process are possible use cases, which we will look at in more detail later.

Checklist:

☑ 3.4.1:   Has each business process been described in more detail with a flow-chart (e.g. UML activity diagram)?

☑ 3.4.2:   Have the use cases been described as abstractly as possible and reduced to the commercial intentions of the external actors?

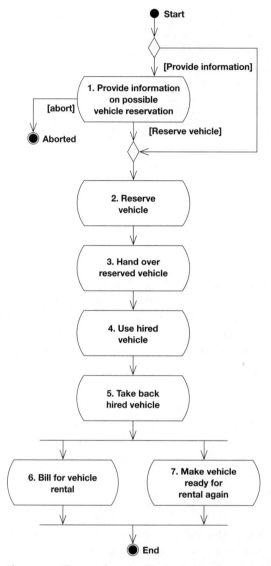

Figure 3.3   The rental reservation business process represented as a UML activity diagram

3.5   Identifying Stakeholders' Interests

Synopsis

- Describe the goals and interests of the individual stakeholders.
- Identify existing problems and weak points from the point of view of the stakeholders.
- Describe the important required system properties from the point of view of the stakeholders.

Describe the interests of the individual stakeholders

You should then try to find out what view the individual stakeholders have of the system, or probably will have in the future. Moreover, you should work out their interests and basic requirements with regard to the system or project that is about to be created.

Different stakeholders have different interests in the system or the software development project. These interests may complement or contradict each other and may not always be obvious. In this connection you should differentiate between the actual, possibly tacit interests of individual people, the interests of the organizational unit to which they belong, and the interests that are expressed officially and publicly.

The representatives of a technical department, whose jobs might be lost following the introduction of the new system, may have an interest in sabotaging the creation of the new system. Others might have an interest in receiving the best possible system in order to reduce their excessive workload or free themselves of tiresome routine activities.

Describe, insofar as you know them, the interests and goals of all the stakeholders (or at least those of all the important stakeholders). To do this, you must ask the stakeholders for this information, or obtain it in some other manner.

Example:

Political requirements

☑ 3.5.1

Call center staff In the opinion of the call center staff the existing system does not adequately support their work, which means they often cannot give customers the level of service they would like.

There are fears that an increase in direct Internet reservations will threaten jobs in the call center.

The call center staff expect the new system to enable them to give customers a better and more attractive service than is possible with an Internet reservation.

Call center management They see it as a problem that the existing system is too slow during peak times.

They see it as a problem that even small deviations from the normal reservation process cannot be properly supported by the existing system, which leads to a considerable amount of time being wasted.

They expect that the new system will reduce the cost per reservation by at least 30% on average.

Checklist:

☑ 3.5.1: Have the interests and goals of all the important stakeholders and contact partners been determined and documented?

3.6 Identifying Business Use Cases

Synopsis

- Identify the business use cases.
- Identify the start and end of use cases with the aid of triggers and results.
- Identify the business use cases to be excluded.

After determining the stakeholders and their interests, you can start identifying and describing the requirements on the system with the aid of use cases.

Identify the business use cases

Definition

A use case describes in natural language a consistent, goal-oriented, chronologically continuous sequence of activities (generally) of an actor, which produces a result of domain-specific value visible to the actor.

What is a business use case?

We use the term "business use case" (or "business case" for short) to designate an abstract form of use case that is independent of the concrete possibilities and requirements for its (IT-related) implementation. Take, for example, the business use case *Reserve vehicle*. This can actually be implemented in several ways, e.g. *Reserve vehicle by phone*, *Reserve vehicle on the Internet*, *Reserve vehicle on site*. These concrete use cases very probably have different processes, requirements, and other details, so should be described separately. We are not concerned with that just yet, we want only to get an overview of the use cases and not yet think about how they can be implemented in practice. We should therefore choose the most general and abstract names possible for business use cases.

Fundamentals ⇨161

Business cases for our example (*see* Fig. 3.4) would be:

- Provide information on possible vehicle reservations.
- Reserve vehicle.
- Complete vehicle rental contract (hand over vehicle).
- Take vehicle back.
- Customer billing.

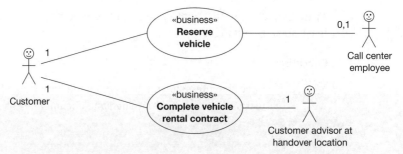

Figure 3.4 Examples of business use cases and their actors

☑ 3.6.1

A use case describes the desired external system behavior from the point of view of the user and thus the requirements that the system should fulfill. It is a description of *what* the system must do, not of *how* it should do it.

What,
not *how*

The size or scope of a use case can be specified relatively precisely. A use case should describe what a user does at a particular time on an application system (e.g. a reservation system) to conclude a commercial event (e.g. the reservation of a Lincoln for Mr. Smith) within a business process.

Identify the triggers and results of the use cases

You must do this so that you can accurately determine where they start and where they end. If you cannot find any clear indications of this, it is likely that you have not yet gone into the domain-specific context in sufficient depth.

☑ 3.6.2

For each business case you should include the following details:

- name;
- short description (1–20 lines of free text);
- actor(s);
- trigger;
- result(s).

Table 3.2 shows two examples:

Table 3.2 Business use case examples

Name:	Reserve vehicle «business»
Short description:	A customer reserves a vehicle for a defined period
Actors:	Customer
Trigger:	Customer would like to reserve a vehicle
Results:	Vehicle reservation, reservation confirmation
Name:	Complete vehicle rental contract «business»
Short description:	A reserved vehicle is handed over to a customer for his/her use
Actors:	Customer, branch office employees
Trigger:	Customer would like to pick up a reserved vehicle
Results:	Rental contract was completed, vehicle keys were handed over

If you are uncertain whether you have correctly specified the actors in the business use case, do not spend too long dwelling on your doubts. In the above use case *Hand over reserved vehicle*, for example, the actor *branch office employees* is doubtful, since the vehicle keys could perhaps also be handed over automatically by a machine. The 80% solution and individual areas of fuzziness can however usually be justified, since it is very probable that these will be clarified during the subsequent development process.

Identify the use cases to be excluded

There are also use cases that cannot or do not need to be supported by the system at all. For example, the use case *Use rented vehicle.* The actor here is the customer or driver of the vehicle. This use case is not relevant to the rental company, since it is handled entirely by the driver and the rental company has no need of system support at this point. It might perhaps be conceivable that the current position of the vehicle could be monitored by satellite navigation, or the current usage data (miles driven, etc.) could be transmitted electronically.

{excluded}
Tagged values ⇨207

The parts of the business process that are not to be supported by the system are also described in this abbreviated form, but are explicitly identified as use cases to be excluded by means of the tagged value {excluded} (*see* Table 3.3). Explicitly excluding the use case *Use rented vehicle* ensures that there are no misunderstandings at this point with regard to the scope of the project.

Table 3.3 Excluded use cases

Name:	Use rented vehicle «business»{excluded}
Short description:	The customer uses the vehicle handed over to him/her within the scope of the rental contract
Actors:	Customer
Trigger:	Customer accepts vehicle keys
Results:	Vehicle was used in accordance with the rental contract

Where does a use case start and where does it end?

This can generally be defined quite clearly. At the start there is always a commercial trigger, a commercial event. For example, a customer would like to conclude a contract. Or a customer would like some information. Or the marketing department would like a statistical evaluation of reservations. On the other hand, activities such as *Enter customer number*, *Save contract*, and so forth are not commercial triggers but steps in a use case.

What is "commercial value"?

At the end of the use case a result has been produced that has "commercial value." That may sound a little stilted, but it describes it very aptly. A commercial result is, for example, a vehicle reservation, a letter to the customer, a business management evaluation, etc. On the other hand, results such as *Contract saved, Customer found/identified* do not have any direct commercial value. If a customer number is used to find (identify) a customer in the system, that is certainly a result, but it does not yet have any commercial value – something still needs to be done with this customer. Perhaps they will be contacted by telephone to clarify a particular situation, or they might be sent a letter – searching for the customer is only an intermediate step in this and therefore does not count as a result that is suitable for a use case.

☑ 3.6.3

No functional
subdivision, no
flowcharts ⇨170

☑ 3.6.4

A process should be subdivided into several use cases if it is clearly interrupted at a given moment, or if clearly identifiable parts are handled by different people.

Use cases are not suitable for functional subdivision, i.e. a use case is not an individual step, it does not describe an individual operation or transaction (e.g. "Print contract," "Generate customer number," etc.) but the largest possible chronologically related process (e.g. "Create new customer").

A use case describes a process. A use case *diagram*, however, is not a process description. A use case diagram does not define any process sequence, etc. There are other ways of doing this, e.g. activity diagrams.

Write scenarios

In the description of their tasks and activities, users are induced by the system analyst's questions to look at their work from a different, less everyday perspective. They are required to report both on (interesting and eventful) peculiarities and exceptions, as well as routine matters of course.

Staff in the application area sometimes have difficulties in describing their activity in an abstract or generalized way. In any case, they should not always be expected to. It is much easier for them to describe their work with the aid of concrete examples.

Summarizing or protocoling the scenarios presented by the users in full length or even in direct speech – more or less as shown below – would obviously involve a lot of work:

☹ *"When the customer comes back and returns the key and the papers, I load in the customer data and check the correspondence with the contract, that is, the items that belong to it and the terms, schedules, and such like, which were agreed. When everything is confirmed, I fill in the return protocol, enter mileage, fuel level, and other notes if needed, and process the invoice."*

Instead, it is usually sufficient to note down such statements by keywords and in a compressed form:

Vehicle return

Customer returns vehicle, keys, and documents.

Consult contract: are items returned completely and have schedules and other conditions been adhered to?

Fill in return protocol: mileage, fuel level, notes.

Then process invoice.

If your users have the time and the opportunity, ask them to come up with scenarios like this (either written out in full or in keywords). Incidentally, this is a standard technique in Extreme Programming (XP), where these scenarios are called *stories*.

Checklist:

☑ 3.6.1: Does the use case describe *what* the system should do, but not yet *how* it should actually do it?

☑ 3.6.2: Have name, short description, actors, trigger and results been noted for each use case?

☑ 3.6.3: Does each use case describe a chronologically continuous and functionally undivided process?

☑ 3.6.4: Have you avoided using a use case diagram to define a process sequence?

☑ 3.6.5: Are all the business use cases stored in their own branch of the package model?

3.7 Describing the Essence of Use Cases

Synopsis

- Identify and describe the commercial essence of all business use cases, i.e. the actual commercial intentions in abstract, technology-independent terms.
- Divide the requirements into "probably stable" and "probably variable."
- For each business use case define the trigger, preconditions, and incoming information.
- For each business use case define the results, postconditions, and outgoing information.
- With each use case describe only a single coherent domain-specific situation, i.e. if necessary divide them up and use «include» and «extend» relationships to unlink them.

Essential use cases
⇨163

Before use cases are concretized and detailed in terms of their content, it is important to work out the actual business purpose in each case. Many details which come to light later relate to very concrete basic conditions and technological realities. From a long-term perspective, these are rarely stable.

Distinguish the probably stable from the probably variable requirements ...

Distinguish the probably stable from the probably variable requirements

In our vehicle rental example the *Reserve vehicle* use case will probably exist for a long time, since it represents a very central aspect of the company's business. However, what can and probably will change over the course of the years is the manner in which this business is actually conducted. For many years vehicles have been predominantly reserved by telephone, but with the spread of the Internet a new channel has been added. The technologies and processes linked to the different variants are sometimes stable only for a few years.

... in order to design software that is easy to expand in the long term.

To avoid having to redesign our software from scratch, or at least modify large parts of it, every time a new technological variant comes on the scene, suitable measures should be taken to make the software easier to adapt at a later stage. The key point in this respect is to differentiate the probably stable elements from those that are probably variable and unstable. It is not always easy to anticipate which parts of the system will be affected by future changes, but it is often possible to identify those elements for which there is a significant probability that they will change.

Determine the actual commercial intention

You can differentiate the probably stable elements from those that are probably unstable by systematically determining the commercial essence. To do this you should investigate each individual use case to establish which individual steps in the process are so essential to the business that they will probably never change. Alternatively, you can break down a use case into individual steps that each represent the actual commercial intention.

A simple example of this: within the *Reserve vehicle* use case it must be clarified on each occasion for whom a vehicle is to be reserved, i.e. it must be determined who the customer is. In the case of a reservation by phone the customer will perhaps give their name and customer number, which is sufficient to identify them.

In the case of an Internet reservation this route is probably not practical, since the customer number and name are insufficiently protected and too easy to misuse. With a phone reservation, control questions could be asked or the caller could be identified by their phone number. With the Internet variant it would probably be more advisable to have customers enter a secret number (PIN).

Imagine various concrete business possibilities...

For the Internet variant the sequence of activities might, for example, look like this:

1. Enter customer number and PIN.

2. Enter desired vehicle type.

3. Enter reservation period.

4. ...

For the variant in which a customer wishes to reserve a vehicle directly at a rental location, step 1 would probably be inappropriate, since in this case the customer could identify themselves using a customer card:

... determine what commercial aspects they have in common...

1. Customer presents their customer card.

2. The employee swipes the customer card through the card reader, thus reading the customer number from the card. If the card is damaged and

cannot be read by the device, the employee manually enters the customer number on the card into the system.

3. ...

... and look for abstract names that match the commercial intention.

Working out the business essence means recognizing what the actual commercial intention is. For a rental company it is commercially irrelevant whether the customer is identified by means of a PIN or a customer card. In our example the actual commercial intention is to find out who the customer is and whether they really are this person. In both cases the customer's identity is established using the customer number. Whether they really are this person is determined in one case by a secret number, and in the other by the possession of a customer card. Finding the commercial essence means finding an abstract designation that matches the actual intention. In our example a possible formulation for the essence might be *Identify customer*.

Essence descriptions

These are mostly very abstract and general formulations. Essential use cases are therefore not really suitable to be used as the basis for implementing a concrete system. On the other hand they do help us to find the core of a business, which allows us to develop systems that are easier to adapt.

In most cases it takes only a few minutes to determine the essence of a use case. After that, we concentrate once more on the practical, concrete situations. These few minutes, however, are well worth it, since they lead to a better structuring of the model.

The essence description is the most compressed and most abstract form of a use case and provides a good overview of the problem area of the overall project.

Some essential use cases are presented and described below for the vehicle rental example. An essential use case consists of a name, a few lines of short description, a list of all the preconditions, incoming data and events, all the postconditions and outgoing data, the actors involved, and a list of the essential activities, i.e. the steps in the process.

Names for actors and roles ⇨35, 164, 225

Essential use cases are very abstract descriptions and often also contain very abstract and sometimes rather clumsy sounding names, for example the actor *Reserver*. This is in the nature of things and is not a problem. A concrete reserver might be a *Call center employee* (in the case of a reservation by phone) or even the *Customer* themselves (in the case of an Internet reservation). The generic term that matches the role of the actor is *Reserver*.

Distinction between business use cases and essential use cases

Business use cases are a good basis for the development of essential use cases, since they are often very abstract already. Essential use cases, however, also describe a process sequence, i.e. the individual steps of the process reduced to its domain-specific essence, which is not the case with business use cases. (*See* Fig. 3.5.)

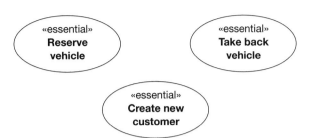

Figure 3.5   Use case diagram with essential use cases

Table 3.4   Essential use case (first version, which may be improved upon)

Name:	Reserve vehicle «essential»
Short description:	A vehicle is reserved for a customer for a defined period
Actors:	Reserver
Trigger:	Customer would like to reserve a vehicle
Preconditions:	
Incoming information:	Customer number and additional customer data, reservation wish
Results:	Reservation, reservation confirmation
Postconditions:	A vehicle was reserved for the customer
Process	1. Identify customer or create new customer
	2. Record reservation wish
	3. Check reservation possibility
	4. Reserve vehicle
	5. Confirm reservation

☑ 3.7.1

In terms of their content, use cases should be structured and delimited in such a way that they represent an individual business situation. In other words, if a use case describes various business situations that themselves might be considered independent use cases, then the use case should in fact be divided up.

In the example *Reserve vehicle* (Table 3.4), the first step in the process is called "Identify customer or create new customer." An independent use case is hiding behind the words "create new customer." It has a commercial trigger (a person would like to be a customer) and an independent result of commercial value (a new customer).

Trigger *Create new customer*

For the *Reserve vehicle* use case we should ask ourselves whether it is really necessary or sensible to branch from within *Reserve vehicle* to the *Creation of new customer*, or whether these two use cases can be unlinked. In the event of a new customer wishing to make a reservation, the use case *Create new customer* would run first, followed by *Reserve vehicle*. In this case we could change the *Reserve vehicle* use case and remove "create new customer" from the first step.

The improved process for the *Reserve vehicle* use case would then look like this:

Process
1. Identify customer
2. Record reservation wish
3. Check reservation possibility
4. Reserve vehicle
5. Confirm reservation

☑ 3.7.3

Check each step of the use case to see if it has a different trigger or result, and if necessary unlink the use cases. Even if it is not quite so easy to unlink them, they should nonetheless be described separately and connected to each other using «include» and «extend» relationships.

«include» and
«extend» ⇨170

The newly identified use case *Create new customer* might look like the example in Table 3.5.

Table 3.5 Essential use case *Create new customer*

Name:	Create new customer «essential»
Short description:	A prospect (a person) is to be created as a new customer
Actors:	Customer service, prospect
Trigger:	A prospect would like to order a service for which they must appear in the system as a customer, i.e. they must have customer status
Preconditions:	
Incoming information:	Customer data
Results:	Customer, confirmation of customer status
Postconditions:	The customer is informed of their customer number and their customer status is confirmed
Process	1. Check preconditions for creating new customer
	2. Record customer data
	3. Check completeness and plausibility of customer data
	4. Create new customer and assign customer number
	5. Confirm customer status to new customer and inform them of customer number

Another example of an essential use case can be seen in Table 3.6.

Table 3.6 Essential use case *Complete vehicle rental contract*

Name:	Complete vehicle rental contract «essential»
Short description:	A reserved vehicle is handed over to the customer at a rental location for their use
Actors:	Driver (as representative of the customer)
Trigger:	The driver would like to pick up a reserved vehicle at a rental location
Preconditions:	A vehicle has been reserved for the customer for the current time at the rental location

Table 3.6 *Continued*

Name:	Complete vehicle rental contract «essential»
Incoming information:	Reservation number Driver's data
Results:	A rental contract signed by the driver
Postconditions:	The driver was identified A rental contract was produced A concrete vehicle was handed over to the driver
Process	1. Identify reservation 2. Check driver's identity 3. Determine concrete vehicle 4. Complete rental contract 5. Hand over vehicle

Always formulate use cases from the point of view of the business operator.

☑ 3.7.2

Make sure that all the descriptions in use cases are formulated from the point of view of the business operator (i.e. the customer, the technical department, the company operating the system) and not from the point of view of their business partners (customers, suppliers, etc.). The following use case is called *Take back vehicle* (Table 3.7) because the business operator (the rental company) is taking the vehicle back. The formulation "Return vehicle" would describe the same situation from the point of view of the driver or customer. Use cases should, however, be described from the point of view of the person or organization that operates the system or the business that the system is designed to support.

Table 3.7 Essential use case *Take back vehicle*

Name:	Take back vehicle «essential»
Short description:	The customer returns a rented vehicle
Actors:	Driver (as representative of the customer)
Trigger:	The driver would like to return a vehicle to a rental location
Preconditions:	The vehicle to be taken back was previously handed over to the customer
Incoming information:	Vehicle Reservation number
Results:	A return protocol signed by the driver with data on vehicle usage and vehicle condition
Postconditions:	The vehicle was taken back
Process	1. Identify reservation 2. Take back vehicle 3. Record vehicle condition and usage data that is relevant for billing 4. Check adherence to contract 5. Acknowledge vehicle return and condition

Checklist:

☑ 3.7.1: Does each use case describe an individual, coherent business situation?

☑ 3.7.2: Is the language in each use case formulated from the point of view of the business operator?

☑ 3.7.3: Does each step of the use case also describe a coherent and unique situation in terms of triggers and results?

☑ 3.7.4: Does each use case describe only the domain-specific essence?

☑ 3.7.5: Are all essential use cases stored in their own branch of the package model?

3.8 Identifying System Use Cases

Synopsis

- Identify the concrete system use cases.
- If applicable, define abstract system use cases.

In the previous section we looked at some essence descriptions of use cases that described the core of a business process in a short, abstract form. As we did so, we did not concern ourselves with any concrete basic conditions, details, or technical aspects.

In this section we shall return to these essential use cases and look at them in more concrete terms. We shall now consider the concrete conditions and requirements, plus those arising from the technical architecture. A single business case will often produce several concrete system use cases. A system use case, furthermore, should describe only those processes that can be mapped on a single technically relevant system unit (e.g. hardware), i.e. processes that relate to more than one system or that run in part on existing external systems should be broken down into several system use cases.

We shall use the *Reserve vehicle* use case as an example. This abstract description will now be compared with the concrete business reality, which yields three concrete cases:

- A vehicle can be reserved by telephone via a call center.
- A vehicle can be reserved on site at a rental location.
- A vehicle can be reserved directly by the customer over the Internet (*see* Fig. 3.6).

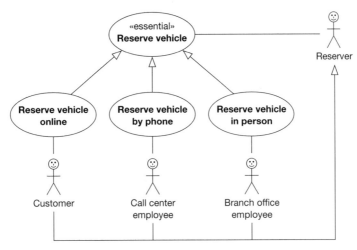

Figure 3.6   Concrete system use cases for *Reserve vehicle*

Differences between
the system use cases
for *Reserve vehicle*
⇨79

In all three cases the business essence is as described in the *Reserve vehicle* essential use case. There are, however, some differences in the details, which have already been mentioned in the discussion of the essential use cases.

First of all, we must create three new use cases that represent specializations of the *Reserve vehicle* essential use case. Figure 3.7 shows the connections.

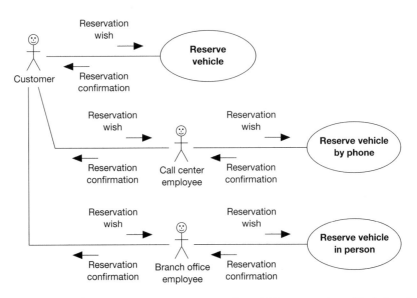

Figure 3.7   The concrete system use cases for vehicle reservation with their actors and the incoming and outgoing data

☑ 3.8.1

We should now describe the concrete expressions of each system use case. If the process and the requirements match the essential use case, they can simply be copied. From a practical point of view this means that the information in the use case header, i.e. name, short description, actors, trigger, results, and process steps, should now be formulated in concrete terms. You can refer to the abstract descriptions of the essence and use them as a template.

☑ 3.8.4

When the individual steps of the essence description are concretized, they will sometimes deviate from the original order. This is because the essence description is abstract and idealized to a certain degree. Moreover, the following further information is now added to the use case description:

- *Stakeholders*. What stakeholders require this use case?

cf. Identifying stakeholders ⇨65

- *Risk*. To what risks does the existence of this use case expose the project (e.g. cost overrun, delays, technical problems, organizational problems, etc.)? How high is the risk?

- *Importance*. How important is the use case (indispensable, important, useful)? What benefit does this use case produce?

- *Expense*. How great is the expense for implementing this use case (in person days)?

- *Stability*. How high is the probability that the use case will be subject to fundamental changes (high, medium, low)?

- *Time, urgency*. What is the deadline for implementing the use case (which iteration or milestone)? What is the most sensible time for implementing the use case (which iteration or milestone)? The individual steps should be formulated as simply and as briefly as possible.

Describe the process in a use case as abstractly and as briefly as possible, but as concretely and in as much detail as is necessary. This means for example that you should not list individual attributes (roof rack, tow bar, child seat, air conditioning, etc.) but refer to them in an abstract and generalized manner (*special features*).

Table 3.8 System use case *Reserve vehicle by phone*

Name:	Reserve vehicle by phone
Specialization of:	Reserve vehicle
Short description:	A vehicle is reserved by telephone for a customer for a defined period
Actors:	Caller, call center employee
Trigger:	The caller would like to reserve a vehicle
Preconditions:	
Incoming information:	Customer number, customer name, caller name, reservation wish
Results:	Reservation, reservation confirmation

Table 3.8   *Continued*

Name:	Reserve vehicle by phone
Postconditions:	A vehicle was reserved for the customer
Process	1. **Identify customer** The caller gives their name, customer number and (if different from the caller) the customer's name. The customer is looked for in the system by means of the customer number; the saved customer name must match the customer name given by the caller
	2. **Record reservation wish** The caller specifies their reservation wish, i.e. vehicle type, reservation period, pickup and return location, and special features
	3. **Check reservation possibility** The system determines whether the specified reservation wish can be fulfilled
	4. **Reserve vehicle** A vehicle is reserved for the customer as desired, and the customer is given a reservation number as confirmation. A concrete vehicle is not reserved, just an instance of the desired vehicle type
	5. **Confirm reservation** The reservation is confirmed to the caller verbally, and they are informed of the reservation number. If required, the reservation is also confirmed in writing, by fax or by e-mail

Here are a few comments on the example in Table 3.8.

- *Short description*: keep the description short, but write enough to ensure that this use case cannot be confused with any other (in this case: who (customer), what (vehicle, reserve), how (by phone)).

- *Actors*: "Caller" is specified as an actor, since it is only in the course of the use case that it can be determined whether the caller is in fact a customer.

- *Trigger*: you could perhaps also add "… and expresses this wish on the telephone," but this is clear from the context. The formulation "Customer/caller phones," on the other hand, would not be sufficient, since the reason for the telephone call is not clear – perhaps they would like to cancel a reservation.

- *Preconditions*: are not specified here, since the use case can occur at any time.

- *Incoming information*: keep it abstract ("reservation wish"); it is not a major problem if details are missing. This category is designed only for sketching the basic situation.

- *Postcondition*: just describe the desired successful case – everything else will follow from the subsequent flowcharts. Once again, keep it as brief as possible.

- *Identify customer*: this is where the caller becomes a customer. In formulating the step, try to bear in mind the facts that distinguish this type of customer identification from other types (e.g. Internet reservation). The concrete requirement that the customer number should be used for the search should be checked with the technical department – perhaps other search criteria are also allowed.

- *Check reservation possibility*: this formulation should perhaps be improved, since the result is not clear. Is the result yes/no? Should just one free vehicle be determined/proposed? Should a list be produced showing all available vehicles? Or should the number of available vehicles be determined? Must all the search criteria included in the reservation wish be met completely and exactly or are fuzzy matches allowed (partial period, similar vehicle type etc.)? You probably do not know these details yet, so note down these questions for your next meeting with the technical department!

- *Reserve vehicle*: maybe you would have called this step "Book vehicle," "Implement reservation," "Secure vehicle for customer," etc., but these are just paraphrases or synonyms of "Reserve vehicle." Do not be afraid to give this step an identical or similar name to the use case itself. Typically there is always a step in the process that has an identical or similar name to the use case, and all the other steps are used for preparation, context delimitation, testing, or evaluation.

Details relating to the risk, importance and expense have been omitted from the example for reasons of simplicity.

Checklist:

☑ 3.8.1: Have you described how each individual essential use case step will actually be implemented in the concrete use case?

☑ 3.8.2: Has each step been described as succinctly as possible, but in sufficient detail so that it cannot be confused with other steps (in similar use cases)?

☑ 3.8.3: Have you used uniform terms and formulations, and avoided synonymous paraphrases?

☑ 3.8.4: Have you specified the stakeholders requesting the use case, the available risk, the importance, the estimated expense, the expected stability, and the time/urgency for each use case?

☑ 3.8.5: Are all system use cases stored in their own branch of the package model?

3.9 Collecting and Studying Materials

Synopsis

- Identify and study materials, objects, examples, and samples from the application domain.
- Assess the materials and objects with regard to their usefulness and relevance for the current project (how up-to-date, reliable, correct, important, etc. are they?).

Materials and objects

Number the
materials

Analysis of the application domain also includes collection and study of materials and objects, at least if you are developing commercial information systems; for technical systems it may not be meaningful or possible. These materials include forms, correspondence, workplace descriptions etc. Ask for examples and samples. Number these documents so that it is easier for you to quote and reference them, e.g. "Material no. 112" or in abbreviated form "M-112." File all the materials in a folder.

In addition, the obvious working objects should be identified or named. These are, for example:

- customer data (M-37, M-38, M-40);
- contracts (M-112, M-117);
- invoices (M-7);
- reservation confirmations (M-67, M-68, M-69);
- vehicle return protocols (M-70);
- garage protocols (M-71);
- vehicle documentation (M-80);
- mobile accessories (child seats, roof racks);
- fixed accessories (air conditioning, tow bar, sun roof);
- vehicle keys;
- customer files;
- parking lots;
- tariff descriptions (M-8);
- contract conditions (M-9);
- and so forth.

Checklist:

☑ 3.9.1:   Have all the example and sample materials been uniquely identified, e.g. with a serial number?

☑ 3.9.2:   Have all the example and sample materials been scanned in, if possible (e.g. in pdf format)?

☑ 3.9.3:   Have all the materials that have not been scanned in been collected in a folder, if possible, or is there at least a note of where they can be found?

→ Mind maps

Now you are spending the whole day with the future users, looking over their shoulders, asking questions, discussing, and making notes with lots of question marks. Later, maybe even in a break, you are back at your desk, sitting there alone and trying to sort thoughts and notes, remembering, and clarifying the questions. One technique to allow you to give free rein to your thoughts is the so-called mind map.

order, and structure. Right-brain thinking is associated more with creativity, associations, fantasy, wholeness, chaos, and so on.

To use our brain potential efficiently, both brain aspects need to be activated and stimulated. The better we succeed in mobilizing both aspects at the same time, the stronger our thinking power is likely to be. To incite the right hemisphere to more activity,

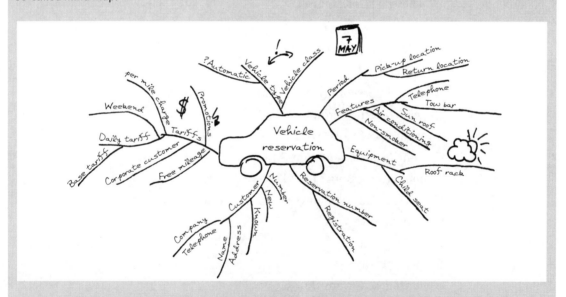

As we all know, our brain consists of two halves. The left hemisphere is associated with more rational aspects. Left-brain thinking can be described with the keywords linearity, precision,

we can use stimulation techniques which, by the way, are generally suited to fix and sort unstructured flowing thoughts. These techniques are quite handy, especially for requirement analysis.

►

So, what will stimulate our right hemisphere? First of all, it is useful to counteract our automatic logical thinking. When we look at a blank sheet of paper in portrait orientation, we view the upper left corner and think in lines that run from left to right. The ordering and sorting requirements of our left hemisphere are satisfied, but the right hemisphere is hardly stimulated – it is getting bored!

Now, if you rotate the paper to landscape orientation, you are inclined to look more towards the center. The horizontal lines are too long to be perceived as such at a single glance. We tend to think more from the middle out. This does not stop our left-brain thinking, but the mechanism is broken. There is something unusual about the sheet of paper; this stimulates our creativity.

A further trick consists of not producing completely formulated sentences but working only with keywords. Therefore not "Our brain consists of a left and a right hemisphere," but only "brain hemispheres." The missing information will nevertheless not get lost! Our creative hemisphere knows the association fields that surround these keywords in the respective context and restores them. The right hemisphere is stimulated and encouraged to produce associations. Reduction to keywords has the additional advantage of recalling quickly more extensive thoughts, facts, and the like.

Try to use small illustrations, drawn abbreviations, symbols, pictograms, colors (colored pens!), and variations and degrees in your form of writing: main concepts in upper case, subitems in lower case. You need not be a great artist; everyone can draw a simple symbol.

More about this subject can be found in the literature (in Beyer, 1993, for example). Make use of these sketches only to gather your associations and do without subsequent elaboration. (Special mind map editors are already available.) Possibilities for developing this technique can be found everywhere – just read a news item or a similar text and then jot down its contents as a mind map.

3.10 Describing the Requirements

Synopsis

- Identify and describe the functional requirements on the system.
- Identify and describe the usability requirements on the system.
- Identify and describe the performance requirements on the system.
- Identify and describe the reliability requirements on the system.
- Identify and describe other requirements on how the system can be modified, expanded, maintained, and administered (supportability requirements).

Requirements can be differentiated according to:

- degree of obligation;
- requirement type;
- degree of detail;
- priority.

Obligation can be divided into the following degrees:

- *Compulsory requirements* must be met without fail, or the product will be considered incomplete and might not be accepted by the client. Compulsory requirements contain phrases such as "The system *must* fulfill ..." or similar.

- *Optional requirements* (wishes) do not absolutely have to be fulfilled, for example if the related costs are considered excessive. Optional requirements contain phrases such as "The system *should* fulfill ..." or similar.

- *Intentions* are requirements that will probably have to be fulfilled in future, for example in later versions. It is important to know the intentions and take them into account to such an extent that subsequent upgrades and adaptations are easy to implement. Intentions contain phrases such as "It is intended that the system ..." or similar.

- *Suggestions* are not requirements but are ideas from stakeholders as to how existing requirements could be (better) solved. Suggestions are often formulated in the subjunctive ("could").

- *Comments* are also not requirements but are notes and explanations on requirements, to make them easier to understand.

The following types of requirements can be distinguished:

- problems;
- goals;
- functional requirements, use cases;
- boundary conditions (laws, standards, etc.);
- quality requirements (usability, reliability, efficiency, supportability, expandability, serviceability, etc.);
- test requirements;
- acceptance criteria.

We shall not include a detailed description of the individual requirement types here, but if you wish to go into this subject in greater depth, read *Requirements Engineering* by Christine Rupp *et al.* (2001).

Can requirements be described with use cases?

Strengths and
weaknesses of use
cases

Use cases represent a special form of requirement description. They require that a particular use case, i.e. a particular typical process, be supported by the system. They are therefore an expression of functional requirements. The strength of use cases is that the requirements are represented from the point of view of users and domain experts and in their language. Their weakness is their low degree of formalization and their fuzziness.

Use cases alone are not sufficient to describe the requirements on a system, but they form a good framework and a starting point. Many requirements, however, do not fit within this framework, or only to a limited extent. Quality requirements, for example those placed on system usability or response times, are often not specific to a use case but are valid system-wide and across many different use cases. Many requirements resulting from business rules, such as "The driver must be 21 before driving the vehicle," also apply to more than one use case. (*See* Table 3.9.)

Table 3.9 Requirements

Req. 1 (compulsory)	The vehicle may only be handed over to the driver if the driver is over 21 at the time of handover
Req. 2 (intention)	It is intended that motorcycles will also be offered for rental
Req. 3 (compulsory)	In at least 80% of cases it must be possible for the call center employee to conclude the telephone vehicle reservation in less than 120 seconds. In all remaining cases in less than 240 seconds

Referencing
requirements in use
cases

It is therefore important that requirements can be defined and administered generally and independently of use cases. These requirements can then be referenced in use cases. In other words, a use case is a compilation of existing general requirements in the context of a domain-specific process.

Functional breakdown
⇨163
Natural language
methods ⇨96

Functional requirements can be described to a large extent in the form of use cases or can be referenced in use cases, since use cases relate to the functionality and the processes to be supported. The context of a use case also offers an initial method of assessing the completeness of the functional requirements.

Checklist:

☑ 3.10.1: Have the requirements been described independently of use cases?

☑ 3.10.2: Can each individual requirement be identified by a unique requirement number?

☑ 3.10.3 Has the degree of obligation been defined for each requirement (compulsory, wish, intention, suggestion, comments)?

Natural language
method checklist ⇨97

☑ 3.10.4   Has each requirement formulation been checked using natural language
methods (see checklist on p. 97)?

3.11 Identifying Business Classes

Synopsis

▪ Identify the most important domain-specific objects, consider them as classes,
and model their structural connections in a class diagram.

▪ Give the classes meaningful names, name their associations and association
roles, and describe, if possible, their multiplicities.

Understandable for
managers and
technical
departments

☑ 3.11.1

☑ 3.11.2

Classes ⇨172

☑ 3.11.3

Association ⇨225
Inheritance ⇨220

A business class describes an object, a concept, a place, or a person from real
business life in a degree of detail that can also be understood by technical
departments and decision-makers (contract, invoice etc.). The classes are
reduced to a large extent to purely technically motivated properties.

The description of the basic structural connections is more important
here than detailing the individual classes and determining which attributes
and operations these classes should have. Accordingly, the result is a simple
class diagram that mainly contains classes without any details, as well as
the relationships between these classes (associations, inheritance) including
their role names and multiplicities. The definition of association directions
is a secondary issue at this point and can be ignored.

Figure 3.7 shows the most important classes from the vehicle rental
example and their connections. Since only very simple notation elements are
used, these diagrams can generally be discussed with technical departments.

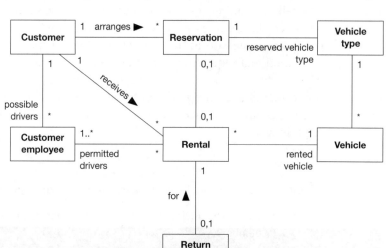

Figure 3.7 The most important domain-specific classes and their relationships
represented as an analysis class model

Business classes are identified by determining the domain-specific central classes of the future class model. Details and finer points can be ignored for the moment. Business classes are usually broken down further during the design process and often lead to several individual classes.

In our case candidates for business classes are customer, reservation, rental and vehicle. At the level of these business classes, the first obvious relationships can be modeled, as shown in Fig. 3.7.

☑ 3.11.4

The multiplicity details in the business class model should at first simply express the permissible quantitative proportions. This does not yet establish that these relationships should subsequently be present in the solution or in these proportions. For example, it is doubtful whether the implementation will contain an association of *vehicle* to *vehicle type*. The 1 to n-association between the two classes reflects only a knowledge of the technical connections that we have acquired from the technical department:

- Each vehicle belongs to one vehicle type.
- A vehicle type may contain any number of vehicles.
- Reservations always relate to one vehicle type (and not to an actual vehicle).
- Rentals always relate to an actual vehicle.

Requirements ⇨190
Constraints ⇨197

In principle, the model allows the rental to reference a vehicle that belongs to a vehicle type different from the one that is defined in the reservation linked to the rental (if available). To what extent and under what conditions this case is allowed is not established in the class model. To do this, corresponding explicit requirements should be defined and/or the model extended with corresponding constraints.

The following items should be examined for each class and, if possible, documented:

- components, subdivision;
- conditions, events, expected/undesirable events;
- life cycle: construction and destruction moments;
- forms of representation, constraints, roles, operations, data types;
- relationships with other objects;
- set specifications/set grid;
- privileges, responsibilities;
- take-over of data from existing systems, and the like;
- overlap of responsibilities with objects and data in other existing systems;
- significance, importance for specific persons, business goals, and so on;
- synonyms, related terms.

Checklist:

☑ 3.11.1: Does the business class have a meaningful name that can also be understood by technical departments and decision-makers?

☑ 3.11.2: Does each business class represent an object, a design, a place, or a person from the real domain context?

☑ 3.11.3: Does the class diagram describe only the structural connections (inheritance, associations, including role names and multiplicities) but not yet any (only a few) additional details?

☑ 3.11.4: Do the multiplicity details in the business class model represent the technically permissible quantitative proportions?

☑ 3.11.5: Are the names of all business classes defined in the dictionary and are the dictionary entries referenced?

☑ 3.11.6: Are the names of all association roles defined in the dictionary and are the dictionary entries referenced?

3.12 Creating a Technical Dictionary

Synopsis

- Create a technical dictionary that defines all the important domain-specific terms.
- Define all the classes of the class model as terms in the dictionary.

☑ 3.12.1

☑ 3.12.2

- Define all the association roles as terms in the dictionary.
- Define all the other important technical objects, concepts, and states of these objects in the dictionary.
- Also define all the important general and domain-specific process words in the dictionary.
- Check all definitions in the dictionary with the standard checklist for natural language analysis.

☑ 3.12.3

While we are getting acquainted with the application domain and develop scenarios, we permanently encounter technical terms of the application domain. These are collected in a technical dictionary or glossary and are carefully and precisely described. On the one hand, this is important to minimize communication problems between developers and users. Often one side quite naturally uses specific terms and carelessly assumes that the other side has exactly the same understanding of these terms.

On the other hand, the same terms are used and interpreted differently even by users and domain experts from within the application domain. As naïve as it may sound, this concerns even seemingly simple concepts such

Supplier
Employee
Customer

as *customer* and *address*. For example, it may turn out that suppliers and employees too may be customers, that customers can be either enterprises or private persons, and so on.

Different people in the application domain may look at the objects denoted by these terms from very different points of view and see completely different distinctions, responsibilities, roles, and attributes. Thus, the definition of terms in a technical dictionary helps developers become familiar with the application domain and calls for confrontation of different interpretations. In many cases, different interpretations can be clarified without contradictions. There may, however, be terms that cannot be unified, and their different and contradictory interpretations are possibly justified. In such cases, the contradictions can at least be documented in the technical dictionary.

Examples of dictionary entries can be seen in the box below. Further conceivable entries in the technical dictionary might be: Condition, Tariff, Invoice addressee, Invoice position, Individual invoice, Monthly invoice, Collective invoice, Partial invoice, Vehicle type, Mobile accessories, Rental object, Fixed accessories, Equipment feature, Rental periods, Transfer, Contract, Availability, and so on.

Also define
important verbs!

☑ 3.12.4

You should also define important process words, i.e. terms that describe a procedure. In general these tend to be verbs. Once again there are often different ways of defining these words, especially if there are different specializations of a process word, for example *reserve*, *pre-reserve*, *reserve without obligation*. In this case, when attempting to formulate the definitions it may emerge that *pre-reserve* or *reserve without obligation* do not make any sense from a technical point of view.

The dictionary is not
a substitute for
requirement
definitions!

☑ 3.12.5

When formulating the definitions, remember that the dictionary is designed only to prevent any possible misunderstandings, confusions, and misinterpretations, and thus to prevent any errors in communication between the people involved. Do not write any more (but also not any less) than is necessary for this purpose. In no case should you attempt to define all the requirements related to a term, even if the dictionary entries often also contain implicit requirements. The dictionary is not a substitute for requirement definitions!

Dictionary entries

Invoice

Each invoice derives from a contract, bills for services, or supplies that have been supplied, and is addressed to a customer. There are single, monthly, partial, and collective invoices.

An invoice has an invoice addressee, a date, an invoice number, and invoice items that list the individual services and supplies to be billed for. Each item contains a description, a quantity, a per-unit and a total amount (item sum). The invoice contains a total sum (sum of all items). The sales tax is displayed separately for each item and all sums.

Around 1,000 invoices are generated each month by each branch office.

▶

Vehicle, reserved

A reserved vehicle is a reserved vehicle type. It is *not* an actual, uniquely identifiable vehicle but only the quantitative reservation of a possible vehicle of the defined type.

Vehicle, actual

An actual vehicle is a vehicle that can be uniquely identified (e.g. by its chassis number).

Customer [general]

A customer is a natural or legal person who can use the services of the vehicle rental company. Before a person can become a customer, their identity must be checked (for example by means of their driver's license). The commercially necessary data, such as name, address, phone numbers, etc., is known for each customer. Each customer has a unique customer number that is assigned by the vehicle rental company.

Customer [marketing]

Customers in the marketing sense are all natural and legal people who have already rented a vehicle from the vehicle rental company, as well as all the people who might intend to do so. For customers in the marketing sense the presence of personal data such as name, address, etc. is not necessary, nor do they need a customer number.

Customer number

A customer number is a globally unique series of characters that uniquely identifies a customer.

Reserve, reserved

Reservation is the procedure of providing a customer with the exclusive use of one or more objects for a particular period. Reservation entails a contract being concluded between the two parties involved, which in the normal case also defines the conditions.

Confirm, confirmed

Confirmation is the procedure of explicitly informing a business partner of a situation or an agreement that is already known to them. It is the verbal, written, or electronic transmission of already known information.

Checklist:

☑ 3.12.1: Is the corresponding business class referenced when a dictionary entry corresponds to a business class?

☑ 3.12.2: Is the corresponding association role referenced when a dictionary entry corresponds to an association role?

☑ 3.12.3: Has each dictionary entry been checked using natural language methods (see checklist below)?

☑ 3.12.4: Are important verbs also defined in the dictionary?

☑ 3.12.5: Is the dictionary entry formulated as succinctly as possible, i.e. only so succinctly that communication errors can be avoided?

☑ 3.12.6: Are important synonyms also defined in the dictionary?

Checklist for natural language analysis:[2]

☑ 3.12.1. *Query process words*. Process words are verbs and verbs made into nouns, e.g. to reserve, to book, information (to inform). For each process word ask the following key questions: who, where, what, when, how. For example "Who reserves?," "What is reserved?," etc. Not all these key questions will be applicable in every case, but they will help you uncover important missing information (so-called linguistic lacunae).

☑ 3.12.2. *Query all comparisons and comparative forms*. Comparisons are formulations containing the comparative forms of adjectives or adverbs, i.e. words such as "better," "faster," "easier," etc. In each case, ask what these comparative forms relate to ("faster than what?"), what reference points exist, how the required property can be measured or compared, and with what level of accuracy the comparison can be made.

☑ 3.12.3. *Query all universal quantifiers*. Universal quantifiers are words such as "all," "never," "always," "each," "every," etc. that are used to describe a quantity or number of something. Ask about the possible exceptions and the associated assumptions: "Does a monthly invoice really have to be issued every month? No, only if the invoice sum is greater than EUR 20.00."

☑ 3.12.4. *Query all conditions, exceptions, and variants*. In formulations that contain words such as "if," "when," "then," "depending on," "insofar as," etc., ask whether these really are all the possibilities or whether there are others. Define each possible variant, draw up a complete list of all the possibilities.

→ Language consolidation

Object-oriented analysis is the unfolding and reconstruction of the conceptual world of the application domain by information technology. This is a multi-facetted and error-prone social process which mostly takes place via linguistic actions, that is, via everyday language. Use cases, scenarios, CRC cards, and the like, are techniques aimed at transforming this analysis into a methodological and systematic process.

Nevertheless, the basic problem remains that different people can talk for a long time about the same object, maybe even using the same terms, and yet have more or less divergent views of that same thing.

Many fundamental assumptions and facts will be withheld from the IT people in this process, because for people from the application area, they are so self-evident and common that they seldom

▶

---

[2] This checklist is based on the comprehensive work carried out over many years by Christine Rupp in the field of natural language analysis (*see* Rupp *et al.,* 2001).

speak about them explicitly. They are much more inclined to talk about exceptions and special cases, and even these are often seen from only one perspective.

Developers and domain experts communicate mainly via natural language and therefore generally not very precisely. The following rules will help you gain more confidence (*see* Irion, 1995).

Try to use active instead of passive formulations

Passive formulations distract and hide the responsible parties. Instead of "*The contract is stipulated*" you should write more clearly "*The branch office stipulates a contract with the customer*" or "*The branch office's customer service attendant hands the customer a copy of the rental contract.*"

Do not use synonyms, homonyms, or tautologies

Try to use a non-equivocal terms. Do not use synonyms for pure linguistic embellishment, but feel free to point out possible synonyms. Example: instead of "*branch*" it is preferable to speak about "*branch office*" if you mean that one, or of "*branching*" if you want to talk about two alternative ways of proceeding.

Use verbs instead of nouns that are not technical terms

In the formulation "*The customer is sent a message about ...*" ("message" used as a common language term), the term "message" is not a technical term but a hidden process. Alternative formulations could be "*The customer service attendant informs the customer that ...*" or "*The

customer service attendant notifies the customer about the fact ...*"

Do not use terms in the plural except where strictly necessary

Formulate your assertions in the singular if a thing occurs only individually in a context. Thus, for example "*The customer returns the vehicle*" instead of "*Customers return vehicles.*" Further example: the term "*kind of business partner*" means the classification, whereas "*kinds of business partners*" means possible expressions, such as supplier, customer, corporate customer, interested party, employee, cooperation partner, and so on.

Try to use qualified terms

Qualification is a restrictive feature and specifies a term; it is usually placed in front of the original term: "*quality check list*" instead of "*check list.*"

Do not confuse information and information vehicle

Example: "*customer file/record*" and "*customer.*"

Be aware of possible misunderstandings with ambiguous terms

It makes no sense and only leads to misunderstandings if terms that are factually incorrect but unequivocal are replaced: the "glove box" may still be called "glove box" because no misunderstanding will arise, although only in very rare cases is it used to hold gloves. "Storage compartment" or something similar would create ambiguity. If a term is really so ambiguous that it might lead to errors in communication, try to find a term that conveys the meaning better and without risks of misunderstanding.

3.13 Developing a Use Case Process Model

Synopsis

■ Break down each use case step in the use case description into one or more elementary activities and model the process flow of each use case with an activity diagram (normal course of events).

■ Model all the anticipated exceptions and branching possibilities for each activity (complete course of events).

■ For each activity, model the required incoming objects and data, plus all the ensuing results (objects, object states).

Essential use cases
⇨163
Concrete use cases
⇨163

Once the business essences and concrete expressions of the individual use cases have been worked out, they can be considered in detail. They are described in such a way that the individual activity steps contain complete details of all their preconditions and postconditions, actors, incoming and outgoing data and events. This can be achieved in several stages:

● *Describe the normal course of events.* The first stage is to create an activity diagram for each use case that represents the normal course of events, i.e. a successful case without any exceptions or variants.

● *Describe the complete course of events.* The second stage is to take the normal course of events and add in all the anticipated exceptions and variants.

● *Describe the object flow.* The final stage is to add the incoming and resulting objects or object states for all the activities.

Describe the normal course of events

☑ 3.13.1
☑ 3.13.2

The individual steps are taken from the use case description and represented as activities in an activity diagram. The normal course of events is noted in the diagram; this is often a predominantly sequential series of events, as shown in the example in Fig. 3.8. If a single step in the use case description is actually masking several elementary individual activities, the activity diagram can be expanded and the activities broken down as appropriate.

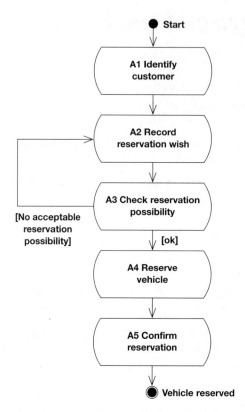

Figure 3.8 Normal course of events for *Reserve vehicle by phone* as a UML activity diagram

Initial and final states

☑ 3.13.3

☑ 3.13.4

Each activity diagram has an initial state and one or more final states. The initial and final states can be given names. Since there are usually several final states (*see* Fig. 3.9), it is a good idea to differentiate them by name. In our example the two final states *Vehicle reserved* and *Vehicle not reserved* may be produced.

Model all the anticipated exceptions and branching possibilities for each activity

☑ 3.13.5

☑ 3.13.6

☑ 3.13.7

Now put each individual activity under the magnifying glass and clarify the possible exceptions and variants. Fig. 3.9 shows this using the example of reserving a vehicle by phone. Up till now (in Fig. 3.8) the activity *A1 Identify customer* only had the outgoing transition *1.1 [ok]* for the normal case. The question is now: what other results are conceivable and possible for the activity on a technical level?

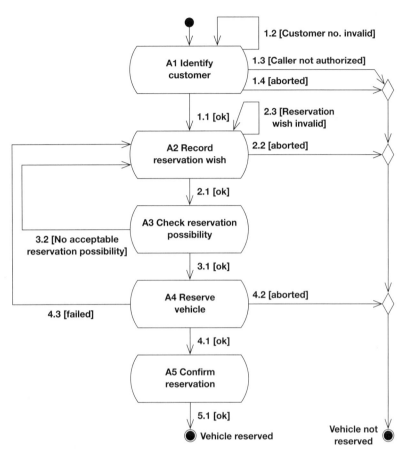

Figure 3.9 Process flow of the *Reserve vehicle by phone* use case with all the anicipated domain-specific exceptions and variants

To answer this we must once again imagine the process (flow of events): a customer calls up, states their name and customer number, and would like to reserve a vehicle. The customer is identified by means of the customer number, i.e. the call center employee uses the customer number to find the customer, sees the customer's name displayed by the system, and compares it with the name specified by the customer on the phone. If the name matches, the customer is considered to have been identified and validated.

What other results might therefore be conceivable for activity A1? One possibility, for example, might be that the customer number specified by the customer is invalid, i.e. no customer exists with this number. This possibility is now included in the diagram as transition *1.2 [Customer number invalid]*.

Another possibility might be that a customer is indeed found for the number, but the name does not match. This possibility is also noted as a further transition: *1.3 [Caller not authorized]*.

We proceed in the same manner with all the activities, until all the technically conceivable situations have been considered. This might be a very large number of variants, but they should nonetheless all be included in the diagram. We are trying to achieve completeness.

What is a domain-specific exception or variant? Does every possible error situation also need to be noted? For example, that the database is unavailable, that memory is low, or that the keyboard has jammed? In this respect we have to differentiate between unplanned problems, technical faults, and general exceptions on the one hand, and process-specific faults, commercially desirable (or at least unavoidable) variants, and so forth on the other hand. Only the process-specific exceptions should be included in the activity model.

These also include the possibilities available to the user in the dialog system for canceling the process. In the example the user can decide to abort the process at activities A1, A2, and A4. The other activities cannot be aborted by the user.

The complete specification of the exceptions and variants can be shown in an activity diagram in a manner that is much clearer and easier to understand than a description of a use case in natural language.

The complete specification of the process flow can also be used to derive all the technically motivated, process-specific test cases. At least one test case is required for each transition, so that all the paths and variants can be run through at least once in the test. In our example the following test cases, among others, are required:

- Enter invalid customer number (A1.2).
- Enter valid customer number (A1.1).
- Enter valid customer number, but name does not match (A1.3).
- User aborts dialog (A1.4).
- Enter invalid reservation wish (A2.3), e.g. enter period in the past.

For each activity, model the necessary incoming objects and data, plus all the ensuing results (objects, object states)

The activity diagram is now transformed into an object flow diagram. When determining the incoming and outgoing objects, it is helpful first to go through the transitions in order and establish in each case which objects have been generated or modified.

What objects are produced if transition A1.1 takes place? This is the OK case for activity A1, i.e. the customer has been identified. Therefore the object *Customer* is noted as a result of activity A1. Since this applies only in the case of transition A1.1, the corresponding transition is quoted. In the case of transitions A1.2, A1.3, and A1.4, no objects are produced or modified (*see* Fig. 3.10).

☑ 3.18.8

Aborting the process
☑ 3.18.9

Deriving test cases

cf. Programmed
test cases ⇨102

☑ 3.13.10

Object flow diagram
⇨255

☑ 3.13.11

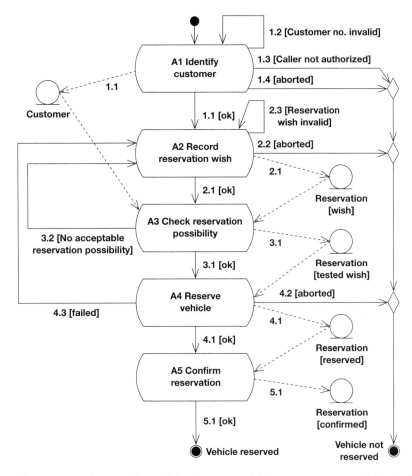

Figure 3.10 Process flow of the *Reserve vehicle* use case expanded to include the assumed and resulting objects or object states

State model ⇨123

☑ 3.13.12

Both newly generated objects (e.g. in A1.1) and the modification of objects (e.g. state alterations such as in A2.1, A3.1, A4.1, and A5.1) are noted. The object states noted here must match those in the corresponding state diagram for the class.

Checklist:

☑ 3.13.1: Is there an activity diagram for each use case?

☑ 3.13.2: Is each use case step represented by at least one activity in the activity diagram?

☑ 3.13.3: Does each diagram have one initial state and one or more final states?

☑ 3.13.4: Does each final state have a meaningful name?

☑ 3.13.5:   Have all the known exceptions and variants been fully noted in the activity diagram?

☑ 3.13.6:   Have all the activities been numbered?

☑ 3.13.7:   Have all the outgoing transitions been numbered (as subitems of the activity numbers)?

☑ 3.13.8:   Have all the process-specific exceptions been taken into account, but not the technical or general exceptions?

☑ 3.13.9:   Have all the user's possibilities for aborting the process been considered?

☑ 3.13.10: Have the incoming and outgoing objects/object states been noted for each activity?

☑ 3.13.11: Have the corresponding transition numbers been noted for all object flows?

☑ 3.13.12: Do the object states used match those in the corresponding state diagram?

3.14   Describing the System Interface

Synopsis

▪ For each use case specify the use case interface, i.e. combine the incoming and outgoing data, objects, and events to create interface descriptions.

Once the processes have been described in detail with the aid of use cases, flowcharts, and object flow diagrams, you should identify the structural elements that are located at the outer boundary of the system. All the interactions, input and output of the system under development, and its environment should be identified and described.

☑ 3.14.1   The interfaces involved can be assigned to each use case step, as shown for example in Table 3.10. At this stage identifying the interface elements involved is more important than their precise allocation to the individual steps.

☑ 3.14.2   Then, describe for each interface:

● name of the interface;

● short description in 2–10 lines of text;

● degree of complexity of the interface (complex | standard | simple);

● exclusion note, if applicable.

Table 3.10 Allocation of the interfaces involved to the individual use case steps

Use case step/activity	Interface elements involved
Identify customer	
Acquire customer number	Customer search dialog
Identify customer	
Record reservation wish	
Record reservation wish	Vehicle reservation dialog
Check vehicle availability	
Determine available vehicles	
Reserve vehicle	
Select vehicle	Vehicle reservation dialog
Reserve vehicle	Vehicle reservation dialog
Confirm reservation	
Confirm reservation	Vehicle reservation dialog
	Generated output: reservation confirmation

If it turns out that an interface does not need to be considered within the context of the project, it should nonetheless be described in the above form, but supplied with an "exclusion note," stating why the interface does not need to be taken into account.

Apart from these general features, other description techniques are useful for adding further details, depending on the type of interface. The first step is therefore to differentiate the various types:

☑ 3.14.3

- dialog interfaces;
- generated output (letters, reports, etc.);
- data interfaces from or to external systems;
- functional interfaces to external systems.

All interfaces and external systems that might be considered by the system under development should be investigated.

☑ 3.14.4

For **functional interfaces** and **data interfaces** the following details should also be documented, if known:

- nomenclature of the external systems in question (program names, transaction names, etc.);
- type of interface: synchronous (functional interface), asynchronous (data exchange, e.g. via files, database tables or queues);
- direction of interface: reading, writing;
- frequency of activation and, if applicable, distribution by time of day, e.g. once a day, approx. 100 times a day, etc.;

- maximum, minimum, and average data volume per activation (in bytes);
- importance of interface (important | standard | secondary);
- possible contact partners, references, documents, etc.;
- special features.

On occasion, the interface analysis will uncover additional use cases and useful dictionary entries.

☑ 3.14.4

Dialog interfaces and generated output can be described in a similar way:

- who uses the dialog/generated output (number, qualification, etc.);
- when and how often the dialog/generated output is used (globally, on average per user, distribution by time of day, days of the week, months, etc.), e.g. once a day, approx. 100 times a day, etc.;
- importance of interface (important | standard | secondary);
- possible contact partners, references, documents, etc.;
- special features.

Some examples of this are shown in Tables 3.11, 3.12 and 3.13.

Table 3.11 Essential dialog description for *Customer search*

Name: **Customer search dialog**
Short description: This dialog allows the user to search for an individual customer with the aid of search terms
Use: All users in the rental locations and in the call center, on average 40 times a day per user
Complexity: Simple
Input fields: Various search terms, e.g. customer number, name, telephone, etc.
Display fields: Customer data (name, address)
Branching possibilities: Customer file, Cancel, Vehicle reservation
Actions: Start search, Select a customer, Delete all search terms

Table 3.12 Essential dialog description for *Vehicle reservation*

Name: **Vehicle reservation dialog**

Short description:
  This dialog allows a vehicle to be reserved for a customer

Use:
  All users in the rental locations and in the call center, on average 25 times a day per user, usage around three times greater between 8 and 10 a.m. on working days than at other times

Complexity:
  Standard

Input fields:
  Vehicle type, handover location, return location, reservation period (DD.MM.YYYY HH)

Display fields:
  Reservation data (vehicle, reservation number, vehicle type, handover location, return location, reservation period (DD.MM.YYYY HH))

Branching possibilities:
  Cancel, End, Customer file

Actions:
  Check vehicle availability, Reserve vehicle, Print confirmation, Cancel reservation

Table 3.13 Essential description of generated output for *Reservation confirmation*

Name: **Generated output – reservation confirmation**

Short description:
  A written communication to the customer, confirming a vehicle reservation

Use:
  Predominantly users in the call center, currently around 5% by post, 55% by fax, and the rest by e-mail. For over 50% of reservations no confirmation is required (verbally only)

Complexity:
  Standard

Output fields:
  Reservation data (vehicle, reservation number, vehicle type, handover location, return location, reservation period (DD.MM.YYYY HH))

Example:
  See material M-67

The required dialogs can be allocated to the individual use cases in use case diagrams. The same procedure can be adopted with external systems, as shown in Fig. 3.11. Consider, for example, the corresponding sections in the *Reserve vehicle* use case in which the dialogs are allocated.

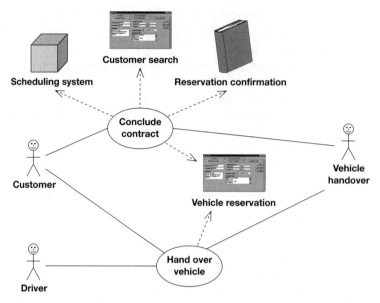

Figure 3.11 Visualization of the dialogs involved in the use cases

Checklist:

☑ 3.14.1: Have the interfaces involved in each use case been established/allocated?

☑ 3.14.2: Has each interface been given a short description and a gradation of complexity?

☑ 3.14.3: Has the type of interface been described (dialog, generated output, functional, data exchange)?

☑ 3.14.4: Have all the interfaces been described in further detail in a manner specific to the type of interface?

3.15 Explorative Interface Prototyping

Synopsis

■ Develop explorative prototypes for the identified interface elements.

Explorative prototypes are in most cases sequences of dialog designs[3] which illustrate previously elaborated use cases. Use cases describe concrete user actions, including potential exceptions and special cases.

---

[3] These are executable, usable dialogs in which data can be entered, but which do not include all features of a finished application, such as help functions, error handling, database storage, performance, robustness, an undo functionality, processes that are unimportant for the use case under consideration, etc.

Dialog designs,
form designs

Explorative prototyping is used for analysis. It is a medium for communicating with future users about the planned application system. Frequently, explorative prototypes are dialog designs. They can, however, also be evaluations, printing samples, form designs, simulations, or calculation rules. The latter could be, for example, realized as spreadsheets and reviewed together with experts from the application domain.

☑ 3.15.1

First, it has to be established which dialogs are needed and on the basis of which use cases they are required. Sometimes, doubts can arise as to whether in a specific situation one or several dialogs are needed, or whether

☑ 3.15.2

in two different situations the same dialog might be used. In such cases, the use cases, i.e. their interfaces, preconditions, postconditions, actors, etc., must be carefully compared. If in doubt, it might be better to opt for the simpler solution, i.e. the one with fewer dialogs. Potentially, this may lead to conflict at a later stage, which suggests a different structure is required. But at least you will know why.

Explorative dialog prototypes show users and specialists actual aspects of the future system. Depending on the users' power of abstraction and imagination and their experience with software systems, you may also get some critical reactions on the dialog designs, such as "this field needs to be shifted further up, and that one is far too small." You as a system analyst, however, might be glad to have identified the dialogs at all, and do not really wish to hear these comments at this stage.

See use case ⇨163

Illustration of use
cases

The development team use the information acquired about the application domain as a basis for the design of dialog sequences. Thus, dialog designs become part of the use cases, since all processes described in the use cases need to be supported by the application system to be developed. All situations described in the use cases can be simulated dialog by dialog with the future users and, as a rule, lead to many more conclusions and questions.

Users' questions,
objections,
suggestions

Now finally, with their future tool in front of them as a sample, users will wish to assess and criticize it concretely. They have their everyday work before their eyes and try to find out how they can cope with it using the new tool. Users' statements frequently point out a lack of specific attributes (data fields) or actions ("And where is the monthly turnover?", "The customer has a PO Box – do I enter it in the street field?", "How can I change the invoice address?").

☑ 3.15.3

All questions, objections, suggestions, ideas, and so on that are brought forward by the users and cannot be immediately clarified need to be protocoled and subsequently evaluated. Thus, when the session is later repeated with new designs, the planned solutions of the previous session's problems will be discussed.

Paper or screen?

Dialog designs can be drawn simply on a piece of paper, but it is better to show them directly on screen. With modern GUI builders, the effort is relatively little. The layout should be fairly detailed and near to the final version. Data fields may remain empty or filled with hard-wired sample values. Buttons and similar dialog elements may remain without any special functionality, but the expected outcomes should be explained. (*See* Fig. 3.12.)

'But the customer has a P.O. Box ...'

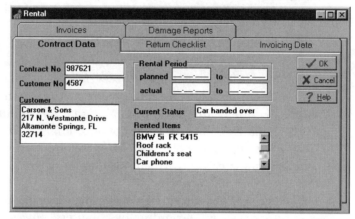

Figure 3.12 Explorative dialog prototype

Prototyping workshops should be well prepared.

Preparing dialog workshops

- Each workshop has a clearly defined subject or deals with a specific aspect previously communicated to all participants. Users should, if possible, contribute sample material (contracts, forms, and so on).

☑ 3.15.4

- Questions should be protocoled, together with the person(s) responsible for clarification of how to handle this problem. A copy of the protocol is later given to each participant.

Before the dialog designs are discussed with the users, they should be discussed inside the development team in order to present the user workshop with a relatively mature version of the designs. It is usually not sufficient to show the identified attributes in a window and add three buttons (such as Save, Cancel, Help). Dialogs cannot be viewed as separate parts, but must be understood as components of a scenario, or a process. The process as a whole must be practical and sensible for the users.

Validation

Prototyping workshops make everybody involved more convinced that the right system is being developed. Misdevelopments are identified at an early stage and can still be corrected at a relatively low cost.

Metaphors

Use metaphors or models when designing the user interface or the visible part of your system. When the dialogs are looked at individually, it may be helpful to view them as users' tools for processing materials. This also influences language use: instead of customer dialog or customer form, we find the *customer file* and, in the same way, the *invoice file* and the *contract file*. Instead of a selection list, we talk about *customer search* or *contract search*. And when a customer has been selected and one of the related contracts has been opened to generate an invoice automatically, the tool is, for example, called *invoice creation* or *invoice creator*. Finally, the invoice is placed into the *out basket*.

If you think this is cheap and mere renaming of things that otherwise would not change, just try it out. At first, the change might feel difficult because the old terms are well established and run-in. But as soon as you have mastered the new, more metaphorical language usage, you will note that you now look at things differently, that you perceive them differently, and therefore arrive at different working results.

In the old-language world, dialog forms were viewed merely as a way of presentation – they were all forms, although the data in the forms could be structured quite differently. In the new-language world, we find tools that have their own, data-independent existence and that have specific semantics attributed to them: they are *searching* and *processing tools*, *out baskets*, *printers*, and so forth. The terms are not only more pictorial and metaphorical, they are also clearer. You would probably not want to extend a *search tool* with the functionality of a *processing tool* because this does not fit into the search tool concept.

Checklist:

☑ 3.15.1:   Has an explorative prototype been created for at least all identical interface elements in the complexity classes *Important* and *Standard*?

☑ 3.15.2:   Do the explorative prototypes contain all the elements specified in the essential interface description?

☑ 3.15.3:   Has each explorative prototype been discussed and agreed with the technical department in prototyping workshops?

☑ 3.15.4:   Is there an agenda and a report for each prototyping workshop?

📖 Suggested Reading

1. Beyer, M. (1993) *Brainland: Mind Mapping in Aktion*, Junfermannsche Verlagsbuchhandlung, Paderborn.
2. Rupp, C. *et al.* (2001) *Requirements Engineering*, Hanser, Munich.
3. Irion, A. M. (1995) *Regelwerk und Qualitätscheckliste zur Bildung von Fachbegriffen bei der Entwicklung und Administration einer normierten Unternehmensfachsprache*, dissertation, University of Konstanz.

chapter 4

Design

When creating a model it is never enough merely to bring together the recorded phenomena – one must always strive for a free invention of the human spirit that gets closer to the heart of the matter. One should not be content with mere observation, but should advance to the speculative method, which searches for the objective form of existence.

A free rendition of an idea from Albert Einstein (Chotjewitz, 1994)

Building on the example of Chapter 3, the process of object-oriented design is discussed, and the application of the individual methodological concepts is shown.

Defining the Application Architecture 114

Identifying Domain Components 118

Developing Component-specific Class Models 120

(Further) Developing State Models 123

Identifying and, if Necessary, Restructuring Component Dependencies 125

Designing Component Interfaces 127

Developing Collaboration Models 129

Developing Process-oriented Component Tests 132

Developing Class Tests 135

Defining Attributes 138

Specifying Dialogs 142

Discussion of Design 145

4.1   Defining the Application Architecture

Synopsis

- Identify the individual elements (layers, components, class types, etc.) of the underlying application architecture, plus the relationships between them, and portray them in a model/diagram.

- Describe the responsibilities, tasks, and special features of each element in the application architecture.

- Describe the principal communication mechanisms with the aid of interaction diagrams, and document the use of design patterns.

What must be designed?

The design process entails developing a draft solution for a given problem, taking into account the specified basic conditions. It is therefore impossible to develop a design without making assumptions about the basic application architecture. The application architecture defines the principal possibilities for and restrictions on potential solutions to the problem. In addition to the application architecture, other basic conditions must be taken into account, e.g. development tools, standards, etc.

Before beginning the first design activities, it is necessary to specify the architecture of the future applications. It determines which kinds of classes and, as a result, which interfaces need to be designed. A well thought-through, clean application architecture also helps to achieve:

- a sensible division of labor and a clear overview;
- long-term flexibility in system development;
- a higher degree of re-usability.

In the literature and in application development enterprises, we can find many application architectures, some of which are very similar to each other, some very different. The architecture outlined here by way of example reflects today's common demands on such architectures. This includes a three-layer client-server architecture with a presentation layer on the client side, the business logic and the application itself on one or more servers, and a centralized data storage system.

This is not a book on application architectures; therefore, without further discussion, one possible application architecture is provided as an example. Figure 4.1 illustrates the principal structure of the application to be developed. The individual internal components are explained opposite.

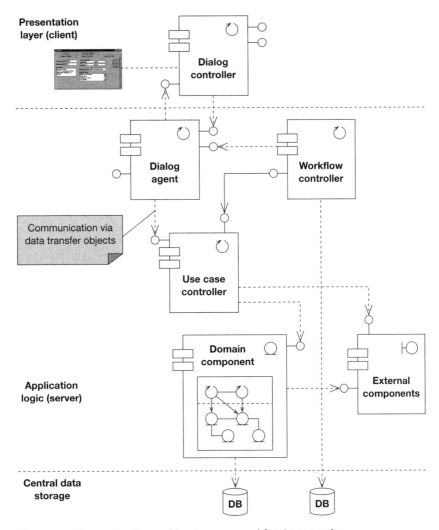

Figure 4.1 The application architecture assumed for the example

Dialogs, dialog controller

Dialogs are the interface with the users. They take care of presentation of information and accept input. The entire system–user communication is initially processed by the dialog control classes. They ensure an adequate representation and formatting of information, but do not process or change the contents of the data. User input is also not processed substantially, but only formally.

A dialog is composed of different individual parts. On the one hand, these are the elements displayed on the monitor, i.e. input fields, selection buttons, and one or more windows in which the dialog takes place. On the other hand, these are invisible elements: usually, there will be a controller which directly controls the presentation and the dialog. The controller generates and initializes the display elements, shows or hides them, highlights them, and so on. Moreover, it directly processes the user input. For example, it will ensure that after the tab or enter key has been pressed, the cursor jumps to the next field. Other input that need not be processed directly, such as pressing the OK button, is forwarded to the interaction control.

Dialog agent

The dialog agent is a special controller that acts as the client's dialog-specific representative on the server. It behaves in a specific manner for each dialog, and optimizes communication with the client-side dialog controller, i.e. it receives events and data/objects and forwards them to the correct domain classes, etc. In addition, it obtains the necessary data for the dialog, bundles it, and sends it to the client. The aim is to optimize client–server communication, i.e. to achieve the minimum level of interaction with the lowest possible volume of data.

Use case controller

A use case controller controls the processes defined in a use case or the associated activity model. The use case controller moderates the interactions between the domain classes or components in accordance with the possibilities defined in the use case. A use case controller can control the process flow of one or more use cases.

The use case controller receives the events coming from the view agent and the workflow controller. It processes the domain-specific content of the information only insofar as it is necessary to determine and to influence the context of the current processing situation, and all the remaining domain-specific tasks are taken care of by the domain components. The use case controller regulates and guarantees communication between the components involved and unlinks their dependencies. It ensures that dialogs are displayed and then removed, that error and status messages from domain objects and the process controller are forwarded to the dialog controller, etc.

«primitive» ⇨54

If dialog agents send data queries to the use case controller, they receive answers in the form of so-called data transfer objects, in which the requested data is compiled as primitive attributes.[1]

---

[1] Yes, I know, data transfer objects are the work of the devil, but in this case there are good reasons for them. See http://www.martinfowler.com/isa

Workflow or process controller

The workflow controller initiates, monitors, and controls processing of a business event from a domain-specific point of view. Use cases represent chronologically connected elements of a business process. If there are chronological interruptions between these elements, possibly lasting hours, days, weeks or more, the current state of processing at the time of the interruption must be saved. The workflow controller is responsible for this.

A workflow controller component is generally composed internally from a set of controller classes, and is persistent.

Domain components

Responsibility for consistency of domain-specific content

See entity model ⇨51

These components represent the actual application domain, the technical view of the application world. They contain and encapsulate the domain classes with their attributes, operations, and constraints of the application world. All elementary domain-specific connections are reflected in these domain objects. They ensure their own internal consistency and correct relationships with other domain objects. However, they do not know anything about the presentation of their data and operations in the dialog layer and they do not know in which elaboration contexts (of use case and workflow control) they are situated.

Entity and control classes ⇨51

A domain component is generally composed internally from a set of entity and controller classes, and is persistent.

Frameworks

In order to use the architecture as consistently as possible for the whole application development, the fundamental relationships of the model, and the required infrastructure, i.e. the communication between the elements, their structure, and so on, are defined in a so-called framework. Frameworks usually provide a multitude of abstract classes from which the concrete classes for the current application layer are derived. Thus, frameworks are, among other things, abstract implementations of the application architecture.

Don't call the framework...

A peculiarity of such frameworks is the transfer of the vertical relationships between the layers, i.e. the control of the fundamental interfaces, to the framework. Communication between layers occurs as far as possible via the classes of the framework. Classes built on top of the framework communicate if possible only within their own layer. When using the framework, the old saying applies: *"Don't call the framework, the framework will call you"* (that is, reversal of control). This is also known as the "Hollywood principle" (*"Don't call us, we'll call you"*).

Checklist:

☑ 4.1.1:   Is there a model of the application architecture?

☑ 4.1.2:   Have the responsibilities and tasks of all the architecture elements been described?

4.1.3: Have the interaction principles and interface properties of the architecture elements been explained?

4.1.4: Has the use of design and architecture patterns been documented?

4.1.5: Is there a prototype to demonstrate the usefulness of the application architecture?

4.1.6: Is the application architecture appropriate for the problem in hand?

4.2 Identifying Domain Components

Synopsis

Analysis class model ⇨92

- Develop an initial component model, based on the analysis class model and the specified application architecture.
- Define a workflow component for each business process.
- Define a use case controller component for each use case.
- Represent each external system by a component.
- Combine related classes in the analysis model to form domain components.

Application architecture ⇨118
Identified business processes ⇨68
☑ 4.2.1

The assumed application architecture is a component-based architecture and provides for a division of the application logic into components.

Define a workflow component for each business process. During the analysis of our rental company example the following business processes, among others, were identified: *Vehicle administration*, *Vehicle rental* and *Customer administration*. These will now each be represented by a workflow component (*see* Fig. 4.2). For reasons of space, we shall not go into any further detail about these workflow components.

Figure 4.2 The workflow components in the example

Identified system use cases ⇨82
☑ 4.2.2

Define a use case controller component for each use case. We now deal with the use cases in a similar manner to the business processes. In this respect, we start with the system use cases that were identified in the analysis, e.g. Reserve vehicle by phone (*see* Fig. 4.3).

Figure 4.3 The use case controller for *Reserve vehicle by phone* as a control component

System use case
model Application
architecture ⇨114

☑ 4.2.3

Analysis class
model ⇨92

☑ 4.2.4

Represent each external system by a component. The principal interactions of the system with the outside world, the actors, are shown in system use case models. Actors may also be external or so-called legacy systems. To implement the interaction with these external systems, the specified application architecture provides that they should be encapsulated as components. In this way Cobol, PL/1, and other non-object-oriented programs can be encapsulated and integrated. For the sake of simplicity, no external systems were identified in our example.

Combine related classes in the analysis model to form domain components. The classes contained in the analysis class model represent the most important starting point for determining the domain components. During further detailing and restructuring each of the classes in the model will probably be subdivided into further classes. For example, the class *Customer* is still very general, there are probably different types of customers, and moreover these customers have addresses, phone numbers, bank accounts, etc. that could themselves be represented by classes in their own right. On the other hand, there may also be common features between the analysis classes; this might be expected, for instance, for the classes *Customer* and *CustomerEmployee*.

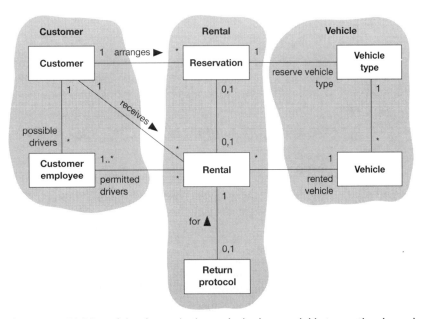

Figure 4.4 Division of the classes in the analysis class model between the planned components

☑ 4.2.5

Components: UML
Fundamentals
⇨272
Introduction ⇨8ff.

Estimate how great the dependencies are between the classes and how closely related they are on a domain-specific level, then group them together as applicable to form components. In our example (*see* Fig. 4.4) this produces the components *Customer*, *Rental* (also includes *Reservation* and *Return Protocol*) and *Vehicle*. As Fig. 4.5 shows, there are as yet no known dependencies between *Customer* and *Vehicle*.

Draw a component model and use dependency relationships to note the dependencies that are known at this stage between the components (Fig. 4.5).

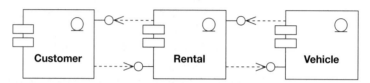

Figure 4.5 A first domain component model

Checklist:

☑ 4.2.1: Can all identified business processes be allocated to corresponding workflow components?

☑ 4.2.2: Can all identified system use cases be allocated to corresponding use case controller components?

☑ 4.2.3: Are all identified external systems represented (encapsulated) by a component?

☑ 4.2.4: Can each class in the analysis model be allocated to a domain component?

☑ 4.2.5: Have the dependencies between the domain components been defined, insofar as they can be determined from the class model?

4.3 Developing Component-specific Class Models

Synopsis

■ Based on the analysis class model (problem description), develop a specific design class model (solution concept) for each component.

■ Use domain-specific keys to represent all the associations to the objects of other components.

■ Define the responsibilities of all component-specific classes, i.e. transform the problem description (analysis) into a solution concept (design) and if necessary restructure the component-specific class model.

Introduction to
responsibilities
⇨24
UML Fundamentals
⇨60

Figure 4.6 Initial class model for the *Rental* component

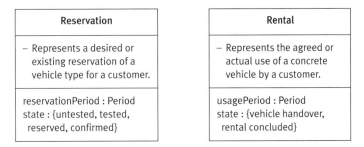

Reservation	Rental
− Represents a desired or existing reservation of a vehicle type for a customer.	− Represents the agreed or actual use of a concrete vehicle by a customer.
reservationPeriod : Period state : {untested, tested, reserved, confirmed}	usagePeriod : Period state : {vehicle handover, rental concluded}

Table 4.1 Responsibilities and important properties of *Reservation* and *Rental*

Introduction to
components ⇨58

☑ 4.3.1

Since components are connected to and communicate with each other in a different way from normal objects (*see* Section 2.16), the cross-component relationships between the classes should be dissolved and replaced by corresponding interfaces suitable for components (factory, observer, and object interfaces). The development of the component interface is described in Section 4.6.

Within a component the relationships between the domain classes can in principle remain intact, but if necessary should be detailed and developed further. In this way, for each component a specific class model is produced that is independent of the class models of other components.

☑ 4.3.1

By way of example, we shall now consider the *Rental* component in further detail. At first, its class model looks like that in Fig. 4.6. To develop this model further, we must now examine and clarify the responsibilities and most important properties of the classes involved (Table 4.1).

It is striking that the responsibilities of *Reservation* and *Rental* are very similar – both imply a relationship to a customer and have a time period. In many cases the reservation period also corresponds to the actual period of usage. Both classes have specific states that are typically consecutive, i.e. they have a chronologically meaningful sequence of states:

☑ 4.3.2

● untested wish (i.e. the wish may be invalid);

● tested wish (wish is plausible);

● reserved (i.e. the quantitative availability of the vehicle has been checked);

● confirmed (the customer has been given a reservation number);

● vehicle handover (the vehicle has been handed over to the customer);

● rental concluded (the vehicle has been returned).

Strictly speaking, there are necessary chronological dependencies between these two state models: the rental must follow the reservation and not vice versa. If a rental takes place after a reservation, the reservation should at least be in the *reserved* state, otherwise it would not have been necessary.

Coherence principle
⇨24

As a result of this chronological dependency, we should check to what extent these classes could be combined, with the responsibility for the chronological sequence of the states being represented by a single class rather than being divided. The corresponding state model is elaborated in Section 4.4; at this point it is simply a question of the design class model of the *Reservation* component.

As soon as we start thinking about combining the two classes, some new questions arise, which make us realize that we have not yet discovered all the requirements:

- If the actual usage period deviates from the reservation period, must both time periods be saved, i.e. so that they can be looked up at a later stage? Or only the chronologically latest period in each case?
- Does perhaps every modification of the period need to be saved?
- Or at least for each state?
- Can the reservation states be skipped and the process start straightaway with the rental? In this case can the desired vehicle type remain undefined? Or does the vehicle type need to be defined only during the reservation states?

For our example we shall simply assume the requirements that are most convenient for us, i.e. only the chronologically latest period needs to be known, the vehicle type must always be defined from the *tested* state onwards, and the reservation states may not be skipped. This produces the class design for the *Rental* component shown in Table 4.2.

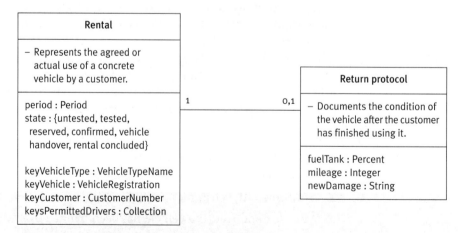

Table 4.2 Class design for the *Rental* component

☑ 4.3.3　　In this model the former associations to objects of other components are now represented by corresponding domain-specific key attributes (*key...*).

Checklist:

☑ 4.3.1:　Have the responsibilities of all classes been checked and detailed?

☑ 4.3.2:　Has the analysis model (problem description) been converted into an appropriate design model (solution concept)?

☑ 4.3.3:　Have all the associations to objects of other components been represented by domain-specific keys?

☑ 4.3.4:　Can all the attributes and operations of a class be assigned to the defined responsibilities?

4.4　(Further) Developing State Models

Synopsis

- Identify the possible domain-specific states for each object.
- Decide how the identified states should be modeled and implemented (e.g. state machine, constraints, state attributes, "state" design pattern, etc.).

Fundamentals ⇨271

If and in what detail states are modeled during the design firstly depends on whether the behavior of an object is considered as sufficiently significant to be modeled. Objects that have only two to three different states which barely influence the behavioral possibilities of that object can usually be designed to a satisfactory degree without modeling.

State-dependent messages

Messages which an object can interpret only in specific states justify the effort of creating state diagrams only to a certain extent. Often it is sufficient to handle such situations independently of state transitions and the like, for example by putting constraints on specific attribute values. If, however, a large part of the messages is state-dependent or more than one or two attributes determine a state, detailed modeling of the state transitions is recommended.

In Section 4.3 the essential states were identified for the *Rental* class. They will now be explicitly described in a state model. As well as naming the individual states, this procedure is primarily about defining which operations can produce state modifications and which operations are state-dependent, i.e. may be executed only in particular states.

☑ 4.4.1
☑ 4.4.2
☑ 4.4.3

For each individual state that has been identified so far, you must now ask: which subsequent states can possibly exist and how can they be reached? In so doing, you refer to your knowledge of the domain, e.g. reservations can be cancelled, as long as the vehicle has not yet been handed over. Or a reserved vehicle is sometimes never picked up. In this event the process is terminated in any case when the reservation period elapses. The state model in Fig. 4.7 takes this knowledge into account.

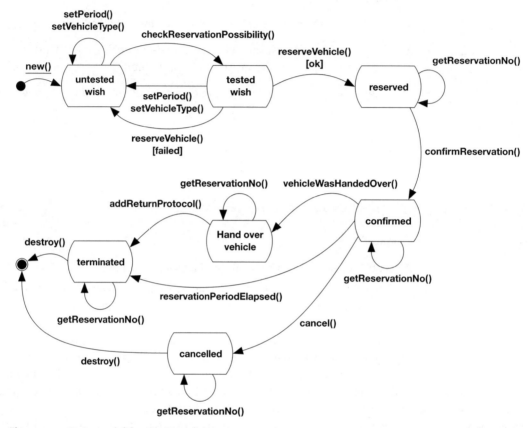

Figure 4.7 State model for the *Rental* class

State-dependent operation

Tagged values ⇨207

☑ 4.4.4

Not all the operations in a class are state-dependent. Theoretically, all the state-independent operations could also be included in the state model, i.e. they would appear as self-referential transitions for each state (in the same way that *getReservationNo()* already appears in many states). This is not usually done, since it would reduce the clarity of the model and the essential knowledge, i.e. the state-specific situations, would be lost. Instead, you can use a special tagged value to identify the corresponding operations in the class definition, for example:

```
setPeriod() {stateRelevant=true}
getPeriod() {stateRelevant=false}
```

Checklist:

☑ 4.4.1:   Have all the technically permissible states of the object been documented?

☑ 4.4.2:   Have the domain-specific implications of the identified states been thought through and taken into account?

☑ 4.4.3:   Have the possible subsequent states and transitions been examined for each individual state?

☑ 4.4.4:   Have all the operations of the class in question been identified as state-dependent or state-independent (e.g. with an appropriate tagged value)?

4.5   Identifying and, if Necessary, Restructuring Component Dependencies

Synopsis

▪ Examine and document the structural connections and dependencies between the components.

▪ Examine and document the dynamic connections and dependencies between the components.

Identified components
⇨118ff.

Examine and document the structural connections and dependencies between the components. The initial component boundaries were outlined in the previous steps. Structural dependencies between the components can also be derived from the associations between the classes in the analysis model. The component model shown in Fig. 4.5 already contains the corresponding dependency relationships.

Object flow diagram
Reserve vehicle by phone ⇨100

☑ 4.5.1

Examine and document the dynamic connections and dependencies between the components. An important criterion for component building is minimizing the interconnection and dependencies between components. The connections arising from the process flow are also significant in this respect. Below we shall return to the object flow diagram of the *Reserve vehicle by phone* use case. Each activity is now uniquely assigned to a component. In many cases, this assignment can be easily decided from a technical point of view. In cases of doubt, however, minimization of interfaces takes precedence.

Object flow diagram:
UML Fundamentals
⇨255

The object flow diagram shown in Fig. 4.8 is now subdivided into two responsibility zones (so-called *swim lanes*), which represent the possible component structure. The process flow of this use case displays only one transition

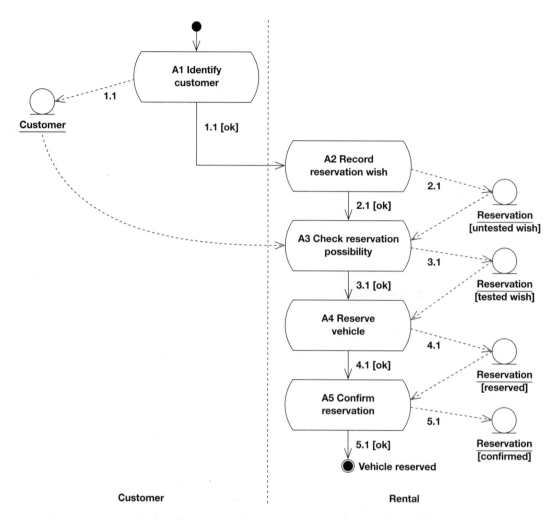

Figure 4.8 Division of the individual activities into domain components

from the control flow of the *Customer* component to the *Rental* component. In this case therefore there are no essential dependencies between the components. The activity *A3 Check reservation possibility* of the *Rental* component needs to be able to access a customer object of the *Customer* component.

Alternatively, the interactions between the components can be examined with sequence or collaboration diagrams.

The interconnection between the components can also be quantified, if required. In our example this produces the following (admittedly trivial) numbers:

Interaction diagrams
⇨256

☑ 4.5.2

Restructuring
☑ 4.5.3

| Control flow changes (inputs) | 1 |
| Accesses to foreign objects | 1 |

If there is a high degree of interconnection, measures should perhaps be taken to reduce this and the components should be restructured.

Checklist:

☑ 4.5.1: Has each activity in the available object flow diagrams been assigned to a single domain component?

☑ 4.5.2: Has the dynamic interconnection of the components been determined by examining the changes in control flow and the accesses to foreign objects?

☑ 4.5.3: Have the components been restructured, if necessary, to minimize the degree of interconnection?

4.6   Designing Component Interfaces

Synopsis

■ Based on the use cases, define the necessary interfaces for each identified component.

Object flow diagram
Reserve vehicle by phone ⇨100

Look at the individual components from the point of view of the use case controller component. For example, let us once again consider the *Reserve vehicle by phone* use case, the object flow diagram of which has just been divided into areas of responsibility (swim lanes).

Application architecture
⇨114

The use case controller component is responsible for controlling this process flow, and it moderates the interactions between the dialog controller, the workflow, and the domain components. The process flow defined in the object flow diagram is definitely implemented by the use case controller component. The use case controller component can therefore formulate the requirements on the interfaces between the neighboring components.

Interfaces: UML
Fundamentals ⇨192

We now develop two interfaces: firstly the interface of the use case controller itself (used by the dialog agent), and secondly the interfaces of the domain components (required by the use case controller).

Use case controller interface

We can now derive an interface description from the activity *A1 Identify customer*. The user (represented on the server side by a dialog agent) enters a customer number, which is received by the use case controller component and then used to load a customer. The result is that the customer data is returned to the dialog agent in the form of a data transfer object *Customer data*. Figure 4.9 shows the design developed up to this point.

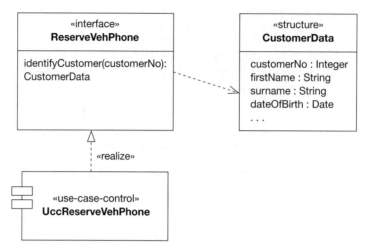

Figure 4.9 Interface provided by the use case controller for the dialog agent

Domain component interfaces

The next step is to consider how the process controller can fulfill its task. It receives the customer number and should load a customer. It must then request data from the customer and use it to generate a data transfer object. From this we can now derive the necessary interface of the *Customer* component, as shown in Fig. 4.10.

☑ 4.6.1

One result of the activity *A1 Identify customer* (see Fig. 4.8) is the *Customer* object. All objects or object states resulting from activities must be located in the interface. The presentation or dialog agent layer does not, however, need a customer object at this point, only individual primitive data elements of the customer, in this case first name and last name. No domain objects are used above the level of the use case controller, only elementary data types such as integer, string, etc. that are combined to form data transfer objects. The use case controller must fill these data transfer objects with data,

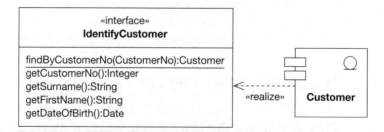

Figure 4.10 Interface of the *Customer* component from the point of view of the *Reserve vehicle by phone* use case

for which purpose it uses the domain objects, in this case *Customer*, and calls *getLastName()* etc. there. *Customer* is the result of the constructor *findByCustomerNo(customerNo):Customer*, as can be seen in Fig. 4.10 in the interface *identifyCustomer*.

The next step is to examine all the other activities in the object flow diagram or use case in the same way and derive the necessary interfaces for the use case controller and domain components.

This is a component-oriented design approach, but in view of the complexity of this subject we must abstain here from any further explanations or details on the modeling of components (EJB keywords, object interfaces, home interfaces, observer mechanisms, persistence, etc.).

Checklist:

☑ 4.6.1:   Are all the objects or object states contained in the object flow diagram located without exception in the described interfaces?

☑ 4.6.2:   Do the described interfaces contain all the operations required for the process controller (use case controller), insofar as they are known?

4.7   Developing Collaboration Models

Synopsis

■ For each use case develop a sequence or collaboration diagram that represents the standard course of events (successful case).

■ Recognize the strengths and weaknesses of the selected design in these situations.

■ For each use case develop 1–3 collaboration diagrams that represent the most important process variants or exceptions.

■ Identify properties that are still missing from the classes in question, i.e. if necessary create new classes, associations, attributes, and operations.

Fundamentals

Collaboration diagrams ⇨256

Sequence diagrams ⇨261

☑ 4.7.1

Collaboration and sequence diagrams illustrate and detail selected situations, i.e. situations that are limited in terms of time and class. They result, among other things, from stimuli at the system boundary (e.g. the dialog layer). Each button triggers an event whose processing can be described by means of a collaboration or sequence diagram. This applies to creation, deletion, and modification of objects or associations, exactly in the same way.

A further possibility for examining the communication between the known objects and components in connection with a use case (here: *Reserve vehicle by phone*) is therefore to develop sequence or collaboration diagrams. Below we shall develop a collaboration diagram.

LIVERPOOL JOHN MOORES UNIVERSITY
LEARNING SERVICES

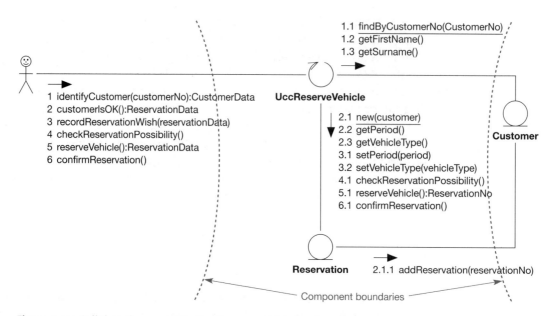

Figure 4.11 Collaboration model for the *Reserve vehicle by phone* use case

UML
collaboration diagram
⇨256

The first step is to take the objects involved and note the existing associations or paths of communication. The messages that the objects send each other in order to carry out their tasks are then shown next to the association lines. In terms of content, the communication follows a concrete scenario, e.g. the standard course of events for the use case. If necessary, additional collaboration diagrams can be created for other important process variants. The messages are numbered in chronological order.

Since the process flow to be examined is only an extract in terms of time and content, it is helpful to define an external actor that kicks off the communication. In Fig. 4.11 it is represented by a stick figure. This actor corresponds to the dialog agent in our assumed application architecture.

The above example runs through the scenario in which the user enters a valid customer number and successfully reserves a vehicle. The process flow begins with message 1 *identifyCustomer()* to the use case controller. To carry out this task, the use case controller must turn to the customer component and search for the customer with the aid of 1.1 *findByCustomerNo()*. The use case controller then gets the first and last name (messages 1.2 and 1.3) from the newly loaded customer and can now use this to generate and return the result structure *CustomerData* required for message 1.

Program code for
identifyCustomer()
⇨133

The creation of the data transfer object *CustomerData* has been omitted from the diagram, since it is trivial and does not need to be considered here. You can however look at it later in the program code.

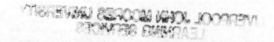
LIVERPOOL JOHN MOORES UNIVERSITY
LEARNING SERVICES

Cross-component
associations ⇨58

Class model cf. fig. 4.4
⇨119

The actor then reports that the customer name is OK (message 2). This marks the start of the next step in the use case. The use case controller generates a new reservation object, with the previously loaded customer being passed as a parameter (message 2.1 *new(customer)*). Since it is necessary that a reservation should always relate to a single customer and that the customer should also immediately create a reference to the reservation (cf. class model), the customer is sent message 2.1.1 *addReservation(reservationNo)*, with the reservation passing as a parameter its number as a unique key. If *Customer* and *Reservation* were objects of the same component, their relationships would be created directly by means of their object identities (in a similar way to message 2.1 with the parameter *customer*). Since, however, component boundaries are being crossed here, only domain-specific keys are exchanged in accordance with the application architecture.

☑ 4.7.3

In this way the two objects *Customer* and *Reservation* can recognize each other. As the result of message 2, the actor finally receives the initial reservation data back (which can then, for example, be displayed as initial values in the dialog). It is apparent that the structure *ReservationData* has not yet been defined. This needs to be created. Since this is just as straightforward as the definition of customer data in Fig. 4.9, we shall refrain from showing it here (it can however be seen in Fig. 4.12).

The process flow is then run through in a similar manner up to the reservation confirmation.

Developing
collaboration diagrams
is an exploratory
activity...

The process flow developed in this way in the collaboration diagram shows only one of many possible processes, since collaboration diagrams are not suitable for displaying all the possible processes in full – unless you were to create a separate diagram for each variant. Since, however, there is often a combinatorial explosion of possibilities, this is unrealistic. You should therefore restrict yourself to 1–3 typical variants (the successful case and the most important exceptions/variants).

☑ 4.7.2

Even if this technique cannot cover all the details, this 80% solution is nonetheless sufficient. The examination of the standard case and some important exceptions produces a quite significant gain in knowledge. Many as yet unknown operations and even some new objects are discovered or created in the course of drawing up the diagram; in this case, for example, the data transfer object *ReservationData*. Developing a large number of additional collaboration diagrams for all the remaining scenarios could not be justified by a cost–benefit analysis, since approximately 80% of the knowledge has already been obtained. The remainder can be acquired during the development of test cases and when programming the operations.

... and once knowledge
has been derived
from them, they have
served their purpose
and are generally no
longer required.

Once you have developed the collaboration diagrams and acquired this new knowledge from them, you can actually forget about them, since each additional detailing and elaboration of the design will immediately render them obsolete.

Checklist:

☑ 4.7.1: Has a collaboration diagram representing the standard course of events been developed for each use case?

☑ 4.7.2: Has a collaboration diagram been developed for the 1–3 most important process variants of a use case?

☑ 4.7.3: Are all the classes, relationships, attributes, and operations used in the collaboration diagrams available, i.e. defined in the class model?

4.8 Developing Process-oriented Component Tests

Synopsis

■ For each use case develop the tests required to test all the defined processes.

■ Recognize which operations and other properties are still missing, in order to develop automated tests.

In fact, instead of "Developing Component Tests" this section could also have been called "Defining and Restructuring Operations," since that is what this step ultimately leads to. The development of automated tests is a design activity. Developing the tests generally produces new insights into the situations to be implemented that you would not gain from a non-test-driven design – or at least not as quickly. In addition, the design must be conceived in such a way that it is subsequently possible to carry out automated tests on it. Where this has not been taken into account from the start, testing requires a great effort or is often possible only in part.

Test-driven design leads you moreover to focus on the result to be achieved, i.e. to produce simple solutions rather than abstract, contrived "reusable" solutions.

Analysis of object flow diagram ⇨103

During the analysis stage the first test cases could be identified on the basis of the use cases or their associated object flow diagrams. At least one test case was required for each outgoing transition of an activity, so that all the paths and variants could be run through at least once in the test. The following test cases, among others, were identified for the *Reserve vehicle by phone* use case:

● Enter valid customer number (A1.1).

See test cases ⇨102

● Enter invalid customer number (A1.2).

● Enter valid customer number, but name does not match (A1.3).

● User aborts dialog (A1.4).

● Enter invalid reservation wish (A2.3) e.g. enter period in the past.

Test the defined
interfaces ⇨104f.

Now develop, i.e. program, the corresponding test classes for these test cases. This should involve testing the interfaces that were defined in the previous steps for the individual components. That sounds simple but may lead you to want to modify the existing interfaces to make them easier to test. This is a typical effect, and is quite desirable, i.e. if necessary you should restructure the existing interfaces.

The tests should, if possible, be automated, i.e. they should just start up, require no user input, check their own results, and be repeated as often as you like.

The following code fragments are based on testing with JUnit[2] using the *UccReserveVehPhone* use case controller as an example. The first step is to produce a rudimentary implementation of the operation to be tested, in this case *identifyCustomer()*. In the simplest case a customer is identified by their customer number, as anticipated in the interface (Fig. 4.9) and the collaboration model (Fig. 4.11). The corresponding operation might therefore look like this:

```
public CustomerData identifyCustomer(customerNo:Integer)
{
    return new CustomerData;
}
```

This operation only returns an empty customer data object and is therefore not yet a complete implementation. But it supplies a valid result, at least formally, and is executable.

The first test operation can now be written. We begin with the first test case *A1.1 Enter valid customer number*. How can *identifyCustomer(customerNo)* be tested? First, a corresponding use case controller should be generated, then you could create a new customer, in order then to find it again with *identifyCustomer(customerNo)*:

```
public void testUccReserveVehicleByPhone() {
        // create use case controller
        UccReserveVehPhone c = new UccReserveVehPhone()

        // create customer to look for
        Customer c1 = new Customer();

        // declare result object
        CustomerData cd = null;

        // A1.1: Look for customer with valid customer no.
        cd = c.identifyCustomer(c1.getCustomerNo());
        assert("No customer found", cd != null);
        assert("Incorrect customer found",
          c1.getCustomerNo() == cd.customerNo);

        . . .
```

___

[2] JUnit is a framework for the automated testing of Java programs.

Test case A1.2 is designed to check that no customer is found if an invalid customer number is entered, whereby we are assuming that 0 is an invalid customer number:

...

```
// A1.2: Look for customer with invalid customer no. 0
cd = c.identifyCustomer(0);
assert("Customer found", cd == null);
```

...

Test case A1.3 is designed to check whether, in the event of an incorrect customer number being entered, another customer number can be input:

...

```
// A1.3: Enter incorrect customer no.
// First create "incorrect customer"...
Customer c2 = new Customer()
// ... then look for "incorrect customer"
cd = c.identifyCustomer(c2.getCustomerNo());
assert("Unexpectedly correct customer found",
  c1.getCustomerNo() != cd.customerNo);

c.customerIsIncorrect(); // user reports difference
```
...
```
// New attempt, this time correct:
cd = c.identifyCustomer(c1.getCustomerNo());
assert(("No customer found", cd != null);
assert("Incorrect customer found",
  c1.getCustomerNo() == cd.customerNo);
```

...

The last test case involved using (i.e. inventing) a new operation *customerIs Incorrect()*. This operation should be included in the interface (Fig. 4.12).

The message *customerIsIncorrect()* informs the controller that the displayed customer is incorrect and the process should not be continued with the next activity. Since this is not a book about software architectures and architecture patterns but "only" about the methodology of analysis and design, we can dodge the question of how the individual states of the process can be checked, i.e. how it can be ensured that particular messages can only be sent if the process has reached a particular state, i.e. a particular activity.[3]

---

[3] OK, let's mention a couple of obvious possibilities: provide a separate interface for each state, apply the state pattern (*see* Gamma, 1996), use a configurable state machine ...

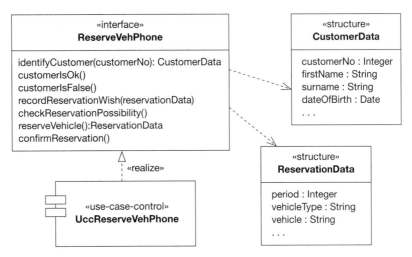

Figure 4.12   Extended use case controller interface

All the other tests can be programmed in a similar way. When all the tests can be completed successfully, you are, in principle, ready. After every change to the code all the tests must be run again. At first, of course, the tests will not yet run successfully, since so far only the interfaces have been defined, but any type of implementation, i.e. functionality, is still missing. In any case, however, the programmed tests should be compilable and executable (even if with negative results). In this way you can check whether all the necessary operations have indeed been defined.

Checklist:

☑ 4.8.1:   Has an automated test been programmed for each identified test case?

☑ 4.8.2:   Are all the automated tests compilable and executable (even if with negative results)?

4.9   Developing Class Tests

Synopsis

▪ Determine which operations in the component interface are to be handled by which class.

▪ Define the preconditions and postconditions of the operations as well as the necessary invariants of the classes.

▪ Develop automated tests for all operations.

The programmed process tests have already uncovered some new operations. The further detailing and implementation of these operations will again yield new operations and the possible need to restructure the existing ones.

Helpful questions for identification of operations include:

- What kind of service is expected from the object (for example, setting of a standard address)?
- Which state transitions might apply to the object?
- When does the life cycle of an object begin, and when does it end?
- For which relations with other objects are add or remove operations required (for example adding a contract)?
- Which information must the object be able to give?
- Which data contents are modifiable? Data changes are carried out via operations which might also take over formal and content checking of the data change.

State diagrams
⇨272

During determination of the operations, you will occasionally gather new insights and a new understanding of relationships between classes. As a consequence, associations, aggregations, and inheritance hierarchies are also adjusted accordingly.

The following items belong to the specification of an operation:

☑ 4.9.3

- *Signature* – describes name, arguments, and return type of the operation.
- *Precondition* – describes the object state that must be given before execution of the operation.

☑ 4.9.1

- *Postcondition* – describes the object state given after execution of the operation.
- *Invariant* – describes the object state that must be present during execution of the operation as well as in general. This includes, among other things, type tests and special value tests for the operation parameters.

☑ 4.9.2

- *Semantics* – describes task and significance of the operation by way of a comment.

In order just to demonstrate the principle, we have included below a simple example for testing the operation *setLastName()*. One invariant is the requirement that the name must be at least one character long. In OCL this would be expressed as follows:

```
context Customer inv:
    self.lastname.length > 0
```

We must now test whether this condition is also met immediately after the creation of a customer (in which the customer is perhaps given the default name "Noname"), whether a valid name will be accepted and an invalid name rejected. In addition, extreme values should be tested. It is assumed that the last name has a maximum length of 40 characters, and if it exceeds this value it will simply be truncated.

```
public void testSetLastName() {
  // Create customer to be changed
  Customer c1 = new Customer();

  // Invariant fulfilled?
  assert("Last name invalid",
    c1.getLastName().length() > 0)

  // Change last name
  c1.setLastName("Goldsmith");
  assert("Last name not modified",
    c1.getLastName() == "Goldsmith")

  // Change last name
  c1.setLastName("Bloggs");
  assert("Last name not modified",
    c1.getLastName() == "Bloggs")

  // Improperly change last name
  c1.setLastName("");
  assert("Last name improperly modified",
    c1.getLastName() == "Bloggs")

  // Last name min. value
  c1.setLastName("3");
  assert("Last name not modified",
    c1.getLastName() == "3")

  // Last name max. value (40 characters)
  c1.setLastName(
    "Goldsmith-Bloggs-Booch-Jacobson-Rumbaugh");
  assert("Last name not modified", c1.getLastName() ==
    "Goldsmith-Bloggs-Booch-Jacobson-Rumbaugh")

  // Last name inadmissible max. value (41 characters)
  c1.setLastName(
    "Goldsmith-Bloggs-Harel-Booch-Jacobson-Rumbaugh");
  assert("Last name improp. modified", c1.getLastName() ==
    "Goldsmith-Bloggs-Harel-Booch-Jacobson-Ru")
```

As this example shows, the code for testing an operation is usually substantially longer than the code for actually implementing it. (However, this is not a book about testing, so the examples are incomplete.)

Checklist:

☑ 4.9.1: Has a test method been developed for each operation?

☑ 4.9.2: Have the semantics of each operation been described?

☑ 4.9.3: Have the invariants, preconditions, and postconditions been described for each operation?

☑ 4.9.4: Are all the operations coherent, i.e. do they only perform a single task?

☑ 4.9.5: Have possible side effects as a result of global variables been ruled out by instead passing the corresponding information as parameters?

☑ 4.9.6: Do overwritten operations behave in a compatible manner to the operations in the superclass?

☑ 4.9.7: Do the operations contain any *switch/case* statements or a series of consecutive *if* statements (indicators of procedural thinking, so-called *fear of polymorphism*)?

☑ 4.9.8: Have the extreme values (minimum, maximum, null, nonsense) of all the parameters been taken into account in order to achieve a robust behavior in all situations?

☑ 4.9.9: Have general and enterprise-specific standards been taken into account?

4.10 Defining Attributes

Synopsis

- Determine the required attributes and assign them uniquely to the existing classes.
- For each potential attribute, ask yourself whether it should perhaps be a class in its own right.
- Divide the attributes into standard attributes, enumerations, and primitive types.
- Determine the required constraints for the attributes.

Fundamentals of attributes ⇨183

Besides the operations, we also need to determine the remaining attributes that have not yet been taken into consideration, that is, we need to take a closer look at the data aspect of the classes. The following questions will help:

- What does the object have to know (generally, short-time)?
- Which information must the object be able to give?
- Which are the attributes used to describe the properties of the object?
- Where does the information come from? What happens to the information in the course of time?

«primitive» ⇨54
«enumeration» ⇨55

As well as the name, data types, initial values, and constraints are specified too, as far as they are known. Besides the usual, system-defined standard data types such as *Integer, Date, Boolean,* and so on, additional fundamental user-defined data types or classes should be created as «primitive» or «enumeration»: *StaffNumber, CustomerNumber, AccountNumber, Currency, ZIP,* and so on.

The found attributes are now thoroughly examined. It has to be considered, for example, whether some attributes had not better be viewed as independent objects. The *Customer* class shown above contains, for example, the attribute *customerGroup* – this attribute would be an appropriate candidate. The attribute becomes the class *CustomerGroup,* and *Customer* is

Attribute or class?

assigned a relationship with this class. Attributes and objects differ insofar as attributes have no identity of their own and can be accessed only via objects. Objects always have their own independent identity, can be accessed and used directly by other objects, and have operations. The questions regarding our above example are:

- Do various domain objects use an identical instance of *CustomerGroup*?
- Do associations lead only to *CustomerGroup,* and there is no association from *CustomerGroup* to a domain class?
- Does a *CustomerGroup* have an independent identity of its own?
- Should the *CustomerGroup* be accessible only by the customer or are there other classes which would like to enter into a direct relation with *CustomerGroup*?
- Does a *CustomerGroup* have to provide special operations of its own that go beyond setting and reading an attribute?
- Is the *CustomerGroup* something that you might handle on its own and that can be used, for example, as a navigation unit?

Figure 4.13 *CustomerGroup* modeled as a domain class

If the last point applies, we would arrive at the model in Fig. 4.13.

If, on the other hand, we consider *CustomerGroup* to be an enumeration, the model would be as in Table 4.3.

Customer
customerNo : Integer firstName : String surname : String customerGroup : CustomerGroup
findByCustomerNo(CustomerNo):Customer getCustomerNo():Integer getSurname():String getFirstName():String getDateOfBirth():Date

«enumeration» **CustomerGroup**

Table 4.3 *CustomerGroup* modeled as an enumeration

Defining enumerations

Consolidate

Find the common
features

An enumeration is a configurable set of values. These are sets of values that
are uniquely defined across the entire application and usually appear as
constant to their users but can in fact be configured. They are employed at
all points where data input is restricted by a predefined set of possible
values. Typically, such sets of values appear in drop-down list boxes.

Examples are sex (male, female), marital status (single, married, divorced,
widowed), type of phone number (phone, fax, mobile), type of address (private, business, holiday, and so on).

Stereotype
«enumeration» ⇨ 55

In class modeling, such sets of values are not noted via associations or the
like, but as attributes with a corresponding type. A particular feature is that
these associations would be directed and of cardinality 1. Thus, if these sets of
values were principally noted as associations, the class models would become
overloaded and unclear. This can be avoided, because the semantic information is relatively small, and such relations are not interesting from a modeling
point of view. Therefore, it is more sensible to note them as attributes.

Since enumerations are a special kind of attribute, it is sensible to define
a stereotype which describes this particular context of usage, for example
«enumeration».

Restructuring

Having a closer look at the attributes to consolidate the present model also
means once again finding common features between the classes, generalizing differences, recognizing dependent and independent properties, and if
necessary further generalizing the classes. With this abstraction, classes will
potentially become usable more universally, both in the current and in
future projects.

Table 4.4 gives some more attribute samples:

Table 4.4 Attribute samples

Street address			
Attribute	*Type*	*Initial value*	*Constraints etc.*
zip	Zip	"00000"	
city	String	"Unknown"	Length = 1 – 30
city2	String		Length = 0 – 30
street	String		Length = 1 – 30
number	String		Length = 0 – 5
Postbox address			
Attribute	*Type*	*Initial value*	*Constraints etc.*
zip	Zip	"00000"	
city	String	"Unknown"	Length = 1 – 30
pobox	String		Length = 1 – 10
Private person			
Attribute	*Type*	*Initial value*	*Constraints etc.*
name	String	"NoName"	Length = 1 – 40
firstName	String		Length = 0 – 30
title	String		Length = 0 – 20
dateOfBirth	Date		dateOfBirth ‹ today
female	Boolean	false	
Employee			
Attribute	*Type*	*Initial value*	*Constraints etc.*
staffNo	Integer	serial no.	staffNo = 1 – 99999
initials	String		Length = 2 – 4

It is fundamentally more advantageous to have a behavior-driven rather than a data-driven design, which is why the activity of *Designing attributes* should only be carried out after the most important operations have been determined. A data-driven design generally gives rise to a small number of central entity classes with a high proportion of control operations and a high overall interconnection of classes. In a behavior-driven design the tasks are more equally divided across the classes, significantly fewer messages are generated, and the classes are interconnected more loosely.

Checklist:

☑ 4.10.1: Have you examined which attribute candidates are a «primitive»?

☑ 4.10.2: Have you examined which attribute candidates are an «enumeration»?

☑ 4.10.3: Have you examined which attribute candidates represent a domain class («entity»)?

☑ 4.10.4: Have the name, type, initial value and constraints been defined for each attribute?

☑ 4.10.5: Have general and enterprise-specific standards been taken into account?

☑ 4.10.6: Can each attribute be assigned to a responsibility of the class? (*See* Checkpoint 4.3.4.)

4.11 Specifying Dialogs

Synopsis

■ Examine the different contexts or use cases in which a dialog or dialog element is used.

■ Design the dialogs in such a way that they can be used in a uniform manner in as many contexts or use cases as possible.

■ Specify all dialog elements according to a standard pattern.

In a systematic process of application development, in particular in major projects, it does not necessarily make sense to devise dialogs completely and immediately. Dialogs are elements with which users are confronted directly; thus, their quality is decisive for positive acceptance of the software and consequently for the whole success of the project.

Dialog contexts

In complex applications, individual dialogs mostly occur in a multitude of contexts. To prevent users from being presented with a separate, different dialog for each processing context, and also in view of the development and maintenance cost, the general aim is to employ dialogs as universally as possible in different contexts.

The simplest contexts are, for example, creating, editing, and viewing data. Usually, a single dialog is sufficient for this purpose. With more complex dependencies in data creation, so-called wizard dialogs have proved a good solution, while in other cases, users are given more freedom.

As well as these trivial dialog contexts, such as creation and modification of data, there are further, mostly domain-related contexts which often also correspond to possible states of their elementary domain objects, such as reservation, contract, invoiced contract, and so on.

Dialogs
Activities
Subsystems
Components

Cf. dialogs involved in use cases fig. 3.11
⇨108

Dialog contexts are the activities of the activity diagrams (or the use cases from which the activity diagrams originate). To view these relationships systematically and be able to deduct requirements from them, it is helpful to associate the identified dialog components with the activities in question. Identification of dialogs has already been shown at use case level (*see* Fig. 3.11 on page 108). This refinement of use cases into activity models is now matched by the refinement of dialogs into dialog components. Since

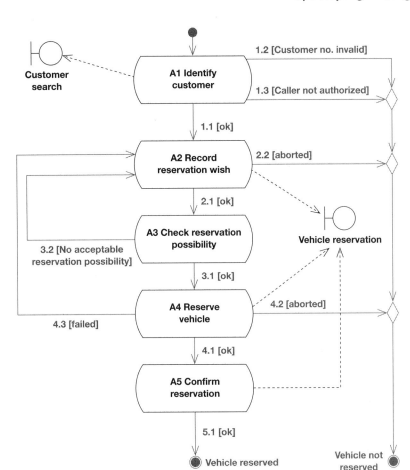

Figure 4.14 Allocation of the dialogs to the activities of the *Reserve vehicle* use case

the activities are already associated with concrete subsystems or components, the association of dialog components with activities implicitly entails an association of dialog components with subsystems (Fig. 4.14).

☑ 4.11.1

When dialogs are supposed to be employed in highly different contexts, the design can be finalized only after all working contexts are known. Otherwise, a dialog is designed and set up for the current environment, and is extended and modified accordingly when it is to be employed in another situation. This may, however, make part of the previously invested effort null and void.

Specifying dialog elements

Dialog specification

☑ 4.11.2

Therefore, it would appear to be best initially only to specify the dialog requirements. This may again happen at two levels. On the one hand, the individual fields and dialog elements need to be specified, for example length and type of the input field *street*. On the other hand, dialog elements can be combined into groups, for example *street*, *place*, and *ZIP* into an *address* group. Such groups can also be called dialog components; they are the smallest technically reasonable combination of individual dialog elements.

The information in Table 4.5 relates to the specification of dialog elements.

Table 4.5   The specification of dialog elements

Question/requirement	Example
What is the field called?	dateOfBirth
Is the field obligatory in principle?	true
Under what condition is it an obligatory field?	age >= 18
How many characters can be entered (minimum and maximum length)?	(length(name) >= 3) and (length(name) <= 40)
Is there an initial or default value?	name = "Anyname"
When or under what condition is the field locked?	date < today
When or under what condition is the field hidden?	date == null
What type of dialog element is it (input box, button, list box, etc.)?	combo box
What checks are carried out when the field is modified and what error message is shown, if applicable?	dateFrom > dateTo: "Negative periods are not allowed"
What checks are carried out when the dialog is terminated and what error message is shown, if applicable?	dateFrom>dateTo: "Negative periods are not allowed"
What short info text (i.e. "bubble help") is shown?	"Zip code"
What long info text (i.e. status line, etc.) is shown?	"Enter a valid zip code"
Is there a predefined set of values, or calculation/selection rules?	{"male", "female", "??"} {select entry from enumerations where type="sex"}
What event is to be triggered (e.g. in the case of buttons)?	ReleaseContract
Under what conditions is this event to be triggered?	date.isValid: EnterDate

Constraints

It should be noted that a large number of formal checks and consistency conditions can already be assured by the dialogs – but only to provide user-friendly and easy-to-handle dialogs. The responsibility for consistency of data and states is ultimately with the domain objects, in which all constraints must be implemented so that they never get into an undefined state. Within dialogs, instead, admitting incomplete and contradictory data is unavoidable, at least temporarily.

In addition to the constraints required by the domain classes, dialogs can enforce further restrictions to guide users in a more directive, that is, restrictive fashion.

Checklist:

☑ 4.11.1: Do you know the different contexts in which each individual dialog will be used?

☑ 4.11.2: Has each individual dialog element been fully specified according to a standard pattern?

→ Some Important Naming Conventions

- Class names, global variables, and class attributes begin with an upper case letter. In compound words, each word begins with an upper case letter, without insertion of underscores.

- Attributes, temporary variables, operations, and parameters begin with a lower case letter. In compound words, all subsequent words begin with an upper case letter, without insertion of underscores.

- Implementation details, in particular type specifications, should not be mentioned in the name of a descriptor.

- Names with semantic content are to be preferred to names with type specifications (sizeOfArray instead of anInteger).

- Names of descriptors should be chosen in such a way that they can be read like a sentence within instructions.

- Operations which return a Boolean as a result should be prefixed with is or has (isEmpty, hasPrinted).

- Names of operations should contain active verb forms and imperatives (deleteInvoice, openCustomerFile).

- Comments should consist of complete sentences and contain active language, naming responsibilities ("Adds the element" instead of "The element is added").

- Operations which return the value of an attribute have the same name as the variable (without the prefix *get*).

- Operations which change the value of an attribute have the same name as the attribute (without the prefix *set*); the parameter describes the expected type.

- Temporary variables should always be used for one purpose only; otherwise, several variables should be declared.

4.12 Discussion of Design

Synopsis

- We shall now look at various design alternatives for a selected section of the example and critically discuss their strengths, weaknesses, and implications.

We shall now make a leap forward in time and imagine that we are one to two iterations further along, and that in the meantime the *Customer* component identified in Section 4.2 has now become a more comprehensive business partner component. The corresponding class model should now be (further) developed. The following terms have appeared in this connection:

- business partner
- customer
- customer file
- contact partner
- supplier
- supplier file
- enterprise
- private person
- bank account
- telecommunication connections (in short: phone number)
- address
- employee.

To begin with, all the listed terms are interpreted as possible classes. But what are their responsibilities and relationships to each other and how can they be suitably represented in a design model? These and other questions will be discussed below.

The terms *enterprise* and *private person* do not exist on their own but only in connection with the terms *business partner*, *customer*, *supplier*, *contact partner*, and *employee* ("A customer is an enterprise or a private person"). The term *business partner* is a generic term for *customer, supplier, contact partner*, and *employee*.

The following terms can therefore be initially considered as classes: *business partner, private person, enterprise, customer, supplier, contact partner,* and *employee*. We shall look at the question of *addresses* later.

Identifying relationships

After having identified the classes, we are now going to analyze their relationships with each other, i.e. their associations, aggregations, and inheritance relationships.

The following discussion contains several examples which violate important design rules. They are intended to show the difficulties that may arise, and how things should not be done. The corresponding illustrations all contain a sad smiley to show that the solution is problematic.

Business partners and their roles

Multiple inheritance
⇨224

Constraints ⇨197

As already mentioned, *business partner* is a generic term for *customer, supplier, contact partner*, and *employee*. Furthermore, the terms *enterprise* and *private person* do not exist on their own but only in connection with a business partner. A customer (as a specialization of the business partner) can be either a private person or an enterprise. The attempt to represent these facts with the aid of inheritance relationships would lead to the class diagram shown in Fig. 4.15.

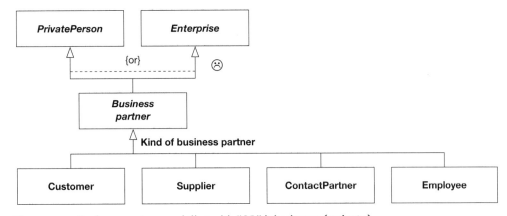

Figure 4.15 Business partner modeling with "OR" inheritance (variant 1)

This model is, however, unsatisfactory: on the one hand, it requires multiple inheritance (even with an exclusive OR); on the other hand, contact partners and employees, although business partners, are always private persons, never enterprises.

Figure 4.16 shows an approach which allows customers and suppliers to be private persons or enterprises. Contact partners and employees, however, are always private persons.

For *customer* and *supplier*, there remains the problem of multiple inheritance. To avoid this, one might think of the following solution which, however, in less trivial cases might quickly lead to a combinatorial explosion of possibilities (Fig. 4.17). Furthermore, the properties to be assigned to the terms *enterpriseCustomer* and *privateCustomer* will supposedly be more or less the same.

Combinatorial
explosion of
inheritance
relationships

Figure 4.18 shows a solution in which *private person* and *enterprise* are each a part (composition) of a concrete business partner. The model takes into account the fact that customer and supplier are either a private person or an enterprise, but never both at the same time. *Contact partner* and *employee*, instead, have always exactly one person object.

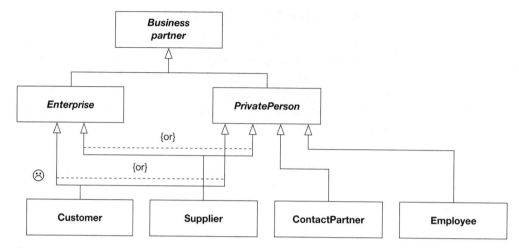

Figure 4.16 Business partner modeling with "OR" inheritance (variant 2)

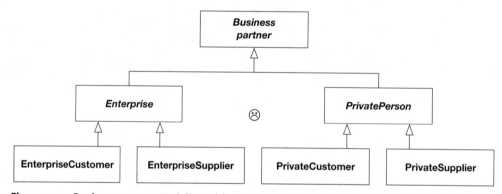

Figure 4.17 Business partner modeling with combinatorial inheritance hierarchy

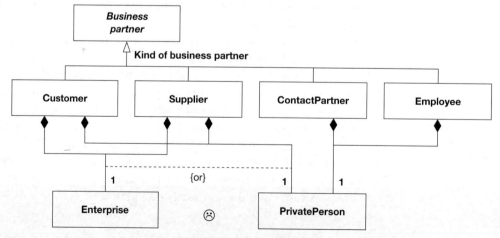

Figure 4.18 Business partner modeling with "OR" compositions

Composition ⇨248

This variation covers the requirements, but would probably become complicated when detailed further. Since *enterprise* and *private person* are not connected with the abstract class *business partner* but with its concrete instances, communication between enterprise and person data and the concrete business partners would have to be located there. This means that the

Redundancy?

required operations – although similar or identical – would have to be maintained redundantly in four concrete business partner instances. This should be avoided for reasons of quality and cost.

OCL ⇨197

The OR constraint between the composition relations between enterprise and private person can also be described by means of OCL expressions. The OR constraint shown above is only a short notation; OCL expressions are usually more precise and therefore preferable. Figure 4.19 shows the corresponding section once again, this time with OCL expressions.

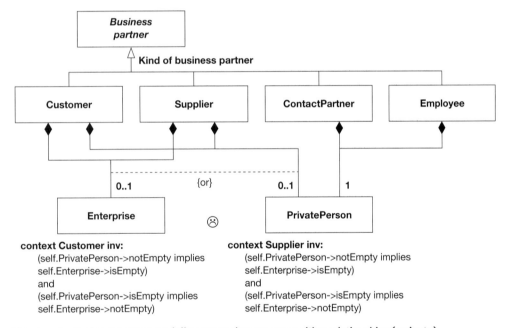

context Customer inv:
(self.PrivatePerson->notEmpty implies
self.Enterprise->isEmpty)
and
(self.PrivatePerson->isEmpty implies
self.Enterprise->notEmpty)

context Supplier inv:
(self.PrivatePerson->notEmpty implies
self.Enterprise->isEmpty)
and
(self.PrivatePerson->isEmpty implies
self.Enterprise->notEmpty)

Figure 4.19 Business partner modeling constraints on composition relationships (variant 1)

Constraints ⇨197

Two constraints each are needed. The first one prevents a customer referring to a private person while simultaneously referring to an enterprise. The second one requires the same if no private person is referred to (Fig. 4.20). Without the second constraint, it would be possible for a customer to be neither an enterprise nor a private person.

In the following solution, again an OR constraint between two composition relations is used. Therefore, we will show once again how this can be converted into the corresponding OCL expressions.

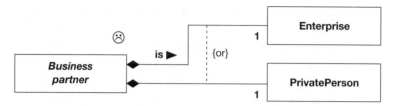

Figure 4.20 Business partner modeling with "OR" composition relationships

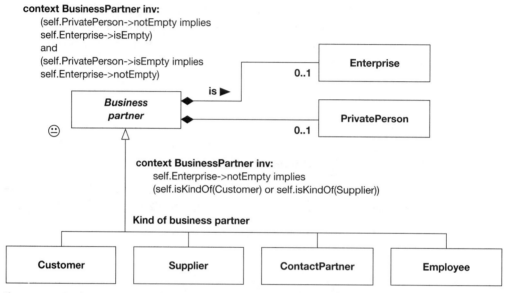

Figure 4.21 Business partner modeling constraints on composition relationships (variant 2)

Figure 4.21 now shows the previously announced better solution. *Private person* and *enterprise* have a composition relation with the *business partner*. The exception that *contact partners* and *employees* are not enterprises is noted as a constraint. This solution covers the requirements, but unfortunately contains a large number of constraints.

A critical check of inheritance

At first sight, the specialization by kind of business partner appears obvious and plausible. A look at the requirements, however, brings this into question. Thus, for example, it was found that suppliers and employees too can be customers. An object can, however, not simply change its class membership (for example from *supplier* to *customer*). Moreover, this would not match the fact, because the concrete business partner is not alternating between being once a supplier and then a customer, but can be both at the same time. However, an object cannot be simultaneously an instance of two classes.

Employee and supplier can be customers
See Analysis
⇨95

The real problem lies in the fact that the kind of view used in modeling is not entirely correct. Business partners cannot be specialized into customers, suppliers, and so on. Instead, customer, supplier, and so on, are possible properties of a business partner. In specific situations, some of these properties come to the fore, for example the customer properties when renting a vehicle.

Specialization vs. role assignment

Customer, supplier, employee, and *contact partner* are therefore not business partner classes but business partner roles. A role defines a special perspective of an object and is a property of the viewer, not of the viewed. The perspective, i.e. the role, initially changes things only for the person viewing or using the object. In our example, it is the car rental agency, or the users of the software to be developed, who perceive business partners in specific situations in a specific role such as supplier or customer. Figure 4.22 takes these reflections into account.

Business partner roles

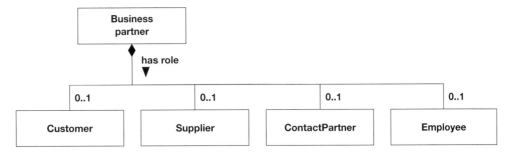

Figure 4.22   Business partner modeling with roles (1st approach).

Yet another – and in connection with our business partner roles the last – variation is based on the actor-role pattern. The design problem discussed here is a classical application for this design pattern. In Smalltalk, its implementation is relatively easy and requires only a few lines of instructions (overwriting of the *messageNotUnderstand:* method). In languages without dynamic type binding and without classes accessible at runtime (such as C++ and Java), it requires a little more effort.

Actor-role pattern

A special feature of this design pattern is that the different partner roles (*customer, supplier, employee, contact partner,* and so on) can forward (propagate) messages to the person to whom they belong. This means that, for example, suppliers can be treated in the same way as an object of the *Person* class. All messages that cannot be directly interpreted by a partner role object (the name of the person, the date of birth of a private person, and so on) are forwarded to the person object (for example a private person) and answered by the latter. The *Partner role* class provides the interface of *Person,* which in Fig. 4.23 is symbolized by the interface lollipop.

Interface lollipop
⇨206

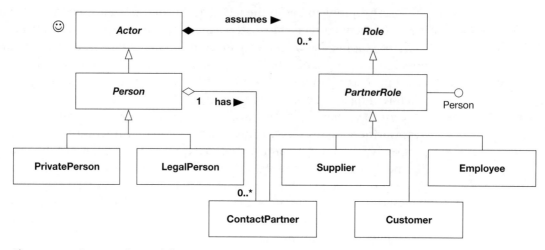

Figure 4.23 Partner roles model

The figure also shows a relationship between *Person* and *contact partner*. Contact partners are needed in particular for legal entities. Frequently, there are also several contact partners (for special domains, and the like) in one enterprise. However, we can also conceive contact partners for private persons, if for example the husband or wife of the actual hirer and driver makes the vehicle reservations.

To prevent a person from being able to refer to itself as contact partner, the following OCL constraint needs to be noted:

ContactPartner
```
self.Person <> self.Actor
```

Bank account, phone number and address

Composition ⇨248

Next, we can integrate the classes *bank account*, *phone number*, and *address* into the class model (Fig. 4.24). This is slightly easier: each of the objects of the three classes is part of a business partner. Each kind of business partner may have an arbitrary number of them (*0..**). All three are perceived as existence-dependent on their respective business partner; that is, we are dealing with composition relations.

A closer examination of the address shows that there are various types of address:

- Street address: address with street, city, and zip code.
- Post box address: address with post office box, city, and zip code.
- Corporate address: corporate address consisting of city and zip code.
- Foreign country address: with no standard structure.

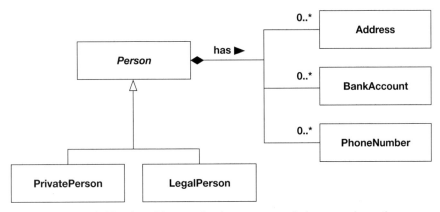

Figure 4.24 Model for the addresses, bank accounts, and phone numbers of a person

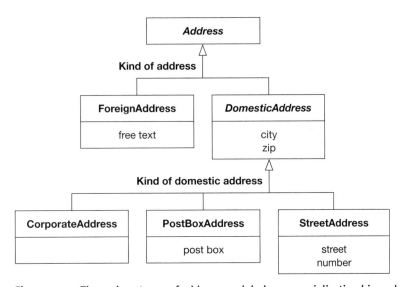

Figure 4.25 The various types of address modeled as a specialization hierarchy

Identifying classes
⇨135

Technical dictionary
⇨94

The basis for our discussion is the model outlined in Fig. 4.25. It is composed of the four concrete kinds of address and two abstract classes *Address* and *Domestic address*.

   This model shows a hierarchical structure of the different kinds of address which, at first sight, looks plausible. The question is, however, whether this solution can be adequately implemented. Adequate in this context means that the implementation cost is reasonable and that the solution is sufficiently robust and flexible. To clarify this, it is helpful not only to look at the data side but also to consider the behavior of such objects and to take their representation into account.

Figure 4.26 shows the four dialog variations. The kind of address is selected by means of radio buttons. Depending on the activated option, specific address fields are shown or hidden. Users can change the type of an address at any time. As long as the address dialog is not terminated, the kind can always be switched. The contents of the fields – even if they are hidden – are preserved. As soon as the dialog is exited, however, only the data of the current kind of address is taken over (Fig. 4.26).

Figure 4.26 The various types of address as displayed in dialogs

Returning to the present class model, the change of kind of address means that the class membership of the address object would need to change – which is not envisaged in Java and C++, and is not common practice in Smalltalk. Precisely speaking, with each change of kind, a new address would need to be created, i.e. a new object with its own identity. The previous old object could be destroyed. Address objects are part of a business partner, so that with each change of object the aggregation relation between *business partner* and *address* would need to be updated. These considerations already show that in order to implement the class model, much effort needs to go into the details.

Figure 4.27 shows a solution whose particular feature is an interface class which is used to hide the internal structure. The solution is based on the *Façade* design pattern, with borrowings from the *State* pattern.

The advantage of this solution is that the owner of an address is always only confronted with one class and one interface. Delegation of the actual attributes and operations is hidden; four interfaces are reduced into one. This also reduces the dependencies between the classes (address and business partner). Internally, the address is structured very pragmatically, i.e. the attributes *city* and *zip* for domestic and other addresses are not factorized out because this would (as we have seen a few pages ago) produce abstract classes

Dynamic
classification

Delegation ⇨33

Interfaces ⇨192
Design patterns ⇨56
Packages ⇨215

with only one or two attributes. The operation *getLetterAddress()* returns a complete multi-line string containing all important components of the address as required, for example, for printing letters, mailshots, and so on.

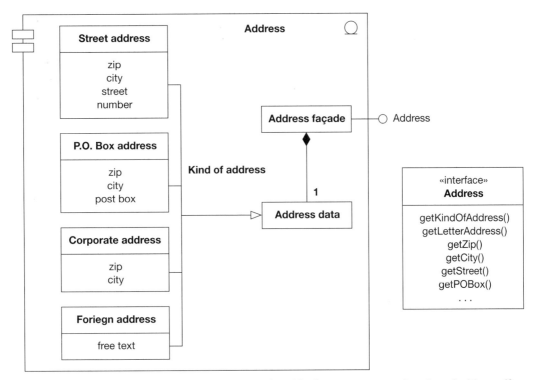

Figure 4.27   The various types of address encapsulated in the component and equipped with a uniform façade

Since in a running system a large number of addresses is to be expected, their structure should not be too complicated. On the other hand, the internal structure is well protected by the interfaces so that modifications and maintenance of the internal representation pose no problems.

Depending on the premises, other solutions may be sensible too. Here, we have merely discussed one possible version.

Checklist:

☑ 4.12.1: Does a subclass support all the attributes and operations of its superclass, i.e. has a suppression of properties been avoided?

☑ 4.12.2: Does each class have a large degree of internal coherence, i.e. have related responsibilities been concentrated in one class?

☑ 4.12.3: Does each class have only a small number of external dependencies, i.e. contracts/interfaces to other classes?

☑ 4.12.4: Has indirect navigation been avoided, i.e. does a class have only limited knowledge of its neighboring classes?

☑ 4.12.5: Have client-server relationships been designed between the classes (cooperation principle)?

☑ 4.12.6: Are the superclasses of an abstract class themselves abstract classes?

☑ 4.12.7: Does a subclass not define any constraints on the properties of the superclass?

☑ 4.12.8: Have you examined the relationships between the classes to determine whether there are any domain-level dependencies or hierarchies between the classes?

☑ 4.12.9: Have you examined inheritance relationships and attempted to replace them by delegation, etc.?

☑ 4.12.10: Have you identified those structures (classes and relationships) which may become unstable in future, and can they be clearly and unambiguously distinguished from those which are assumed to be stable?

☑ 4.12.11: Can the class structure survive without a combinatorial explosion of relationships, even in the event of future extensions?

☑ 4.12.12: Have separate operations been provided instead of operation modes?

☑ 4.12.13: Does the code for each operation generally cover less than a page? Otherwise you might as well go back to Cobol, PL/1, etc.

☑ 4.12.14: Have you defined uniform and appropriate names, types, and parameter sequences?

☑ 4.12.15: Have domain classes (e.g. *Vehicle* class with *serial number*, *owner*, *color*, etc.) been separated from expression classes (e.g. *VehicleType* class with *model number*, *length*, *number of doors* etc.)?

📖 Suggested Reading

1. Gamma, E., Helm, R., Johnson, R., Vlissides, J. (1995) *Design Patterns: Elements of Reusable Object-Oriented Software*, Addison-Wesley, Reading.

chapter 5

UML Fundamentals

This chapter gives a detailed explanation of the individual diagrams and model elements used in OOAD (which are derived for the most part from UML).

Introduction 158

Types of Diagrams 160

Use Case Diagrams 161

Class Diagrams (Basic Elements) 172

Class Diagrams (Relational Elements) 219

Behavioral Diagrams 250

Implementation Diagrams 272

5.1 Introduction

This chapter describes all the necessary theoretical principles and model elements that were used in the example in Chapters 3 and 4 or that are important in general. Most of them belong, directly or indirectly, to the UML. Where they relate to necessary extensions to the UML, this has been indicated.

What is UML?

The Unified Modeling Language is a language and notation for specification, construction, visualization, and documentation of models of software systems. UML takes into account the increased demands on today's systems, covers a broad spectrum of application domains, and is suitable for concurrent, distributed, time-critical, socially embedded systems, and many more.

History ⇨3

UML in its current version 1.4, which is the basis for this book, can be seen as an industry standard. Almost all tool manufacturers and authors already support UML or have announced their intention to do so. The Object Management Group (OMG) has declared UML as its standard. It was developed under the direction of Grady Booch, Ivar Jacobson, and James Rumbaugh (the "Amigos") of Rational Software. Many other enterprises, such as Digital Equipment, Hewlett-Packard, i-Logix, ICON Computing, MCI Systemhouse, Microsoft, Oracle, Texas Instruments, and Unisys, have actively participated in its development and support UML.

Who stands behind UML?

UML is a language and notation for modeling, but it is intentionally not a method. The Amigos do not undervalue the importance of a method, but consider it as something different. A method needs to consider the specific framework and conditions of the application domain, the organizational environment, and much more. UML can serve as a basis for different methods, as it provides a well-defined set of modeling constructs with uniform notation and semantics.

Which method is used here?

The method underlying the analysis and design chapters of this book is use case driven, architecture-centered, and evolutionary, with a view to development of interactive business information systems as they can be found in particular in service and commercial enterprises. This also influences the following explanations of UML, which is why some elements, such as distribution diagrams, receive slightly less attention.

Focus of this chapter

UML includes a multitude of model elements and details. To facilitate getting acquainted with the subject, special and, in practice, less significant elements of the UML are marked as "*advanced UML*." Moreover, to ensure a compact and simplified access, the UML metamodel has been left out of the discussion.

5.1.1   Suggested Reading

Up-to-date information on the continuing development of the UML:
   http://www.omg.org/uml/
Publications by the original developers of the UML:
   Grady Booch: *UML User Guide*, Addison Wesley, 1999.
   Jim Rumbaugh: *UML Reference Manual*, Addison Wesley Longman, 1999.

5.2 Types of Diagrams

The following sections provide detailed explanations of all model elements of UML, ordered by the types of diagram in which the elements are used. Some elements can be part of different diagrams; these are explained in the context of the diagram in which they primarily occur.

The following diagram types are introduced:

Example ⇨161
- *Use case diagram* – shows actors, use cases, and their relationships.

Example ⇨223
- *Class diagram* – shows classes and their relationships with each other.
- Behavior diagrams:
  - *Activity diagram, object flow diagram* – shows activities, object states, states, state transitions, and events.

Example ⇨259
  - *Collaboration diagram* – shows objects and their relationships, including their spatially structured message exchange.

Example ⇨263
  - *Sequence diagram* – shows objects and their relationships, including their chronologically structured message exchange.

Example ⇨272
  - *State diagram* – shows states, state transitions, and events.
- Implementation diagrams:

Example ⇨218
  - *Component diagram* – shows components and their relationships.

Example ⇨273
  - *Deployment diagram* – shows components, nodes, and their relationships.

5.3 Use Case Diagrams

This section explains in detail the elements of the Unified Modeling Language used for the representation of use case diagrams.

5.3.1 Use Case Diagram

Definition
A use case diagram shows the relationships between actors and use cases.

Description

Business processes, business events

A use case diagram describes the interaction between a set of use cases and the actors involved in these use cases. It therefore represents both context and structure for the description of how a business event is handled.

A business event is, for example, the written damage report of a person with home insurance. The business process (for example "Damage claim home insurance") describes the entire process of handling such an event. Potentially, the business process also includes activities which are not directly supported by software or the application to be developed (for example "Visit to the premises by a loss adjuster").

Explanation of use cases ⇨163

There are various types of use cases, various types of actors, and various types of relationships between these model elements. They will be explained individually in the following sections.

Not process diagrams

It should be noted that use cases do not represent a design approach, and that they do not describe the internal behavior of the system, but are a tool for requirement determination. Use cases should not be used for functional destructuring; they are not process diagrams, data flow charts, or functional models.

Use cases support communication with future users, the customer, the technical department, and the like. Use cases describe external system behavior, that is, *what* the system is supposed to do. *How* this comes into being – i.e. which system design and which implementation contribute to this external system behavior – are questions to which use cases provide no answer.

Example
Figure 5.1 shows those parts of a *Magazine circulation* business process supported by software within an enterprise. Each incoming magazine is first registered by the library before its content is analyzed by an employee. The articles the analyzer has found to be of interest are entered into the system as summaries. Subsequently, the magazine is circulated among the employees, which is not considered in the use case diagram because it is not to be supported by the system under development. However, magazine circulation requires a circulation note to be produced. This note is attached to the magazine and contains the names of the employees currently reading the magazine. Creation of this note is to be supported by the system. Finally, after the last reader has returned the magazine to the library, it is archived in the library.

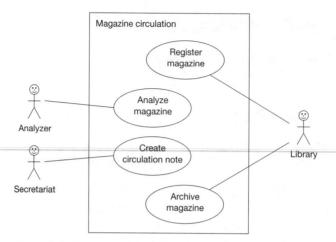

Figure 5.1   Use cases of the *Magazine circulation* business process

Activity diagrams
⇨250

The four use cases in this example, read from top to bottom, suggest that there is a sequence, but this is not present and not intended on the part of the UML. (If you nonetheless try to infer a sequence, you will probably run into problems.) The diagram merely describes what use cases there are and who is involved in them. The representation of process flows and sequences is described in Section 5.6.1.

Notation

A use case diagram includes a set of use cases which are represented as individual ellipses, and a set of actors and events that are involved (actors). The use cases are joined by straight lines with the classes involved. A frame around the use cases symbolizes the system boundaries (Fig. 5.2).

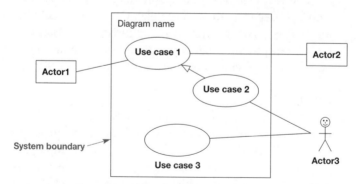

Figure 5.2   Notation elements of the use case diagram

The names of the use cases can either be placed within the ellipse or underneath it. The latter variant makes it possible to draw ellipses that are always the same size, irrespective of the length of the name, which is why it is preferred by some tools.

5.3.2 Use Case

Related terms: scenario, script.

Definition

A use case describes a set of activities of a system from the point of view of its actors which lead to a perceptible outcome for the actors. A use case is always initiated by an actor. In all other respects, a use case is a complete, indivisible description.

Description

Business processes, business events

A use case is a description of a typical interaction between a user and a system, i.e. it represents the external system behavior in a limited working situation from the point of view of the user. It describes requirements for the system – what it should do, but not how it should do it. A use case can have different variations. A very specific variation of a use case is called a scenario. A use case describes a set of possible scenarios. The context of a use case is usually limited by the actions a user carries out on an application system in one operating cycle in order to process one business event of a business process.

Scenarios

The following rules should be observed:

- At least one actor is involved in each use case.
- Each use case has a domain-specific trigger.
- Each use case produces a relevant domain-specific result for the actors, i.e. a result of "commercial value."

Various types of use cases may be distinguished:

«essential»
Essential
Use case

- *Essential use cases «essential».* An essential use case is described in an abstract, generalized, simplified, implementation-independent, and technology-neutral manner. It concentrates on the actual domain-specific intention and therefore represents the shortest and most abstract form of use case description.

Normal
Use case

- *Normal (pragmatic) use cases.* A pragmatic use case is a standard use case that, in contrast to an essential use case, may also contain non-domain-specific basic conditions and assumptions.

«secondary»
Secondary
Use case

- *Secondary use cases «secondary».* Secondary use cases are use cases that do not possess the aforementioned required properties of a domain trigger and a domain result but which have been produced by a functional subdivision of existing use cases, i.e. for example by the application of include and extend relationships.

Observe granularity

No functional decomposition!

When subdividing a use case into several smaller use cases, you should ensure that each use case has a domain trigger and produces a domain result. Use cases that are not initiated by an actor and that do not lead to a perceptible result for the actor are incorrect or incomplete, or they have been produced by a functional decomposition. In this case they should be identified as secondary use cases.

5.3.3 Actor

Related terms: stakeholder, event, external system, dialog, boundary, control, entity.

Definition

An actor is an entity located outside the system that is involved in the interaction with the system described in a use case. An actor may be a person, e.g. a user, but may also be another technical system, e.g. SAP, the operating system, etc.

Description

Actors = roles

Actors are, for example, the users of a system. As actors, however, it is not the person involved who is perceived but the roles they assume in the context of the use case. Thus, if a person appears in several roles (for example *customer advice* and *order reception*), several corresponding actors are noted in the use case diagram.

Events
External systems

Actors possess associations to use cases if they are involved in the processes described in the use cases. Actors can also have relationships to each other. On the one hand, they can have association relationships, if you wish to portray that actors interact among each other, which generally does not represent any direct requirements on the system to be produced, but which makes clear the overall situation and the context of the use case. Associations between actors can be used in exactly the same way as associations between classes, i.e. they may be directed, possess multiplicities, have relationship names, and also represent aggregations or compositions, although in most cases this will not be necessary or meaningful. On the other hand, actors can have generalization/specialization relationships, in order to represent a hierarchical structure and abstraction between them.

Customer

«actor»
Actor: person involved in the use case
role of the person in the use case context

Scheduling system

«actor»
Actor: other (technical) systems involved
in the use case, or their role

Time event

«actor»
Actor: external system involved in the use
case that triggers a time event (e.g. timer
of the operating system)

Figure 5.3 Actors do not have to be people

Notation and Example

Actors can be represented in different ways: as textual stereotypes, visual stereotypes, or in a mixed representation (Fig. 5.4).

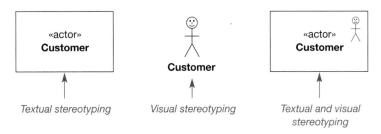

Textual stereotyping   Visual stereotyping   Textual and visual
stereotyping

Figure 5.4 Various ways of representing actors

Since it may be confusing to portray actors that represent other technical systems as stick figures, there are other visual stereotypes, for example a cube for representing technical systems or a clock icon for representing a time event (usually triggered by a technical system, for instance the operating system).

Stereotypes ⇨ 209

Actors describe the roles of parties involved in the use case. These roles may be generalized or specialized.

Since use cases are employed to record system requirements in the form of typical processes seen from the user's point of view, acceptance and comprehension of the symbols and concepts used is decisive. In practice, it might therefore be sensible to use simpler or more intuitive representations, such as a clock icon for a time event (see above).

5.3.4 Use Case Description

A use case describes a set of activities of a system from the point of view of its actors which lead to a perceptible outcome for the actors. A use case is always initiated by an actor.

A use case describes a typical working process. The process is composed of (usually consecutively numbered) individual steps. These steps are also known as activities. Since the description is purely textual, noting down dependencies between individual steps is a very long-winded task. Often, for example, the sequence of steps present in the use case is typical, but not mandatory. Some steps may even be skipped in specific situations. Such interrelationships can be textually described only with great effort and remain nevertheless hidden in the text.

A graphical representation of such processes is easier to produce and to understand. Therefore, use case diagrams are often detailed and illustrated by behavior diagrams, for example by activity diagrams and, in specific cases, also by sequence, collaboration, or state diagrams. This is mostly done with a view to the design, in other words, to the description or analysis of the necessary internal system behavior resulting from the use case.

Use cases may also be illustrated with dialog designs or prototypes. This is of greater interest for users and technical departments: processes are visualized and thus communicated in a substantially more concrete way, which provides an additional possibility of validating use cases.

The interrelationships between different use cases can be represented in use case diagrams. Activity diagrams too can be employed to cover several use cases at a time.

Notation

A use case is graphically represented by an ellipsis that bears the name of the use case.

For each ellipse, there is a text that describes the use case in more detail. Such texts may be keyword summaries or more extensive descriptions. They may be informal, but some content-related structuring is recommended.

Each use case has a unique name. Use cases may additionally be numbered for quick identification in diagrams and in their textual form. The following list shows a sample structure of a use case:

Uc No. Name of use case	
Actors: ...	Rules: ...
Trigger/preconditions: ...	Services: ...
Results/postconditions: ...	Requirements: ...
Invariants: ...	Contact partners: ...
Non-functional requirements: ...	Modification history: ...
Process description: ...	Notes/open questions: ...
Exceptions, error situations: ...	Dialog samples, references: ...
Variations: ...	Diagrams: ...

Actors ⇨164

- *Actors*
  Actors (roles) involved in the use case. This corresponds to the relationships between use case and actors noted in use case diagrams.

- *Preconditions, trigger*
  State of the system before the use case occurs.

- *Postcondition, results*
  State of the system after the use case has been successfully gone through.

- *Invariants*
  Conditions which, in the context of the use case, must always be satisfied.

- *Non-functional requirements*
  Important constraints for design and implementation, such as platform and environment conditions, qualitative statements, response time requirements, frequency estimates, priorities, and so on.

- *Process description*
  Description of the use case, possibly structured into numbered individual items. This is the proper kernel of a use case.

- *Exceptions, error situations*
  Description of the exceptions and error situations that may occur in the context of the use case. These are not technical errors but domain-related or user errors, such as lack of users' access rights, impossibility of plausible filling in of input fields, and the like.

- *Variations*
  Deviations and exceptions from the normal process and description of alternative processes for these cases.

- *Rules*
  Business rules, domain-specific dependencies, validity and validation rules, and so on, which are of importance in the framework of the process. Often, activity diagrams are a more suitable alternative for describing such interrelationships.

- *Services*
  List of operations and, where required, objects which are needed in the context of the process (used as a transition towards class design).

- *Requirements*
  References to or specification of requirements relating to more than one use case, non-functional requirements, and other requirements that are not covered by the use case description.

- *Contact partners, other stakeholders, sessions*
  List of persons with whom the use case was elaborated or discussed, date and time of such sessions, and so on; if required, list of people still to be talked to, roles and functions assumed by the people involved, and so on.

- *Modification history*
  A list of the various versions of the use case description, showing in each case the date, author and contents/object of the changes that were made.

- *Notes/open questions*
  This is, for example, the place for documentation of important design decisions. Sometimes, several competing designs exist for a use case. Therefore, the reasons that led to the decision for one alternative or the other should be briefly protocoled; otherwise, at a later stage, the discussion starts again on whether the other alternative would have been a better choice [...].

- *Documents, references, dialog samples or patterns*
  Sample dialogs, screen shots, dialog prototypes, expression and form samples, instructions, manuals, and all other materials which illustrate the use case, and which were used in discussions with the users and so on, or were somehow part of the context.

- *Diagrams*
  Sequence and collaboration diagrams which represent the internal system behavior resulting from or needed for the use case. Class diagrams which show the static model structure resulting from or corresponding to the use case. Activity and state diagrams which show the system-internal dependencies and state transitions in connection with this use case.

Example

The following use case description shows an example for the paying out of money by an automated teller machine (ATM). The underlined terms indicate references to the corresponding glossary entries, which are not defined here:

Name	**Pay out money from an ATM**
Short description	An <u>ATM</u> is to <u>pay out</u> to an <u>authorized user</u> an <u>amount of money</u> required by the <u>authorized user</u> and the <u>amount of money</u> is to be <u>debited</u> from the associated <u>account</u>.
Actors	Authorized user, account management system
Trigger	The authorized user inserts a card into the ATM.
Precondition	The <u>ATM</u> is ready to accept a <u>card</u>.
Result	The <u>authorized user</u> has received an <u>amount of money</u> that has been <u>debited</u> from his/her <u>account</u>. The <u>authorized user</u> has been given his/her <u>card</u> back.
Postcondition	The <u>ATM</u> is ready to accept a <u>card</u>.
Essential process	1. <u>Identify authorized user</u>
	2. Determine <u>amount of money</u> required
	3. Check possibility of paying out the money
	4. Debit <u>payment</u> from <u>account</u>
	5. Transmit <u>amount of money</u>

5.3.5 Use Case Relationships

In UML, three types of relationships between use cases are defined:

- **«include»**
  The «include» relationship (which replaces the «uses» relationship in UML 1.1) is used to denote that another use case occurs inside a use case. This construct is therefore suited to extract identical sections occurring in several use cases in order to prevent redundancy. The «include» relationship does not cause any properties to be inherited.

- **«extend»**
  The «extend» relationship, on the other hand, is used to show that in certain circumstances or at a specific point (the so-called extension point) a use case is extended with another use case. The «extends» relationship in UML 1.1 had a slightly different meaning. It pointed to a use case that extended another use case. Now, however, the use case that represents the extension points to the use case that is to be extended. Moreover, by specifying the extension point you can describe the exact place at which the extension case is to be integrated.

  The extension is always dependent on a condition that should be noted as a constraint next to the «extend» relationship or at the extension point. The «extend» relationship is therefore suitable for:
  - highlighting optional system behavior;
  - separating optional system behavior from the standard behavior;
  - documenting the conditions of optionality.

  The «extend» relationship does not cause the properties of the use cases involved (e.g. actors) to be inherited. Since, however, the «extend» relationship is similar to the specialization relationship, this is occasionally practiced.

- **Specialization/generalization**
  Generalization allows sub use cases to inherit behavior and semantics from super use cases, in analogy with the generalization relationship between classes. In other words, sub use cases can partially overwrite the inherited behavior and add further behavior. (*See* Fig. 5.5.)

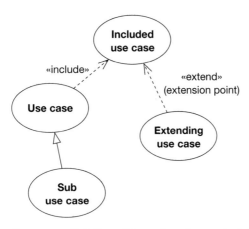

Figure 5.5 Notation of the various forms of relationship between use cases

Generalization ⇨220

The stereotypes *«include»* and *«extend»* are useful but dispensable model constructs that often lead to an excessive functional subdivision of use cases. For this reason, many modelers refrain from using them.

5.4 Class Diagrams (Basic Elements)

This section explains the individual basic elements of the Unified Modeling Language for the representation of class diagrams – each of them structured into definition, description, notation, and example.

5.4.1 Classes

Related terms: type, object factory.

Objects ⇨181
Attributes ⇨183
Operations ⇨186

Definition
A class is the definition of the attributes, the operations, and the semantics of a set of objects. All objects in a class correspond to that definition.

Description

Type ⇨286

Often, the term type is used instead of class, where it should be noted that type is the more general term. A class contains the description of structure and behavior of objects it generates or which can be generated using it. Objects are produced by classes and are the units that act in an application. The definition of a class is made up of attributes and operations. The behavior of an object is described by the possible messages it is able to understand. For each message, the object needs the appropriate operations. Message and operation are often used as though they have an identical meaning, although this is not correct.

Difference
message/operation
⇨40

As well as attributes and operations, a class includes the definitions of potential constraints, tagged values, and stereotypes.

Notation
Classes are represented by rectangles which either bear only the name of the class (in bold) or show attributes and operations as well. In the second case, the three rubrics – class name, attributes, operations – are divided from each other by a horizontal line. Class names begin with an upper case letter and are singular nouns (collective classes or similar may be in the plural form, if required).

Attributes are at least listed with their name, and may additionally contain specifications of their type (that is, their class), an initial value, and potential tagged values and constraints. (*See* Fig. 5.6.)

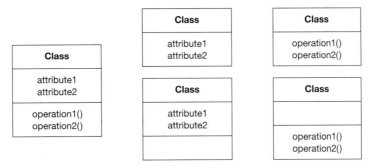

Figure 5.6 Various methods of notation for attributes and operations

Operations are also noted at least with their name, and additionally with their possible parameters, class and initial values of these parameters, and potential tagged values and constraints.

In the top rubric (class name) we find, above the class name and enclosed in guillemots, the class stereotypes (for example *«DomainClass»*), while below the class name and enclosed in braces, we find the tagged values (for example *{abstract}*). The class name can be prefixed with the name of a package, with a double colon separating package and class names. (*See* Figs. 5.7 and 5.8.)

Abstract classes ⇨178

Package ⇨215
Attributes ⇨183
Operations ⇨186

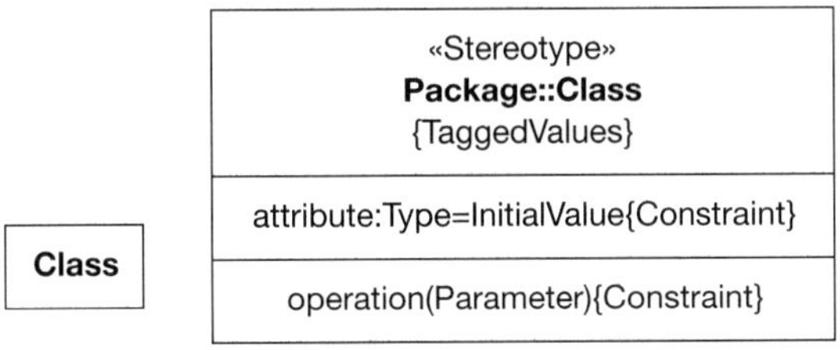

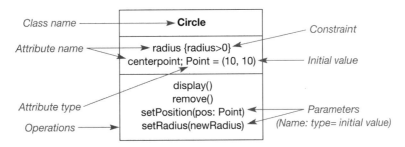

Figure 5.7 Notation possibilities for classes

Figure 5.8 Example of a class

Further rubrics may be inserted, for example to group properties with the same stereotypes (*see* section 5.4.10).

Grouping by
stereotypes ⇨209

Packages ⇨215

Example

A class *Circle* might, for example, include the attributes *radius* and *position* together with the operations *display()*, *remove()*, *setPosition(pos)*, and *setRadius(newRadius)*. No package name is specified in the illustration, but it might read *Graphics::Circle*. The constraint *{radius > 0}* requires the value of the attribute *radius* to be always greater than 0. A circle with a negative radius or with a radius equal to 0 is not allowed. The specification of the initial value (*10, 10*) for the attribute *center* means that when an instance is generated, the value of the attribute is preset to this value.

Metaclass

ADVANCED
UML

Class operations, see
⇨186

In Smalltalk (and also in CLOS), classes too are simply objects – they can be sent messages, and they can include (class) attributes. In C++, class attributes and operations can be emulated by declaring them as *static*. However, in C++ classes cannot be treated like objects. An example for a class message or a class operation is *new*, which is used to create a new instance of a class. In Smalltalk, for example:

```
newObject:= Class new.
anEmployee:= Employee new.
```

Classes of class objects are called metaclasses and, similarly to a normal class, noted with the stereotype *«metaclass»* (Fig. 5.9).

Stereotypes ⇨209

«metaclass»
CustomerClass

Figure 5.9 Metaclass

In Smalltalk, classes are principally instances of their metaclasses. The metaclasses themselves are instances of the class *MetaClass*, which in turn is an instance of the class *MetaClassClass*. The latter, however, is again an instance of the class *MetaClass*, which brings the cascade to an end.[1]

In UML, class operations need not be noted within the metaclass; they may also be contained in the class itself, where they are underlined in order to distinguish them from normal operations. The same applies to class attributes. (*See* Fig. 5.10.)

Class operations
⇨186

Class attributes
⇨183

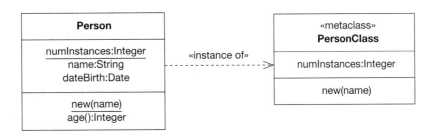

Figure 5.10 Instantiation relationship

---

[1] The representation relates in this case to Enfin Smalltalk. *See* Wallrabe, 1997.

Parameterized Classes

Related terms: generic class, template, bound element.

Template

Definition

A parameterized class is a template equipped with generic formal parameters, which can be used to generate common (that is, non-parameterized) classes. The generic parameters serve as placeholders for the actual parameters which represent classes or simple data types.

Description

In a parameterized class, no concrete class is defined but only a template for generation of classes. These templates are usually a type of macro technique which has no special function, apart from text replacement. In statically typed languages, parameterized classes are an important means for writing re-usable code. C++ and Eiffel support parameterized classes.

Bound element

A class generated with the aid of a parameterized class is called a bound element.

Example

A typical application are collection classes, i.e., classes in which a set of objects can be stored. A possible example is the following waiting queue template (C++):

```
template <class Element>
class WaitingQueue {
  public:
    void add(Element* i);
    void remove(Element* i);
    ...

};
```

This waiting queue can be parameterized for different types of elements, for example for patients in a waiting room or cars in a traffic jam:

```
class Patient;
class Car;

...

WaitingQueue<Patient> WaitingRoom;
WaitingQueue<Car> TrafficJam;
```

Notation

Refinement relation
⇨248

In the graphical notation, parameterized classes are represented in the same way as classes, with an additional dashed rectangle in the upper right-hand corner that shows the parameters. Classes generated with the aid of a parameterized class have a refinement relation with the stereotype *«bind»* to the parameterized class (Fig. 5.11).

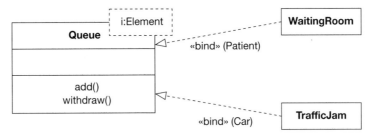

Figure 5.11 Template class with refinement relationship

Another notation variation is shown in Fig. 5.12, in which the parameterized class is shown without the *«bind»* relation (see p. 176: "Description").

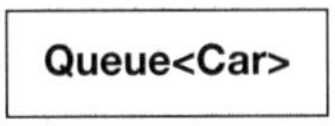

```
Queue<Car>
```

Figure 5.12 Template class in abbreviated form

References

Template-based programming is a programming paradigm in its own right – *see*, for example, Alexandrescu, 2001.

Abstract Classes

Related terms: virtual class.

Definition

Classes ⇨172

An abstract class is never used to generate object instances; it is intentionally incomplete and thus forms the basis of further subclasses which can have instances.

Description

Abstract classes often represent a general term, a generic term for a set of concrete terms. Thus, *vehicle* can be an abstract generic term for *bicycle*, *car*, *truck*, *train*, and *airplane*. Real instances exist of the concrete terms *bicycle*, *car*, and so on, but there is no such thing that would be simply a *vehicle*. *Vehicle* is merely an abstraction, a generalization.

Superclass
Inheritance ⇨220

An abstract class is always a superclass. An abstract class that has no subclasses makes no sense. Either it is superfluous, or it lacks a concrete class as subclass.

Notation

An abstract class is represented in the same way as a normal class, but in addition, the tagged value *abstract* is written below the class name. Alternatively, the class name can also be set in italics. As usual, attributes, operations, constraints, and so on can be part of the class (Fig. 5.13).

Tagged values
⇨207

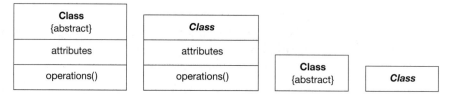

Figure 5.13 Various notation methods for abstract classes

For handwritten presentations, it is somewhat time consuming to mark classes as abstract. On the one hand, it is difficult to produce handwritten italics. On the other hand, you need to know beforehand whether a class is abstract; later marking-up is not possible. In the old Booch notation, you could add an "A" in a triangle standing on its top, which was easier for handwritten notes because it used up less space. In line with the old Booch notation, I often use the short form *{A}* to mark a class as abstract (Fig. 5.14).

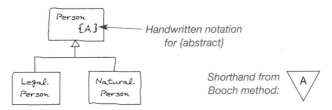

Figure 5.14 Handwritten notation of abstract classes

Example

Discriminator
⇨220

The class hierarchy shown in Fig. 5.15 represents the abstract superclass *GeomFigure*. In practice, a geometric figure will always be a triangle, a circle, or a rectangle, and this is why these are its concrete subclasses. The discriminator in this context is the *figure shape*.

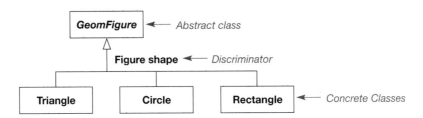

Figure 5.15 Class hierarchy with abstract superclass

Utility Classes

Related terms: function collection.

Classes ⇨172

Stereotypes ⇨209

Definition

Utility classes are collections of global variables and functions which are combined into a class and defined there as class attributes and operations. The stereotype *«utility»* marks a class as a utility class.

Description

Utility classes are not true classes but collections of global variables and functions which are, however, noted in the form of a class.

Notation and Example

Class attribute
⇨183
Class operation
⇨186

Utility classes are noted in the same way as normal classes but have the stereotype *«utility»* (Fig. 5.16). They contain class attributes (global variables) and class operations (global functions/operations).

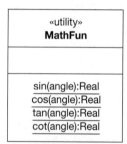

Figure 5.16   Utility class

Utility classes allow procedural facts to be expressed in an object-oriented way. They frequently occur in connection with hybrid programming languages such as C++, which also contain procedural modes of expression. In object-orientation, they are usually not needed; thus, the trigonometric functions shown in the example would fit well as common operations into the corresponding numerical classes.

5.4.2 Objects

Related terms: instance.

Definition

Classes ⇨172

An object is a unit which actually exists and acts in the current system. Each object is an instance of a class. An object contains information represented by attributes whose structure is defined in the class. An object can receive the messages defined in the class, i.e. it has appropriate operations for each message defined. The behavior defined through the messages applies equally to all objects of a class as well as to the structure of their attributes. The values of the attributes, however, may change individually from object to object.

Attributes ⇨183
Operations ⇨186

Description

Instance

An alternative term for *object* is *instance*. A class contains the definition of objects, i.e. their abstract description. The behavior of an object is described through the possible messages it can understand. For each message, the object needs appropriate operations. Message and operation are often used synonymously, although this is incorrect.

In *multiple classification*, an object is simultaneously an instance of more than one class (a fairly theoretical case, not contemplated in C++, Java, and Smalltalk). In Smalltalk, however, you can achieve the same effect via the actor-role design pattern.

«disjoint» (dynamic classification)

In *dynamic classification*, an object can become consecutively an instance of more than one class (mainly possible in Smalltalk, but again a fairly theoretical case).

Notation

Objects are represented by rectangles which either bear only their own name, or which in addition show the name of their class, or the values of specific or all attributes. If attribute values are indicated, the rectangle is subdivided into two rubrics separated by a horizontal line. To differentiate it from the class notation, the name of the object is underlined; furthermore, the object name usually begins with a lower-case letter (Fig. 5.17).

Figure 5.17 Notation possibilities for objects

Collaboration
diagrams ⇨256
Sequence diagrams
⇨261

Attributes are shown with their names and an exemplary value or their current value in the actual context. Operations are not shown because they have no object-individual manifestations and are identical for all objects of a class. In collaboration and sequence diagrams, the concrete message exchange between objects is shown instead.

Instantiation relationships, i.e. class-object relationships are represented by a dashed arrow. The object points to its class (Fig. 5.18).

Dependency
relationship ⇨246

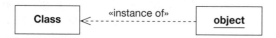

Figure 5.18 Instantiation relationship

Example

See class ⇨172

Figure 5.19 shows an object of the name *aCircle*, which is an instance of the *Circle* class. It is described by the two attributes *radius* and *center*, with the radius having a value of *25* and the center (*x,y*) a value of (*10,10*).

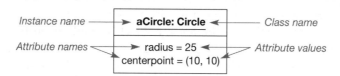

Figure 5.19 Example of an object

5.4.3 Attributes

Related terms: data element, instance variable, variable, member.

Definition

An attribute is a (data) element which is contained in the same way in each object of a class and is represented by each object with an individual value. In contrast to objects, attributes have no identity of their own outside the object of which they are a part and are completely under the control of these objects.

Classes ⇨172
Objects ⇨181

Description

Each attribute is at least described by its name. In addition, a data type or a class, plus an initial value and constraints, may be defined. The definition of the attribute type is programming language dependent: in Smalltalk, the value of an attribute is again an object; in C++ it can also be a pointer, or a composite, or an elementary data type (for example integer). Usually, the type or class of an attribute is indicated.

Instance variable

In languages with dynamic binding (such as Smalltalk), in which attributes (instance variables) are not fixed to one type, the class specification describes which class membership may be expected for the attribute, even though the language remains noncommittal.

Constraints ⇨197
OCL ⇨197

Constraints can be used in addition to the type specification to further restrict the value range or value set of the attribute, or to make it dependent on other conditions. Constraints cannot always be adequately included within the class rectangle and should therefore be noted separately. Most CASE tools, for example, provide extra specification dialogs for attributes; if necessary, more extensive constraints can be recorded as comments. The following is a simple OCL example for a constraint on the *Circle* class regarding the possible values of the *radius* attribute:

```
context Circle inv: radius > 0
```

Tagged values
⇨207
State diagrams
⇨265

Tagged values can be used to specify additional special properties. Thus, for example, the tagged value *{readonly}* indicates that an attribute may only be read.

Optional and mandatory attributes can be differentiated by specification of the appropriate multiplicity:

Optional and
mandatory attributes

Multiplicity
specification

Dynamic Arrays
Composition

```
optionalAttr : Class[0,1]
mandatoryAttr : Class[1]
```

Multiplicity specification should only be noted when they are not [1], which is the default value, that is, normally all attributes are mandatory. Sets (for example dynamic arrays) can be noted with [*], which means that we are dealing with a composition (that is, the elements of the set have their own identity), which should therefore be used, or in other words, modeled.

Derived attributes. A particular variation are the so-called derived attributes. Inside an object, these are not represented physically by a value but are calculated automatically. The calculation prescription is specified in the form of a constraint. For derived attributes too a type can be indicated. Specification of an initial value does not apply; indication of a tagged value is usually dispensable too.

Derived
attributes

Caching
Performance

Class attributes

Visibility mark:
public, protected,
private

Access restriction

Derived attributes are principally not directly modifiable. Since attributes should in no case be directly modifiable, derived attributes can also be realized by means of appropriate operations. Derived attributes should only be derived from object-internal elements and do without accessing neighboring objects. Otherwise, it is preferable to define appropriate calculation operations.

Definition of derived attributes is useful to indicate that intermediate storage (caching) of values is sensible at that point. Usually, this is done wherever calculations must not be repeated unnecessarily, for performance reasons.

Class attributes (class variables) do not belong to an individual object, but are attributes of a class (for example, in Smalltalk). This means that all objects of a class can access such a common class attribute. Class attributes can, for example, be used to count or number the generated objects of a class. With each newly generated object of a class, for example, a counter is incremented.

Visibility. Depending on the programming language, the external visibility of attributes can be restricted. In Smalltalk, this is superfluous, because attributes can only be addressed by the object itself; any external access is only possible via operations. In C++, the access possibilities can be declared as follows:

- *public*: visible and usable for all.
- *protected*: access is allowed to the class itself, its subclasses, and the classes declared as *friend*.
- *private*: only the class itself and the classes declared as *friend*[2] can access private attributes.

Attributes should be used only by the class in which they are defined. Other classes (superclasses, subclasses, and associated classes) should always use operations to access them (*private*).

---

[2] *Friend* is a mechanism in C++ with which a class can grant access rights to selected other classes.

Notation

Attribute names begin with lower-case characters and class names with uppercase ones, while tagged values and constraints are enclosed in braces.

```
Stereotype Visibility attributeName:
   Package::Class Multiplicity = InitialValue {TaggedValues}
```

Class operations
⇨172

Derived attributes are marked by a prefixed slash (/). Class attributes are underlined, and (C++) visibility specifications, such as *public*, *protected*, and *private* are marked with "+", "#" and "–." *Public*, *protected*, and *private* marks can also be assigned to class attributes.

```
+publicAttribute        /derivedAttribute
#protectedAttribute     classAttribute
–privateAttribute
```

Inside a class, attributes are separated from the class name by a horizontal line and are thus located in the second category within the class rectangle.

Examples

```
name : String = 'Unknown'
birthDate : Date
radius : Integer = 25 {readonly}
/age : Integer {age = today – birthDate}
defaultName = 'Noname'
–versionNo : Integer
–counter : Integer
time : DateTime::Time
dynamArray[*]
name : String[1]
firstName : String[0,1]
firstNames : String[1..5]
```

5.4.4 Operations

Related terms: method, service, procedure, routine, function, message.

Definition

Message
Operation
Method

Operations are services which may be required from an object. They are described by their signature (operation name, parameters, and, if needed, return type).

A *method*[3] implements an operation; it is a sequence of instructions.

A *message* passes an object the information on the activity it is expected to carry out, thus requesting it to perform an operation.

Description

Signature
Parameters
Attributes
⇨183

A message consists of a selector (a name) and a list of arguments, and is directed to exactly one receiver. The sender of a message is as a rule returned exactly one response object. Inside a class definition, an operation has a unique *signature* composed of the name of the operation, potential parameters (arguments), and a potential return value (function result). The parameters of an operation correspond in their definition to the attributes, i.e. they bear a name and, where needed, additional indications of type and default value.

Constraints ⇨197

Operations may be provided with *constraints* which, for example, describe the conditions to be met at the call or the values the arguments may have. The arguments of operations can be identified with the keywords *in*, *out* and *inout*, depending on the direction of the data in the operation: only into it, only out of it, or both in and out.

Type = {in, out, inout}

Tagged values
⇨207

Tagged values can be used to describe additional special features. Tagged values are, for example, {abstract} to indicate an abstract operation, or {obsolete} to indicate that this operation exists only for compatibility with previous versions and should no longer be used otherwise.

Abstract
operations

Abstract classes ⇨178

Abstract operations are operations which are represented only by their signature and whose implementation takes place only in a subclass. In C++, abstract operations are also called purely virtual operations. Abstract operations can exist only in abstract classes. Abstract operations that are not repeated and implemented in a subclass make no sense.

Operations that have no side effects, i.e. that do not change the state of the object or other objects, can be marked with the stereotype «query».

Difference
message/operation
⇨40

Objects communicate with each other by exchanging messages. Each object understands exactly the messages for which there is a corresponding operation (which is the reason why the terms message and operation are often used synonymously – this is, however, incorrect). However, in classes that define an object, this operation may be defined multiply.

---

[3] Differently from these definitions, the terms *operation* and *method* are often used synonymously or according to the definition of the programming language used.

Notation

The signature of an operation looks like this:

```
Stereotype Visibility operationName
    (Type argument : ArgumentType = DefaultValue, ...):
    ReturnType {TaggedValues}
```

Example for the *setPosition* operation in the *Circle* class:

```
+ setPosition(in x : Integer = 1, in y : Integer =
1):
    Boolean {abstract}
```

The name of the operation begins with a lower-case letter. Arguments have names that begin with a lower-case letter and are described further by specifying a data type or a class, if required. In this case, argument name and type are separated by a colon. Default values may be specified for arguments, although this is only sensible when using programming languages with optional parameter passing. The body of an operation contains the implementation code and is therefore programming language specific.

Tagged values are enclosed in braces. Abstract operations are either set in italics or assigned the tagged value *{abstract}*:

```
display()
display() {abstract}
```

Constraints ⇨197
OCL ⇨197
Abstract
operations

Constraints on operations should be noted separately. The following is an example of an OCL constraint on this operation:

```
context Circle::setPosition(x : Integer, y : Integer)
    pre: (x > 0) and (y > 0)
```

**ADVANCED
UML**

Class operations (for example in Smalltalk) are indicated by underlining, while the external visibility of operations is marked by prefixed special characters:

Visibility mark

```
classOperation()
+publicOperation()
#protectedOperation()
-privateOperation()
```

In C++, *public* means visible and usable for all, *protected* allows operations to be accessed by the class itself, its subclasses, and classes declared as *friend*, while *private* means that only the class itself and classes declared as *friend* are allowed access.[4]

---

[4] The meanings of these keywords in C++ and Java do not match completely; the best thing to do is use the meaning from the actually employed programming language.

Smalltalk

In programming languages that cannot differentiate operations with regard to their access possibilities, operations are instead given names that begin with *private* (for example *privateShowAt*). This naming convention is mostly sufficient (... and what you really should never use are *veryPrivate* operations). In the class model, granting of access rights is uniform and language independent: access restrictions are noted as tagged values.

Tagged values
⇨207

Examples

See class ⇨172

```
getPosition(x, y)
getPosition(out x : Integer, out y : Integer)
resize(byFactor : Real): GeomFigure
+addPhoneNumber(phoneNumber : String, type : CallType = #Fax)
payIn(in amount : Amount):Amount
#release():ContractStatus
«constructor» create()
```

5.4.5 Responsibilities

Related terms: task, purpose.

Description

Before classes are modeled in detail, it is useful to define the responsibility of the class. Although these definitions are in fact relatively fuzzy and abstract descriptions in natural language, they concern one of the most important object-oriented principles, the principle of responsibility.

All domain-specific situations represented in object-oriented models should ultimately be allocated to a single class. Operations, attributes, business rules, constraints, associations, etc. should always be allocated to a single class that is responsible for them. A class should, if possible, only be responsible for a single domain-specific situation, or for as few different situations as possible.

Notation and Example

What a class is responsible for can be noted in a special section in the class symbol, as shown in Table 5.1.

Table 5.1 Notation of the responsibilities of a class

Delivery
Responsibilities
– describes and administers quantity and type of objects to be delivered – describes and administers the destination and recipient – documents current status and progress so far of the delivery

5.4.6 Requirements[5]

Definition

Requirements are statements about the performance to be supplied. They describe the scope of the functions and performance of a product, for example the software that is to be developed.

Description

Requirements describe not only the functionality of a system (what is to be created?) but also in what way (with what level of quality?) the behavior of the system is to be provided to the user. The following two statements represent these two different classes of requirement:

- The system is to be protected by a password from unauthorized access.
- The system must have an availability of 99.9%.

The first requirement concerns a statement on the function of the system – this type of requirement is called a *functional requirement*, while in the same way the second requirement is termed *non-functional*.

Representation

Requirements can either be documented formally (e.g. in the form of diagrams or in formal language) or in prose.[6] The prose form is preferred in practice, since many authors and domain experts have only a limited knowledge of standardized description languages. On account of the large number of different participants in the analysis phase, a description of the requirements in prose is often the only common notation that will be understood and accepted by all the people involved. Only when the requirements are subsequently converted into an object-oriented model do we return to a (semi-)formal representation.

Irrespective of how they are represented, the requirements should be:

- unambiguous;
- complete and free of contradiction;
- implementable;
- testable;
- and formulated in a manner that can be understood by all the participants in the project.

---

[5] This section is based on formulations that were kindly made available to me by Chrisitine Rupp (Sophist Group). (*See* Rupp, 2001.)

[6] The term prose for the method of representing a requirement relates to a description in natural language (e.g. in English). Prose is distinguished from verse by the fact that it primarily emphasises the efficient transmission of information.

That this is not always the case can be seen from the above example ('The system is to be protected by a password'). If you analyze this requirement more closely, numerous questions arise: Are there conventions for the password? Is there only one password for all users or one per user? Who assigns the password? Are there different groups of rights (admin, user, reader etc.) for which a user needs different passwords? The answers to these questions will determine what sort of functionality will be implemented.

5.4.7 Interfaces, Interface Classes

Definition

Interfaces describe a selected part of the externally visible behavior of model elements (mostly of classes and components).

Interface classes are abstract classes (more precisely, types), which define abstract operations exclusively.

Description

Interface class

Interfaces are specifications of the external behavior of classes (or other elements) and contain a set of signatures for operations that classes (or others) wishing to provide this interface need to implement. They are marked with the stereotype *«interface»*. Their operations need not be explicitly marked as *{abstract}* because this is mandatory.

Tagged value
⇨207

Common classes that wish to implement an interface need to provide all the operations defined in the corresponding interface class. A common class can implement several interfaces and, in addition, contain further properties. In other words: an interface usually describes a subset of the operations of a class. Between implementing class and interface class there is a realization relationship (a dashed inheritance arrow with the stereotype *«realize»* – *see* Fig. 5.20).

Realization
relationship ⇨248

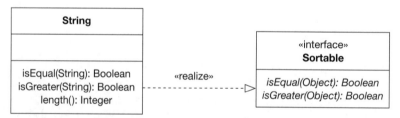

Figure 5.20 *String* realizes the *Sortable* interface

Extension of
interfaces

Interface classes can extend other interfaces, that is, inheritance relationships between interface classes are possible. These relationships are marked with the stereotype *«extend»*. Care must be taken to ensure that only abstract operations are added. This extend relationship should not be confused with the extend relationship in use cases.

Use cases ⇨163

It is illegal to restrict the semantics of the interface superclass. All invariants must be kept. Additional invariants are allowed. It is also possible to specify restrictions for parameters and return types.

Multiple inheritance
⇨224

An interface class can extend several other interfaces, i.e. it can have several superclasses. In contrast to multiple inheritance in common classes, this is unproblematic because only sets of signatures are combined (Fig. 5.21).

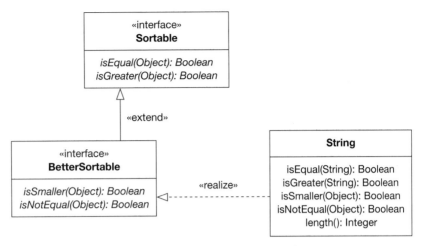

Figure 5.21 Extension and realization of interfaces

Common classes can implement several interfaces; however, it should be ensured that the different interfaces do not contain homonymous signatures because it would be very risky if their semantics too were defined identically. In any case, the interfaces to be implemented must be free of contradictions within each other. This can, for example, be achieved by factorizing out common features of the interface classes.

Interface references in associations

At the ends of associations (i.e. next to the roles of an association) references can be made to interfaces in order to indicate that the only accesses permitted via this association are those defined by the specified interface.

To make the interface concept even more powerful, you can, for example, specify the following additional constraints for each signature defined in an interface:

- *Precondition* – description of the conditions to be satisfied prior to the call of the operation, which may (tacitly) be assumed by the operation.
- *Postcondition* – description of the conditions to be satisfied by the operation after having terminated.
- *Invariants* – description of the conditions which must always be satisfied.
- *Exceptions* – list of exceptions that may be triggered by an operation.

Constraints ⇨197
OCL ⇨197

For the notation of these constraints, OCL expressions in the following form may be used, for example:

```
context InterfaceName
    inv:   ... (Boolean expression for invariant)
    pre:   ... (Boolean expression for precondition)
    post:  ... (Boolean expression for postcondition)
    throws: ... (list of exceptions)
```

Notation

Interface classes are noted in the same way as common classes, except that they bear the stereotype *«interface»*. They do not need a department for attributes because they contain only operations. Operations in interface classes define only signatures; they are abstract and should therefore be set in italics.

As shown in Fig. 5.21, interfaces can extend other interfaces; for this purpose, an inheritance relationship is drawn with the arrow pointing towards the interface to be extended.

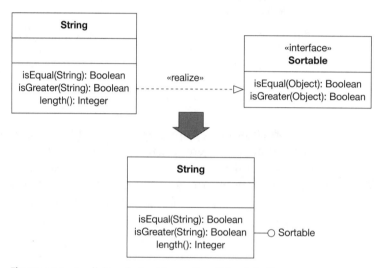

Figure 5.22 Explicit and short form of realizing interfaces

The fact that a class implements an interface can be represented in two ways. On the one hand, a realization relationship can be noted, as shown in Fig. 5.22. The realization relationship looks like an inheritance relation, but the line is dashed. If your modeling tool does not support this, just take an inheritance relation and mark it with the stereotype «realize». The other possibility of representing the implementation of an interface is the so-called interface "lollipop." Interfaces are noted with the lollipop symbol (a small empty circle joined by a line to the class that provides the interface). Next to it, the name of the interface is shown; it corresponds to the name of the corresponding interface class.

Both variations are equivalent. The notation with the realization relationship offers the possibility of reading the operations required by the interface class. The lollipop variation is a short notation; the operations required by the interface are not directly visible, only the name of the interface class is shown (*see* Fig. 5.25).

Dependency relation
⇨246

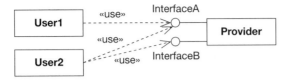

Figure 5.23 Use-dependencies of an interface

Exploitation of an interface by other classes can be noted by means of a dependency relationship (dashed arrow) with the stereotype «use» towards the interface class. Usage of an interface presumes that the user knows the interface provider, that is, usually there is also an association, for which the dependency relationship is not a replacement.

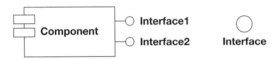

Figure 5.24 Interfaces as a lollipop symbol and standing alone

Lollipops without sticks

As well as classes, components can provide interfaces, with the same conventions applying to their notation. An interface can also be noted as an individual circle (i.e. a lollipop without a stick). Whenever an interface is indicated in abbreviated form (circle or lollipop), it means that the interface class is specified in full somewhere else.

Example

Further examples
⇨33, 128, 247

Figure 5.22 shows that the class *String* implements the interface *Sortable*. Both notation variations are equivalent. The *Sortable* interface requires two operations: *isEqual()* and *isGreater()*. Objects which have these two operations can be sorted. The *String* class satisfies the requirements for this interface because it has the two required operations.

Figure 5.25 shows the class *String* which provides an interface named *Sortable*. This interface is used by the class *SortedStringList* which is noted by the dashed relationship with the interface symbol. This means that *SortedStringList* uses the properties of *String*, which are defined in the interface class *Sortable*.

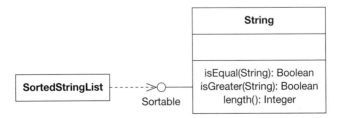

Figure 5.25 Example of an interface dependency

The definition of interfaces is helpful to explicate and reduce coupling between classes. Thus, in the above example, *SortedStringList* as the interface user is only dependent on two operations of the *String class*. All other operations of the *String* class could be changed without impairing sortability – a fact one would only have obtained with an intensive study of the *SortedStringList class*.

In strongly typed languages such as Java, modeling of such dependencies is usually of no importance because the compiler carries out the necessary type checks. In languages with dynamic typing such as Smalltalk, this may be of interest for a restrictive handling of interface and type export.

5.4.8 Constraints-Object Constraint Language (OCL)

Related terms: assertion, restriction, integrity rule, condition, tagged value, stereotype, invariant.

Definition

OCL

A constraint is an expression which restricts the possible contents, states, or the semantics of a model element and which must always be satisfied. A constraint may consist of a stereotype or of tagged values, a formal Object Constraint Language expression, a semi-formal or a free formulation (note), or a dependency relationship. Constraints in the form of pure Boolean expressions are also called *assertions*.

Description

Integrity rule

A constraint describes a condition or integrity rule. It can describe the legal set of values of an attribute, specify pre- or postconditions for messages or operations, request a special context for messages or relationships, constrain structural properties, define a specific order, put a chronological condition, and the like.

Feature ⇨207
Stereotype ⇨209
Note ⇨212
Dependency ⇨246

Constraints are formulated freely (as free text or a formula-like/semi-formal description) or they are noted more stringently as tagged value, stereotype, or dependency. Constraints request or prohibit specific properties. Depending on the possibilities of the modeling tool, they can be appended to arbitrary notation elements, amongst others to attributes, operations, classes, and all kinds of class relationships.

Constraints represent additional semantic information on a model element. Freely formulated constraints, however, generally remain uninterpreted, i.e., they are used by designers as information storage and bookmarks, but their contents are, for example, not converted automatically into code.

Constraints and tagged values overlap somewhat in their use. Tagged values cannot be formulated freely but are specific key/value pairs. In contrast to freely formulated constraints, in most cases they directly influence code generation. Thus, if a corresponding tagged value can be defined instead of a constraint, this should be preferred with a view to a more precise meaning and to code generation. This liberty is intentional and allows pragmatic adaptation to the capabilities of the modeling tools.

Notation

Constraints are enclosed in braces when appended directly to a model element, or introduced by the keyword *context* in OCL style:

```
{ Constraint }
context ResponsibleModelElement inv:
  Constraint
```

Object Constraint Language (OCL)

The Object Constraint Language is a simple formal language that allows additional semantics to be added to UML models which, with the remaining UML elements, can be either not expressed at all or only insufficiently.

The OCL grew out of an attempt by IBM to describe the business rules for insurance applications, etc. and has its roots in the Syntropy method (*see* Cook, 1994). The OCL formalism is based on set theory and is very similar to the Smalltalk language and to predicate logic.

This section does not provide a complete OCL reference but explains only the most important elements. An extensive description can be found in Warmer, 1999.

Self and Context

OCL expressions are usually initiated by a context for a specific instance in the form:

```
context Object inv:
  self.property
```

In this case *self* is a specific instance of context and *"inv:"* stands for invariant. An alternative to writing *"context ... inv:"* is simply to underline the context object, as shown in the examples below:

```
Person
  self.age
Enterprise
  self.employee->size
Enterprise : e
  e.employee->size
```

In the last case an alias (*e*) is introduced for the context object (*enterprise*).

Named Constraints

The constraints can also be given their own names; an example of the necessary syntax looks like this:

```
context Object inv constraintName:
  ...
context Person inv ageOfMajority:
  self.age >= 18
```

Apart from invariants, you can also specify preconditions and postconditions, for which the keywords *pre* and *post* are used. As well as classes, constraints can be applied to operations, etc.:

```
context Type::operation(p1 : type1): ReturnType
  pre: parameterOk: p1 = …
  post: resultOk:  result = …
```

By the way, *result* is a predefined keyword with which you can query the result, i.e. the return value, of an operation. The precondition and postcondition in the above example have also been supplied with freely selectable names (*parameterOk* and *resultOk*).

A further possibility for the formulation of OCL expressions is the use of so-called sub-expressions with the keyword *let*:

```
context Vehicle inv isNewCar:
  let age : Integer =
                Date.now.year — self.purchaseDate.year in
  age <= 2
```

Examples

Accessing
attributes

The first two examples define restrictions on the values of attributes (employee, boss, and person are classes, salary and age are attributes):

```
employee.salary < boss.salary
person.age > 18
```

Accessing sets

The next expressions represent set operations. Set operations begin with an arrow "->":

```
person.addresses->isEmpty
  "tests whether the set of addresses is empty"
person.addresses->size
  "determines the number of addresses for the person"
employee->select(age > 30)
  "supplies the subset of all employees who are
  older than 30"
```

When navigating along associations, the role name of the opposite class is used for accessing the opposite side of the association. If no role name is noted, the class name can be used.

Dependency ⇨246

Subset constraint. The example in Fig. 5.26, which shows associations between the classes *Project* and *Employee*, asserts that the project leader is recruited from the set of project members.

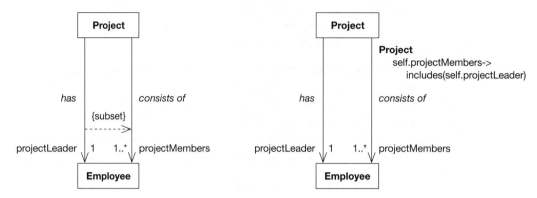

Figure 5.26 Constraint with dependency relationship and OCL expression

Subset constraint

The OCL expression

```
context Project inv:
    self.projectMembers->includes(self.projectLeader)
```

means that the set operation *includes()*, applied to the set of project members with the project leader as an argument, must return *true*. In this case, *self* is an instance of the class *Project*.

OCL ⇨197
Further examples
⇨148f.

In older publications on the UML one finds examples of graphically noted constraints, for example a dependency arrow with the constraint *{subset}*. This type of constraint should be avoided since it can only be used to represent simple cases and is not suitable for more complex constraints.

Consistency
constraint

Consistency. The example in Fig. 5.27 is similar. Here it is stated that an invoice belongs to the same customer as the contract on which it is based. This ensures that the customer receives only invoices for existing contracts. The association between *Invoice* and *Customer* is redundant in this example; therefore, its consistency must be defined by means of a constraint. Usually, one tends to avoid redundant relationships. However, where they are necessary or sensible, problems resulting from the redundancy can be handled with the aid of such consistency constraints.

The OCL expression also makes clear who is responsible for consistency, namely the context which initiates the expression and to which *self* refers, in this case the instances of the *Invoice* class.

OR constraint
see 148

OR. Another example for constraints between relationships can be seen in Fig. 5.28, which asserts that a person has either domestic or foreign country addresses (thus, an exclusive OR, or XOR). Persons having both domestic and foreign country addresses are excluded. This example is admittedly somewhat artificial. OR constraints for associations are not properly regarded as elegant design and should be used sparingly;-)

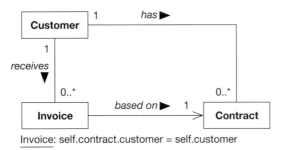

Invoice: self.contract.customer = self.customer

Figure 5.27 Example of a consistency constraint

Figure 5.28 OR constraint noted graphically

As mentioned above, graphical constraints are usually suitable only for simple cases, while OCL expressions can be used for any degree of complexity, which is why OCL constraints are preferable. The OR constraint as an OCL expression reads as follows:

```
context Person inv:
   listDomesticAddresses->isEmpty xor
   listForeignAddresses->isEmpty
```

Value constraint

Values. In Fig 5.29, constraints are put on the possible values of the attributes of the *Rectangle* and *Triangle* classes. In the rectangle, all values must be greater than 0; in the triangle, it is stated that values can only assume constellations that are valid for triangles.

Rectangle
a {c > 0}
b {b > 0}

Triangle
a {c–b < a < b+c}
b {a–c < b < a+c}
c {a–b < c < a+b}

Figure 5.29 Value constraint noted directly

The expression noted in the attribute section of the class rectangle

```
{a > 0}
```

is an abbreviated way of writing

```
context Rectangle inv: a > 0
```

Order constraint

Order. In the next example (Fig. 5.30), an order is stated: the list of names is sorted by the last names of the persons. "Ordered" is not a predefined expression and is also difficult to express with OCL. If you wish, nonetheless, to achieve a halfway formal expression, you could place the actual constraint as a comment in natural language in an OCL context:

```
context Seminar inv:
    "The elements in the list of participants are
    to be sorted by Person.lastName"
```

Aggregations ⇨241

Figure 5.30 Order constraint

Formula constraint

Formulas. Another example for the use of constraints is the definition of calculation rules for derived attributes. Figure 5.31 shows the class *Person*, in which the age represents an attribute derived from the date of birth and the current date. Derived attributes are marked with a prefixed slash. On the left-hand side the constraint is written directly after the attribute; on the right-hand side it is put in a note. Both forms of notation are allowed.

Person
dateBirth : Date /age {age=today-dateBirth}

Figure 5.31 Calculation formula for a derived attribute

Enumeration

Enumerations are also enclosed in braces, for example:

```
color : {red, blue, green}
```

or described more precisely

```
context color inv:
  (self = #red) or (self = #blue) or (self = #green)
```

However, enumerations can usually be avoided and should be described, instead, by a class (here, the *Color* class).

Gerontological constraint

To conclude this section, we introduce another example with a constraint on an aggregation (Fig. 5.32). It shows a collection of people who take part in an off-shore duty-free shopping spree. To ensure that the OAPs remain together, it has been established that participants must be over 65: a duty-free shopping tour is an aggregation of elderly people.

Figure 5.32 Knee rugs are optional

The question arises where and how such constraints, and in particular object-transcendent constraints, should finally be implemented. An important factor is to determine the responsibility for satisfying the constraint, i.e., to answer the question as to which class has to bear the responsibility. In the *customer/contract/invoice* example discussed earlier, the OCL expression tells us that it is the invoice.

In the above example, the responsibility question is also easy to answer. As we can see from the navigation direction, the *ShoppingSpree* class is responsible for the aggregation. Thus, this is where the constraint should be located. The *ShoppingSpree* class will provide an operation for adding further people to the set of participants, for example *addParticipant(participant:Person)*. Within this operation, the age needs to be checked. Here is an outline of the conversion into Java:

```
Class ShoppingSpree {
    private Vector participantSet;
    public void addParticipant(Person : participant)
{
    if (participant.age > 65} {
        participantSet.addElement(participant);
    }
    . . .
```

Since participants cannot become younger, this form of conversion is alright. It should be noted that in this example the constraint is checked only when adding a new participant but that the constraint must also be maintained at any later point in time – this is required by the OCL constraint in the illustration but is not enforced by the above Java implementation.

Predefined OCL Basic Types and Operations

The following basic types are predefined in the OCL:

Type	Example
Boolean	true, false
Integer	1, 2, 23, 12045
Real	3.14, 0.266
String	'Starship'
Set	{55, 23, 47}, {'red', 'blue', 'yellow'}
Bag	{55, 23, 47, 5}, {12, 8, 8}
Sequence	{1..10}, {8, 17, 25, 26}

Set, *Bag*, and *Sequence* are subclasses of *Collection*. *Set* is a set in which no element occurs more than once, while in a *Bag* elements may occur any number of times. *Sequence* is a *Bag*, except that the elements are ordered.

The following evaluation order applies:

1. Dot operations (".") have the highest precedence.

2. Unary operators ("not").

3. Binary operators ("+", "and").

4. Among binary operators, the usual order applies: dot before plus and minus, from left to right, and so on.

5. Bracketing "(" and ")" forces a different order.

The following operations are predefined for the basic types:

Integer, Real		
Expression	Type of result	Description
$i_1 = i_2$	Boolean	Returns true if i_1 and i_2 are equal
$i_1 + i_2$: Integer	Integer	
$i_1 + i_2$: Real	Real	
$r_1 + i_1$	Real	
r_1 round	Integer	

Boolean		
Expression	**Type of result**	**Description**
a and b	Boolean	Returns true if a and b are true
a or b	Boolean	Returns true if at least one of the two values a and b is true
a xor b	Boolean	Returns true if exactly one of the two values a and b is true
not a	Boolean	Returns the negation of a
a implies b	Boolean	(not a) or (a and b), i.e. if a is true, b shall also be true
if a then a1: OclExpr else a2: OclExpr	a1.type	If a is true, expression a1 is evaluated, otherwise a2
a = b	Boolean	Returns true if a and b are equal

Collection		
Expression	**Type of result**	**Description**
s1 = s2	Boolean	Do s1 and s2 contain the same elements?
s.size	Integer	Number of elements of s
s.sum	Integer or Real	Sum of all elements of s, provided they are numerical
s.includes(e)	Boolean	Is e an element of the set s?
s.isEmpty	Boolean	Is the set empty (size=0)?
s.exists(Expr)	Boolean	Does the set s contain an element for which the expression returns true?
s.forAll(Expr)	Boolean	Does the expression return true for all elements of the set?

Set		
Expression	**Type of result**	**Description**
s1.union(s2)	Set	Union of s1 and s2
s1.intersection (s2)	Set	Intersection of s1 and s2
s1–s2	Set	All elements of s1 not contained in s2
s.include(e)	Set	All elements of s plus the element e
s.exclude(e)	Set	All elements of s without the element e
s1.symmetric Difference(s2)	Set	All elements of s1 and s2 that do not occur simultaneously in s1 and s2
s.select(Expr)	Set	Subset of s composed of the elements for which the expression returns true
s.reject(Expr)	Set	Subset of s composed of the elements for which the expression returns false
s.collect(Expr)	Bag	Bag of the results of the expression applied to all elements of s
s.asSequence	Sequence	Returns s as a sequence
s.asBag	Bag	Returns s as a bag

Bag		
Expression	**Type of result**	**Description**
b1.union(b2)	Bag	Union of b1 and b2
b1.intersection (b2)	Bag	Intersection of b1 and b2
b.include(e)	Bag	All elements of b plus the element e
b.exclude(e)	Bag	All elements of b without the element e
b.select(Expr)	Bag	Subbag of b composed of the elements for which the expression returns true
b.reject(Expr)	Bag	Subbag of b composed of the elements for which the expression returns false
b.collect(Expr)	Bag	Bag of the results of the expression applied to all elements of b
s.asSequence	Sequence	Returns b as a sequence
s.asSet	Set	Returns b as a set

Sequence		
Expression	**Type of result**	**Description**
s1.append(s2)	Sequence	Sequence s1, followed by the elements of s2
s1.prepend(s2)	Sequence	Intersection of s1 and s2
s.first	Element.Type	First element of s
s.last	Element.Type	Last element of s
s.at(i)	Element.Type	i-th element of s
s.include(e)	Sequence	All elements of b plus the element e inserted at the end
s.exclude(e)	Sequence	All elements of b without the first occurrence of the element e
s.select(Expr)	Sequence	Subsequence of b composed of the elements for which the expression returns true
s.reject(Expr)	Sequence	Subsequence of b composed of the elements for which the expression returns false
s.collect(Expr)	Sequence	Sequence of the results of the expression applied to all elements of s
s.asBag	Bag	Returns s as a bag
s.asSet	Set	Returns s as a set

5.4.9 Tagged Values

Related terms: property string, feature, characteristic, constraint.

Definition

Keyword/value pairs

Tagged values are user-defined, language- and tool-specific keyword/value pairs which extend the semantics of individual model elements with specific characteristic properties.

Description

Tagged values add specific additional properties to existing model elements. In the same way that attributes describe the properties of a class in more detail, tagged values can further specify the properties of an arbitrary model element (for example, of a class or an attribute). They detail the semantics of a model element and, in many cases, influence code generation. Some tagged values have been explicitly designed to control code generation, mostly on the basis of specific design or code patterns.

Although tagged values can be assigned completely arbitrarily, it is sensible, for example in a project or an enterprise, to agree on a limited and well-defined set of tagged values for a tool. In view of the relationship with code generation, this usually happens automatically.

Constraints ⇨197

Abstract
classes ⇨178

Abstract
operations ⇨186f.

Probably, the most frequently used tagged value is *abstract* (unless it is not defined as a freely formulated constraint, which would also be possible), which marks abstract classes and abstract operations. For attributes, the property *query* may be sensible if they can only be read but not modified. In operations and attributes, the keyword *private* can indicate that the element should not be used, while the keyword *obsolete* indicates that the element in question exists for compatibility with older versions only and should no longer be used. It is also possible to specify information on the author or the version number of a class as a property.

Code generation

In the examples mentioned above, connections to code generation are obvious: usually, abstract classes and operations must also be declared as abstract or virtual in the program code, and the same applies to private operations and attributes. For read-only attributes, at most a read operation is generated, but not an operation for setting the attribute value.

Thus, tagged values are a very powerful and easy-to-handle tool for definition of semantic details and automatic conversion of design patterns.

Stereotype ⇨209

The difference with the stereotype consists in the fact that a stereotype extends the metamodel by a new element. Tagged values, instead, allow individual instances of existing model elements (for example, a specific operation) to be extended by specific properties.

Notation

Tagged values consist of a keyword and a value and are enclosed in braces either individually or as an enumeration. They can be attached as a kind of label to all model elements, for example to associations, classes, attributes, and operations.

If the value is a *Boolean* which is *true*, it may be omitted; thus.

```
{transient=true}
```

is identical with

```
{transient}
```

Instead of braces, tools may also use other kinds of marking up, such as colored highlights, italic type, and so forth.

Examples

{abstract}
{readOnly}
{private}
{obsolete}
{version=2.1}
{Author=Tara King}
{transient}
{persistent}

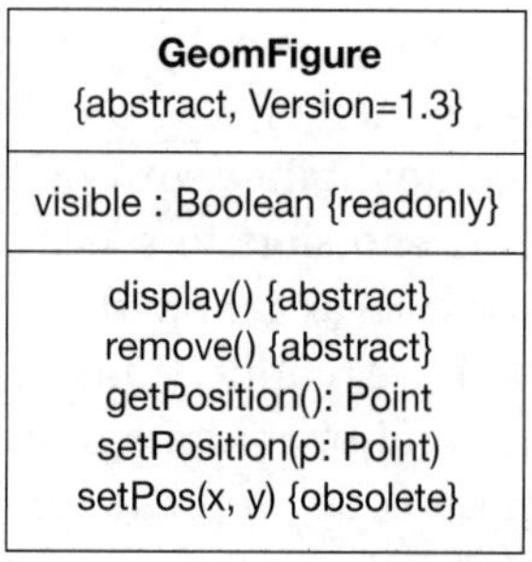

GeomFigure {abstract, Version=1.3}
visible : Boolean {readonly}
display() {abstract} remove() {abstract} getPosition(): Point setPosition(p: Point) setPos(x, y) {obsolete}

Figure 5.33 Tagged values

5.4.10 Stereotypes

Related terms: usage context, constraint, tagged value.

Definition

Metamodel
extension

See feature ⇨207
Constraint ⇨197

Stereotypes are project, enterprise, or method-specific extensions of pre-existing model elements of the UML metamodel. According to the semantics defined with the extension, the model element to which the stereotype is applied is semantically directly affected.

In practice, stereotypes mainly specify possible usage contexts of a class, a relationship, or a package.

Description

Stereotypes classify the possible uses of a model element. This does not mean modeling of metaclasses, but ascribing specific common features to one or more classes. One might object that multiple inheritance serves the purpose; however, stereotypes are once again different because they have no type semantics, they are neither types nor classes. Instead, they allow a semantic/conceptual and sometimes visual differentiation and give hints on ways of use, connections with existing application architectures, development environments, and so on.

Code generation

A model element can be classified with more than one stereotype (since UML 1.4). The semantics and visual representation of the element can be influenced by assignment of stereotypes. In practice, this is realized for example by modeling tools which vary their code generation in function of stereotypes. Stereotypes should not be freely and arbitrarily invented and assigned by individual developers, but should be defined in a project, enterprise, or tool-related fashion.

Attributes and operations too can be provided with stereotypes. This allows attributes and operations to be subdivided into appropriate groups within the class (see example on the next page). Relationships may also be classified by means of stereotypes.

The difference between stereotypes and tagged values lies in the fact that with a stereotype, the metamodel is extended by a new model element. With tagged values, in contrast, individual instances of existing model elements (for example a specific operation) are extended by specific properties.

Tagged value
⇨207

According to Joos et al. (1997) four types of stereotypes can be distinguished:

Use case diagrams,
actors ⇨164

- **Decorative stereotypes**
  These may be used to make tools and diagrams look more colorful and visually appealing, for example actors and the like in use case diagrams.

- **Descriptive stereotypes**
  These are stereotypes which are mainly used to describe contexts of usage and which represent a kind of standardized comment, for example, to associate classes to specific architecture layers (*«entity»*, *«control»* etc.). See Fig. 5.34.

Interface class ⇨192

● **Restrictive stereotypes**

These stereotypes mean formal restrictions to be applied to existing model elements. They define restrictions on existence or non-existence of specific properties, thus extending the metamodel.

The most prominent exponent is UML's predefined stereotype *«interface»*, whose restriction consists in the fact that classes marked as such are abstract classes and must only contain abstract operations. (Although in this example the metamodel looks different and the «interface» stereotyping is only used for the purpose of notation.)

● **Redefining stereotypes**

These are metamodel modifications which would allow the fundamental concepts of the original language (UML) to be violated and which should therefore be avoided.

Descriptive and restrictive stereotypes are sensible on the whole; decorative stereotypes make sense as long as they are used in homeopathic doses. New stereotypes should principally be defined, i.e. invented only with extreme care and not without need.

Many stereotypes are already predefined in UML. Self-created and tool-specific stereotypes are problematic as they may be used to double-cross the standardization of UML. Yet another problem may arise with the modification of (the meaning of) stereotypes because no version concept exists for the resulting stereotypes.

Notation

The stereotype is placed before or above the element name (for example a class name) and enclosed in French quotes or guillemots («»).

Alternatively, special symbols may be used (decorative stereotypes), as shown in Fig. 5.34 with the stereotypes *«actor»*, *«control»*, *«boundary»* and *«entity»*. Furthermore, tools are free to use specific color or other visual highlighting.

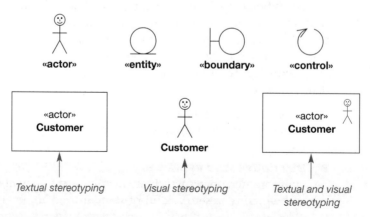

Figure 5.34 Stereotypes

Examples

Stereotypes can, for example, be used to indicate the meaning of a class in the application architecture, such as:

«presentation», «process», «domain class».

Further examples:

«model», «view», «control», «exception», «primitive», «enumeration», «signal», «complete», «incomplete», «overlapping», «disjoint», «implement», «include», «extend».

«DomainClass» Circle
position visible
display() remove()
«Information» isVisible()
«AttributeAccess» setPosition(newPos)

5.4.11 Notes

Related terms: annotation, comment.

Definition
Notes are comments to a diagram or an arbitrary element in a diagram, without any semantic effect.

Description
Notes enable annotations, comments, explanations, and additional descriptive text to be made to any UML model elements, e.g. to classes, attributes, operations, relationships, etc.

Notation, Example

Example
Constraint ⇨199

Notes are represented by earmarked rectangles containing text. Optionally, a line or a dependency relationship may be drawn from the rectangle to the diagram element to which the note refers, for example to an attribute.

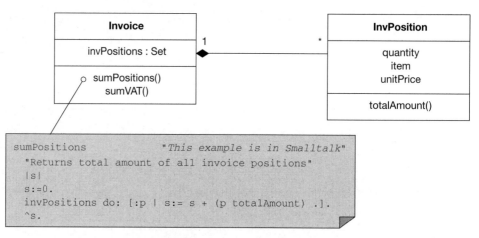

Figure 5.35 Annotating model elements

5.4.12 Collaboration, Mechanism

ADVANCED
UML

See design patterns
⇨280

Related terms: pattern, design pattern notation.

Description

In this context, *collaboration* means that several elements together create a behavior which is more comprehensive than the sum of all the elements. If the essence of this collaboration is represented in an abstract way, similar to design patterns – that is, independent of a specific application area – we call it a *mechanism*.

Design patterns describe frequently occurring design problems and well-proven solution approaches to such problems. A design pattern describes the problem structure, the solution, when and with which consequences the solution can be applied, and so on. The solution is then usually implemented individually, i.e. tailored to fit. Class models and the like are substantially easier to understand when one knows where design patterns have been employed. Therefore, it is sensible to document this in the model in an appropriate manner.

Notation and Example

The application of a design pattern is noted by means of a dashed ellipse which contains the name and, where needed, additional source references. Dashed arrows whose ends are marked with the individual roles are drawn from this ellipse to the classes affected by the design pattern.

Figure 5.36 shows the composite pattern by Gamma (1996), which is usually employed for part list structures. The present case deals with products (for example, a home insurance) made up of individual product elements (such as theft, glass, bicycle, and so on).

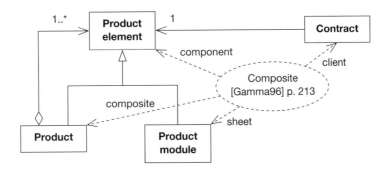

Figure 5.36 Notation of the *Composite* design pattern

5.4.13 Subsystems

Related terms: package, component, category.

Definition

A subsystem is part of a complete system that is defined to the outside by an interface and that hides the structure and collaboration of its individual parts.

In contrast, a package is a loose collection of model elements that is not necessarily defined by an interface and that does not encapsulate the structure and collaboration of its parts. In contrast to a subsystem, a component is instantiable and in principle interchangeable (substitutable).

Description

The demarcation between subsystems, components, and packages follows the features described in the above definition. Furthermore, these elements may be distinguished with regard to their intended purpose.

A package merely represents a namespace and is a means of clearly structuring a large number of model elements, in a similar way to directories in operating systems. The package structure can be formed on the basis of any criteria you like, e.g. based on domain-specific interrelationships or from technical viewpoints (configuration management, authorizations, compilation units, etc.). A component is instantiable in the same way as a class and encapsulates complex behavior, in order to form units that have a high level of coherence from a domain-specific point of view.

The purpose of subsystems is domain-specific system partitioning on a relatively coarse level; a subsystem might be composed, for example, from a set of components and classes.

Notation and Example

A subsystem is represented like a package, but is marked with the predefined stereotype «subsystem». The visual representation of a «subsystem» is a fork-like symbol (Fig. 5.37).

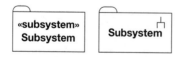

Figure 5.37 Notation variants for a subsystem

5.4.14 Packages

Related terms: category, subsystem, component.

Definition

Gaining an overview

Packages are collections of model elements of arbitrary types which are used to structure the entire model into smaller, clearly visible units. A package defines a namespace, that is, the names of the elements within a package must be unique. Each model element can be referenced in other packages, but it belongs to exactly a single (home) package. The package can in turn contain packages. The top package includes the entire system.

Description

Packages may contain different model elements, for example classes and use cases. They may be hierarchically structured, that is, contain packages in their turn. In this respect, the entire system is itself a package. Figure 5.38 is taken from the Rational Rose modeling tool which structures packages in the form of a tree used to navigate through the model.

Figure 5.38 Packages represented in a tree structure

Packages are built on the basis of logical or physical relationships. Existing libraries, subsystems, and interfaces all form individual packages. Even the model of the application to be developed may itself be subdivided into logical packages when it becomes too large. Packages provide a better overview of a large model; they serve for internal model organization and, except for the namespace, do not define any further model semantics.

A model element, for example a class, can be contained in several packages – the sets may overlap but each class has its home package. In all other packages, it can only be quoted in the form

Dependency ⇨246

        PackageName::ClassName

This creates dependencies between the packages: one package uses classes of another package.

A good architecture leads to few dependencies between packages. Besides the improved clarity of view, packages are also suitable working entities for project management and organization.

Notation and Example

Stereotypes ⇨209

A package is represented as a folder (Fig. 5.39). Inside this symbol, the name of the package is noted. If model elements are shown inside the symbol (classes or embedded packages), the name is written on the file tab; otherwise in the large rectangle. Above the package name, stereotypes may be noted.

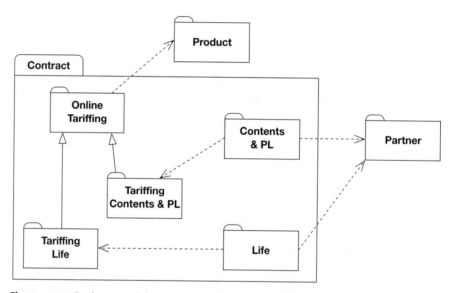

Figure 5.39   Package model

Dependency ⇨246

The dependencies between packages are noted by a dashed arrow which points towards the independent package. The dependencies between packages must correspond to the underlying navigation definitions of classes and associations.

Generalization ⇨220

Besides the dependency relations, it is possible to represent generalization relations between packages if the model elements contained in the packages are generalizations or specializations of elements contained in other packages.

5.4.15 Components

Related terms: package, subsystem, module, application module, class.

Definition

A component is an executable and interchangeable software unit with well-defined interfaces and its own identity. A distinction should be made between component definitions (e.g. "person") and component instances (e.g. "Gabby Goldsmith").

Description

See introduction ⇨58

A component is instantiatable in the same way as a class and encapsulates complex behavior, in order to form units that have a high level of coherence from a domain-specific point of view. In contrast to a class, a component should also be fundamentally interchangeable (substitutable). One technical platform for components is, for example, Enterprise Java Beans (EJB).

A component usually consists internally of a set of classes. Components generally supply different types of interfaces to the outside:

- **Factory services** for generating and loading new component instances. With EJB these might be called, for example, *findByName(name)*, *findByKey(key)*, etc.

- **Observer services** for setting up event notifications on an abstract, i.e. anonymous level. These might be called, for example, *addChangeListener*, *addVetoableChangeListener*, *removeChangeListener*, etc.

- **Object services** for providing domain-specific operations, e.g. get and set operations, but also complex operations. These might be called, for example, *getCustomerNo()*, *setCustomerNo(customerNo)*, *updateDailyBalance ()*, etc.

The internal implementation is independent of the interfaces supplied to the outside. Object services in particular can be structured internally in a way that is completely different from their external representation. Each component therefore makes a type system available to the outside and is usually implemented internally by a set of classes. Components generally have their own persistence mechanisms, independent of other components.

Notation and Example

Physical
architecture

A component is noted as a rectangle with two small rectangles on its left side (Fig. 5.40). The name of the component and, if applicable, its type is written inside the rectangle. In addition, the component can itself contain further elements (objects, components, nodes).

Figure 5.40 Components with interfaces and a runtime object

The dependencies between the individual modules are represented by corresponding dependency relationships (dashed arrows) (Fig. 5.41).

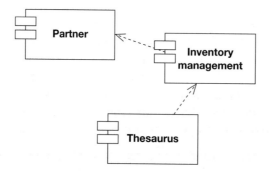

Figure 5.41 Dependencies between packages

5.5 Class Diagrams (Relational Elements)

This section gives a detailed description of the individual elements of the Unified Modeling Language used for representation of static modeling features, each subdivided into definition, description, notation, and examples.

Here is a brief overview of the various types of relationships, together with references to the sections in which they are explained in further detail:

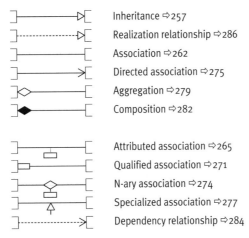

Inheritance ⇨257

Realization relationship ⇨286

Association ⇨262

Directed association ⇨275

Aggregation ⇨279

Composition ⇨282

Attributed association ⇨265

Qualified association ⇨271

N-ary association ⇨274

Specialized association ⇨277

Dependency relationship ⇨284

5.5.1 Generalization, Specialization

Related terms: inheritance, concretization.

Definition

Mechanism
(Inheritance)

Inheritance is a programming language concept, an implementation mechanism for the relationship between superclasses and subclasses by means of which attributes and operations of a superclass also become accessible to its subclasses.

Structuring principle
(generalization,
specialization)

Generalization and specialization are abstraction principles for hierarchical structuring of the semantics of a model. Generalization (or specialization) is a taxonomic relationship between a general and a special element (or vice versa), where the special element adds properties to the general one and behaves in a way that is compatible with it.

Description

Superclass
Subclass

In generalization or specialization, properties are structured hierarchically – properties of general significance are assigned to more general classes (superclasses), and more special properties are assigned to classes that are subordinate to the general ones (subclasses). Thus, the properties of the superclasses are bestowed on the subclasses, i.e. subclasses inherit properties from their superclasses. Therefore, a subclass contains both the properties specified in itself and the properties of its superclass(es). Subclasses inherit all the properties of their superclasses, can overwrite and extend them, but not eliminate or suppress them.

Discriminator

Differentiation into superclasses and subclasses is often performed by means of a distinctive feature (or characteristic) called *discriminator*. The discriminator denotes the aspect relevant for hierarchical structuring of the properties. This is not given per se but as the result of a modeling decision. For example, one might categorize vehicles on the basis of the discriminator *KindOfPower* (*combustion engine, electrical, horse power*), but also on the basis of *LocomotionMedium* (*air, water, rail, road*).

Whether a discriminator is chosen and, if so, which one, depends on the semantic contents of the generalization relation. If the subclasses can be seen as elements of a defined enumeration (air, water), the discriminator usually suggests itself. It is helpful to bring the discriminator explicitly to mind during modeling, and to integrate it into the graphical or textual model description. Thus the discriminator becomes a documented design decision.

Partition

The entirety of subclasses based on the same discriminator is called a partition.

Within the class hierarchy, the attributes and operations are located in exactly those classes in which they actually represent a property of the class. This may also be an abstract property. In other words, an attribute or

Delegation ⇨33

an operation is not located in a class with the sole purpose of guaranteeing its reuse in derived subclasses, although this is usually the effect of this kind of hierarchical structuring. The same applies to optimization and normalization effects known from data modeling (ERM). The decisive factor is the presupposed semantics and the responsibility assigned to the classes.

Implementation inheritance

Implementation inheritance. Specialization relationships are based on the substitution principle that states that under all circumstances it must be possible to use instances of subclasses in place of instances of the superclass. If this principle is violated and it is a question of pure implementation inheritance, the inheritance relationship is marked with the stereotype *«implementation»*. Implementation inheritance is understood to be the purely technical and pragmatic reuse of properties of the superclass without any further conceptual intentions; from a conceptual point of view this is often problematic.

Specification inheritance, Substitution principle

Specification inheritance. So-called specification inheritance, on the other hand, is based on the substitution principle. For operations that are overwritten in subclasses, the rule is that they may not have any stricter preconditions than those in the superclass, while the postconditions must be at least as strict as those in the superclass.

Contravariance principle for operation parameters

Equally, the definition ranges in the parameters of the subclass operations may not be restricted, i.e. in the subclass operations the parameters have the same types or are supertypes. For the return values of the operations the rule is that they must have the same type as those of the superclass operation or must be a subtype thereof.

Specialization inheritance

Specialization inheritance. The most widespread form of inheritance, however, is probably specialization inheritance, which is also known as *is-a* inheritance: a circle *is a* geometrical figure. In this case the instances of the subclass represent a subset of the instances of the superclass. With specialization inheritance the definition and value ranges and the pre- and postconditions of operations are in general restricted or intensified.

Covariance principle

Notation

The inheritance relation is represented by means of a large empty arrow pointing from the subclass to the superclass (Fig. 5.42). The arrows may alternatively be drawn directly from the subclasses to the superclass, or combined to a common line. The direct arrows allow for a more flexible layout and can also be easily drawn by hand. The combined arrows emphasize the collectivity of the subclasses, namely that they are specializations of a superclass on the basis of *one* discriminator.

In the direct arrow variation, the inheritance relations to which the discriminator applies are either joined by a dashed line which is then labeled with the name of the discriminator, or each individual inheritance arrow is

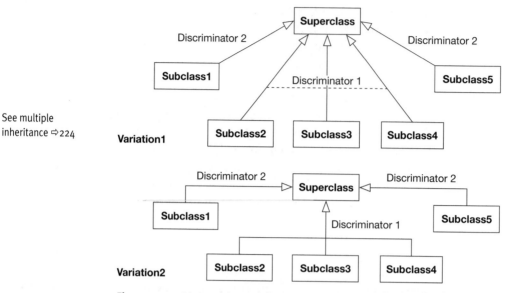

Figure 5.42   Direct and tree-type notation of inheritance relationship

See multiple
inheritance ⇨224

Constraints ⇨197

labeled with the discriminator. If the specification of discriminators is omitted, it is unclear whether the subclasses are independent specializations or the outcome of a common discriminator.

The discriminator is a virtual attribute of possible concrete objects. It does not appear as an attribute in any of the classes, but it is implicitly contained in the relation between superclasses and subclasses: the names of the subclasses created through this discrimination would be the attribute values of the implicit discriminator attribute.

Example

Discriminator:
figure shape

In a screen display window, circles, rectangles, and triangles are supposed to be displayed and moved. The concepts of *circle*, *rectangle*, and *triangle* can be generalized and very generally denoted as *geometric figures* (Fig. 5.43). The classes *Circle*, *Rectangle*, and *Triangle* would therefore be specializations of the common superclass *GeomFigure*; the discriminator would be the *figure shape*. In the abstract superclass, the operations *display()* and *remove()* are marked as abstract, i.e. all geometric figures have these operations, but they are only implemented in the concrete subclasses.

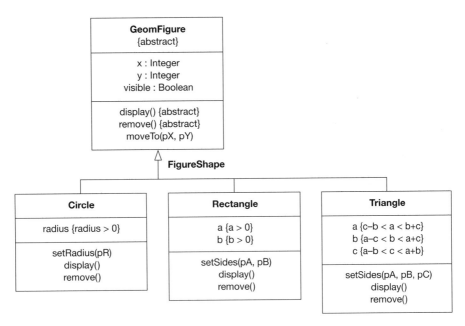

Figure 5.43 Example of inheritance

See discussion
⇨28

The attributes *x*, *y*, and *visible* are part of all geometric figures and are therefore located in the superclass. The *radius* and the sides *a*, *b*, and *c*, in contrast, are special properties of the concrete geometric figures. The concrete attributes are equipped with the necessary constraints for the geometric figure in question. For example, in a circle, the radius must not be equal to or less than zero, and in a triangle, the sum of any two sides must be greater than the remaining third side.

Multiple Inheritance

The previous section showed simple inheritance with the aid of the geometric object example. Each class has at most one superclass. In multiple inheritance, a class may have more than one superclass. Instead of a class hierarchy, in this case one could speak of a class heterarchy.

Not all programming languages need or support multiple inheritance (Smalltalk and Java, for example, do not). It should also be viewed with a fairly critical eye, as it creates problems. What happens if different superclasses contain homonymous properties (which obviously may behave differently)? Of which superclass will the subclass take the property? This conflict can as a rule be avoided only by addressing the property in a fully qualified way, i.e. including the denomination of its superclass.

Conflicts in multiple inheritance

Further conflict situations may be constructed. For example, the two superclasses that possess a common subclass could in their turn be derived from a common superclass, so that a property would be passed on in two directions and then combined again through multiple inheritance. Here, too, the property may be overwritten in any intermediate class lying between the two. An alternative to multiple inheritance is delegation.

Delegation ⇨33

Consider an example for multiple inheritance: a pig is both a mammal and a terrestrial animal. It therefore inherits the properties of the *Mammal* class and the *Terrestrial* class (Fig. 5.44).

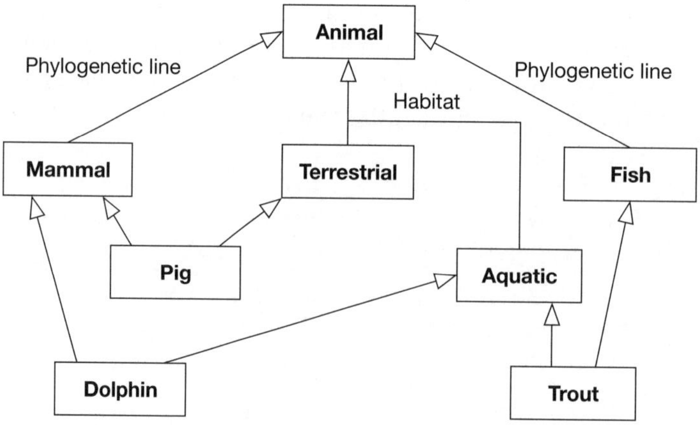

Figure 5.44 Multiple inheritance

5.5.2 Association

Related terms: aggregation, composition, link, object connection, relation.

Aggregations ⇨241
Compositions ⇨244

Definition

As a relation between classes, an association describes the common semantics and structure of a set of object connections.

Description

Object connections
[*links*]

Associations are needed to enable objects to communicate with each other. An association describes a connection between classes. The concrete relation between two objects of these classes is called *object connection* or *link*. Thus, links are the instances of an association.

Recursive
association

Usually, an association is a relation between two different classes. In the main, however, an association may also be of a recursive nature; in this case, the class has a relation with itself, where it is usually assumed that two different objects of that class are linked. However, even three or more different classes can be involved in an association. Special variations of an association are aggregation and composition.

Aggregation ⇨241
Composition ⇨244

Temporary
links

Usually, an association is valid for the entire life span of the involved objects, or at least for the duration of a business event. However, it is also possible to model associations that are valid only temporarily. For example, because an object is the argument of a message and is only locally known to the receiving object inside the corresponding operation. In this case, the stereotype *«temporary»* should be used.

Visibility specifications
⇨187

Cardinality:
number of elements
Multiplicity:
Range of allowed
cardinalities

The multiplicity of an association specifies the number of objects of the opposite class to which an object can be associated. If this number is variable, the range, that is minimum and maximum, is specified. If the minimum is 0, the relation is optional.

Roles,
constraints

Each association can be given a name which should describe the relation in more detail (usually a verb). On each side of the association, role names can be used to indicate which roles the individual objects assume in the relation. Constraints may be used to restrict the relation under specific aspects (Fig. 5.45).

Customer — 1 ——— 1 — CustomerAccount ◇— 1 ———— * — AccountingPosition
+ account   –accpos

Figure 5.45 Association/aggregation with multiplicities, role names, and visibility marks

Apart from role names, visibility marks can also be applied to each side of the association. For example, if an association is declared as private (-), the object itself, i.e. the operations of the object, can use the association, but adjacent classes will not be given any access.

Notation

Reading direction

Relations are represented by a line drawn between the involved classes. At the respective ends, the multiplicity of the relation can be indicated. Each relation should be given a name (set in italics) which describes what this relation consists of or why it exists. To be able to read the class names and the name of the relation in the correct direction, a small solid triangle pointing in the reading direction can be drawn next to the relation name.

Attributes ⇨183

Interface ⇨192

Relation names can be noted for both reading directions. At each end of a relation, additional role names can be specified (naming conventions as with attributes). A role name describes how the object is seen by the opposite object in the association. Next to the role, the name of an interface can also be specified for a class. The class must then implement this interface. Access via the association will then be restricted to the possibilities defined in the interface.

Furthermore, an association can be described in more detail by means of constraints, tagged values, and stereotypes.

Constraints ⇨197
Tagged values ⇨207
Stereotypes ⇨209

Classes can be joined by direct lines, that is, the shortest way, or by lines following a rectangular grid. This is a matter of personal taste or the drawing capabilities of the design tool.

Multiplicity

On each side of the association, the multiplicity is noted as an individual number or as a value range. Value ranges are noted by specifying the minimum and the maximum value, separated by two dots (for example 1..5). An asterisk * is a wildcard and means "many." Different alternatives are listed, separated by a comma.

Directed association ⇨237

One-way associations or directed associations, in which only one side knows the other but not vice versa, are described in the section on directed associations.

Example

Figure 5.46 shows a relation between a company and its employees. The relation is read as follows: "1 company employs * employees." The asterisk * stands as a wildcard for an arbitrary number of instances.

Figure 5.46 Example of an association

In addition to relationship names, role names may be appended to the relation, since objects of such classes often interact with each other in specific roles. In this case, the company plays the role of employer, while the employee is the employee. In practice it is often easier to find meaningful role names than relationship names. Precisely when relationships are called "has" or something similar, you should look for informative role names.

Roles

Further examples of multiplicity specifications are:

1	exactly one
0, 1	zero or one
0..4	between zero and four
3, 7	either three or seven
0..*	greater than or equal to zero (default, if the specification is omitted)
*	ditto
1..*	greater than or equal to one
0..3, 7, 9..*	between zero and three, or exactly seven, or greater than or equal to nine

Associations are usually realized by assigning appropriate reference attributes to the classes involved. In the above example, the class *Employee* would receive an attribute *employer* as a reference to an object of the class *Company*, and the class *Company* would get an attribute *employee* with a collection object (or a subclass) for referencing the *Employee* objects. Some modeling tools use the role names of the relation for the corresponding automatically generated attributes. Therefore, role names often correspond to the corresponding attributes.

Attributed Association

 Related terms: association attributes, association class.

Definition

An attributed association is a model element which has both the properties of a class and an association. It can be viewed as an association with additional class properties (attributed association) or as a class with additional association properties (association class).

Description

Besides the forms of association described until now, there is yet another one in which the relation itself has attributes. An attributed association suggests itself in cases where attributes are found which can be associated neither to one nor to the other class, because they are a property of the relation itself.

Association class

The properties of the relation are modeled as a class which is notationally attributed to the association. Semantically, association and association class are identical, i.e. the name of the association class corresponds to the name of the association. The instances of the association class are the concrete object relations between the (normal) classes involved in the association.

A peculiarity of attributed associations is that two involved objects may at most have one relation with each other. This will be explained further below with the aid of an example.

Notation

Attributed associations are represented in the same way as normal associations. In addition, via a dashed line that starts from the association line, a further class is assigned, the so-called association class. Otherwise, the association class is noted like a common class.

Examples

Implicit association classes

The association between employee and company of the previous section can, for example, be extended in a way that information on employment periods can be taken into account (Fig. 5.47).

The attributes which describe these periods belong neither to the class *Company* nor to the class *Employee* but are part of the relation between those two. In the same way, operations could be part of association classes. Since the instances of the association classes are identical to the concrete object relations, they cannot exist on their own but are dependent on the two actual objects involved.

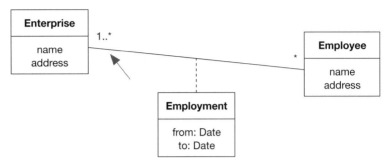

Figure 5.47 Association attributes

Occasionally, we also speak of implicit association classes; implicit because the class does not describe independent objects and needs not bear a name (associations do not require names). Obviously, in this case it is very sensible to specify a name. The names of the association and the association class are always identical.

Special semantics of multiplicity

What makes attributed associations so special is that two involved objects can at most have one relation with each other. The multiplicities specify that a company may have $0..*$ employees and that an employee must at least be employed by one company. In real life an employee may have worked several times, in different periods, for a company. In an attributed association like the one shown above, this is not possible! Any two involved objects may have only one relation with each other. Thus an employee cannot have two relations with the same company. If this is required, an attributed association is not suitable.

Qualified association
⇨233

Figure 5.48 shows an example in which the special semantics of the attributed association are required. Each employee is assigned specific abilities combined with a degree of competence. Here, an employee can be assigned an ability only once, because the employee cannot have the same ability with different degrees of competence; one would always choose the higher degree (this example is, by the way, taken up again in the section on qualified associations).

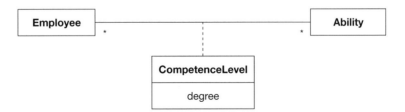

Figure 5.48 Attributed association with meaningful semantics

In the design process, such relations are usually broken up, and the association class becomes a proper class (Fig. 5.49). It must, however, be ensured that the special semantics of the attributed association are maintained, i.e. replaced by corresponding constraints.

Please also note the transfer of the multiplicities.

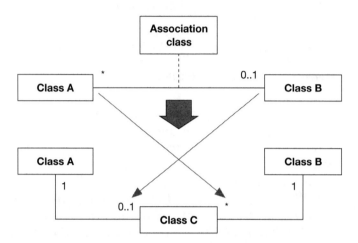

Figure 5.49 Transformation of an attributed association into standard associations

Warning

Attributed associations should be avoided since they are not object-oriented. Even the notation of a single bidirectional association is something that cannot be represented in this form in object-oriented models, since the responsibility for each situation should always be allocated to one class. In this way a bidirectional association is really only a shorthand way of indicating two individual, opposing directed associations.

See directed association ⇨237

If you extend a bidirectional relationship by an association class, remembering that a bidirectional relationship only represents a shorthand for two directed associations, the question arises: to which of the two directed associations does the association class actually relate?

The use of attributed associations therefore leads to the obscuring of responsibilities and is unsatisfactory from a semantic point of view, which is why it is preferable to use associations that have been resolved or converted into standard associations.

Association Constraints

If it is required that an association satisfies specific conditions, these may be noted, enclosed in braces, as constraints next to the association line. The constraints may have an arbitrary content and may be formulated freely, semi-formally, or formally (as OCL expressions).

OCL ⇨283

The following example takes up the situation discussed in the previous section. It was required that each employee can be assigned an ability only once (with a corresponding degree of competence). The constraint shown in Fig. 5.50 makes use of the fact that in a *Set*, an element may only be contained once (in contrast to the *Bag*). Thus, even if the sets are identical, no ability occurs twice.

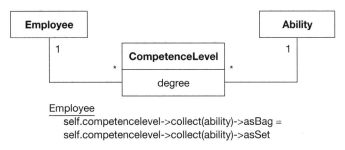

Employee
    self.competencelevel->collect(ability)->asBag =
    self.competencelevel->collect(ability)->asSet

Figure 5.50 Constraint on the uniqueness of degrees of competence

The attributed association *"Enterprise employs employees"* as shown already in the previous section is shown in Fig. 5.51 as a broken-up variation with two common associations. Here, the constraints are to ensure that the employment periods of an employee do not overlap. This has just been freely formulated. The constraint gives no information on how this should be implemented.

Ordered association

**ADVANCED
UML**

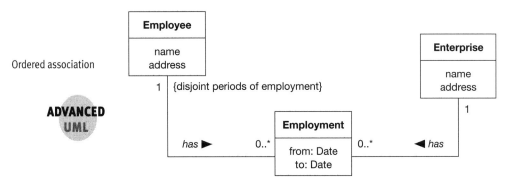

Figure 5.51 Constraint noted in natural language

Here, an OLC expression could be more precise. Why don't you try to formulate it!

Another example is the *{ordered}* constraint which specifies that the objects inside the relation are ordered. The way this order is implemented is usually not mentioned. Another possibility is sorting the objects: *{sorted}*. The constraint may also describe by which attributes the objects are ordered or sorted, for example *{ordered by contract date}*. Complex sorting rules should be noted as separate constraints.

Constraints, further examples ⇨199

The section on constraints contains further examples of constraints inside and between associations.

Qualified Associations

Related terms: associative array, dictionary, qualifying association, partitioned association.

Definition

A qualified association is an association in which qualifying attributes are used to subdivide the referenced set of objects into partitions, whereby the specified multiplicity relates to the permissible set of objects of a partition.

Description

Relations in which an object can associate *many (*)* objects of the opposite side are usually implemented by means of a container object in the initial object. This could, for example, be a dictionary (associative array, look-up table in a database, or the like). In a dictionary, access is carried out by specifying a key. The qualified association is the UML counterpart to the programming construct dictionary. Further explanations are given below with the aid of an example.

Notation

The qualifying attribute used for the association is noted in a rectangle attached to the side of the class that accesses the target object via this qualifier (Fig. 5.52). Several attributes may be specified in this rectangle. The notation corresponds to that of attributes in classes; however, the specification of default values does not apply in this case.

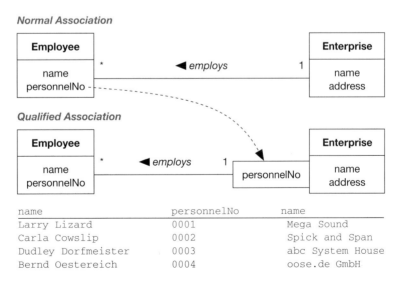

Figure 5.52 Qualified association

LIVERPOOL JOHN MOORES UNIVERSITY
LEARNING SERVICES

Example

Figure 5.52 shows employment of people in an enterprise. Besides their names, employees have their personnel numbers. From the normal association shown on top, it can be seen that each employee belongs to a single enterprise and that an enterprise has a set of employees.

In the qualified association, the sets of employees are partitioned (divided into subgroups). Partitioning is carried out on the basis of the specified qualifying attribute, in this case the personnel number. All employees of an enterprise who have the same personnel number belong to one partition. Since personnel numbers within an enterprise are normally unique, the cardinality on the side of the employee is set to 1. An enterprise may nonetheless have any number of employees, but they must all have different personnel numbers.

Employees of different enterprises may also have identical personnel numbers without, however, landing in a partition, because partitioning is enterprise-specific.

e.g. attributed
association ⇨228

Figure 5.53 shows a further variation of an example that has already been discussed in the section on attributed associations. In the example shown below, an employee may have abilities (Oh!), where each ability is assigned exactly one degree of competence. This excludes the possibility of specifying several contradictory degrees of competence for one ability. Furthermore, the association is directed, i.e. the competence levels know nothing about the employees' abilities.

Figure 5.53 Example of qualified association

Derived Associations

Related terms: calculated association, derived element.

Definition

A derived association is an association whose concrete object relations can be at any time derived (calculated) from the values of other object relations and their objects.

Notation

Derived associations are noted just like common associations, except that their name is prefixed with a slash (/). The derivation rule can be noted as a constraint.

Description and Example

Constraints ⇨197

Figure 5.54 shows a derived association, i.e. this relation is not stored but is calculated when required. Thus, through a detour via the *Department*, each *Employee* is assigned one *Enterprise*. The */works for* association marking this fact can therefore be derived (calculated). This situation should not be confused with the *Customer–Invoice–Contract* examples in the section on constraints, where actually existing redundant associations were supposed not to contradict each other.

Derived associations often also represent subsets of normal associations.

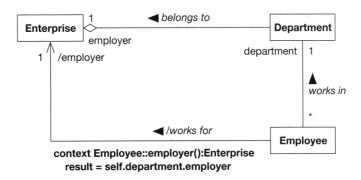

Figure 5.54 Derived association as a subset specification

N-ary Associations

 Related terms: ternary association.

Definition

An n-ary association is an association in which more than two association roles are involved.

Description

Ternary association

As well as the usual binary relations, and apart from attributed associations, there are ternary and n-ary associations, in which three or more classes (more precisely: association roles) are equally involved. An association role is represented by a class. A class may also be multiply involved in an n-ary association (Fig. 5.55).

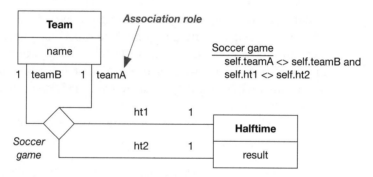

Figure 5.55   n-ary association

Since programming languages generally do not support n-ary associations, and the most common programming languages do not even possess a direct way of representing standard associations,[7] they must be implemented at the design stage. Irrespective of this, I recommend that in practice you should not use n-ary associations, on account of the many possible semantic detail problems, but should instead use standard associations to describe the situation you wish to represent.

If possible, do not use any n-ary associations

---

[7] Associations are generally implemented in a class by adding a collection and a series of standard operations (*add...*, *remove...*, *count...*, etc.) for processing this association. The adherence to the specified multiplicities is usually handled within these standard operations.

Directed Associations

Related terms: unidirectional association, navigability.

Definition
A directed association is an association in which you can directly navigate from one of the involved association roles to the other, but not vice versa.

Notation
A directed association is noted in the same way as a common association, with the exception that on the side of the class towards which navigation is possible, it shows an open arrow head. Multiplicity and role names are only relevant on the side of the association towards which you can navigate.

Description and Example
Figure 5.56 shows an association which can only be navigated in one direction. In this example, the invoice can access the address, but the address does not know with which invoices it is associated.

Unidirectional and bidirectional relations

Figure 5.56   Directed association

Inverse association

All associations are unidirectional, i.e. are directed associations. Bidirectional associations are actually two inverse associations, as shown in Fig. 5.57.

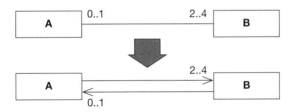

Figure 5.57   Association versus relation

Confusion with
relational
connections

Thus, object-oriented associations have different semantics as compared with relational connections in Entity Relationship Modeling, where bidirectional relations are assumed. Particularly OO rookies with a "relational background" often continue to perceive associations with relational semantics.

Thus, if in object-oriented associations only one association line without navigational direction is drawn (upper relation between *A* and *B* in Fig. 5.57), this is practically only a simplification and short notation. In reality, we are dealing with two independent relations. For one relation, class *A* bears the responsibility; for the other, class *B*. Different semantics or distribution of responsibilities would both violate the encapsulation principle and reduce possibilities of reuse.

If no direction is indicated, associations are by default bidirectional.[8]

[8] ... writes Grady Booch in any case (see Booch, 1999, p. 72). One also finds other interpretations in the literature, e.g. that associations without direction details in analysis models are not bidirectional but underspecified.

Specialized Associations

Related terms: generalized association, association generalization, association specialization, association inheritance.

Definition

A specialized association is an association with which an existing relationship is specialized, i.e. there is a specialization relationship between two associations.

Description and Notation

In the UML specialization relationships are not only allowed between classes but also for other elements, e.g. associations. A specialized association is a standard association that also possesses a specialization relationship to another association. In an analogous way to the use of specialization or inheritance with classes, in this case the specialized association (subassociation) inherits from the more general association (superassociation).

The specialized association does not produce any additional object relationships, i.e. there is only one object link between the instances whose classes possess the super- and subassociations. The subassociation is almost always an association between two classes that are themselves subclasses and whose superclasses have the association from which the subassociation is derived (see example).

Although specialized associations are sometimes described in other UML publications, I would advise you against using them. Restrictions on the superassociation can generally be expressed by other means, e.g. by OCL constraints, which are usually also clearer and more precise. In connection with specialized associations there is a series of questions that are difficult to answer, e.g. can association inheritance be applied in a meaningful way if the associated classes do not possess an inheritance relationship? According to what rules can directions, visibility, role names, role-specific interfaces, multiplicities, stereotypes, constraints, etc. be refined, restricted, or extended? Can there be multiple inheritance between associations? Are there abstract superassociations? To what extent do CASE tools support this construct? etc.

Association specialization is problematic and avoidable

Example

In Fig. 5.58 the relationships between the instances are restricted by the specialized association in such a way that *NaturalPerson* and *ContactPartner* may be connected, as may *LegalPerson* and *Supplier*. Relationships between *LegalPerson* and *ContactPartner*, however, are excluded.

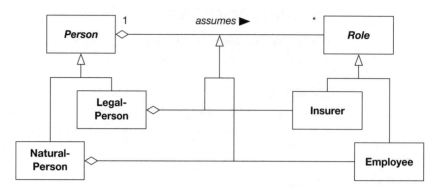

Figure 5.58 Specialized association

Figure 5.59 and the associated OCL expressions show that these situations can also be described without specialized associations. If a graphical notation is nonetheless desired, there is also the possibility of using derived associations instead of specialized associations, in addition to the OCL expression.

See derived associations ⇨235
OCL ⇨197

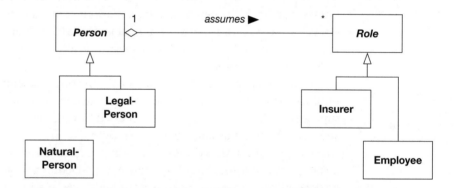

Figure 5.59 Specialized association constrained by OCL expressions

```
context r : Role inv:
  r.person.roles->includes(r)
context r : Supplier inv:
  r.person.isKindOf(LegalPerson)
context r: ContactPartner inv:
  r.person.iskindOf(NaturalPerson)
```

5.5.3 Aggregation

Related terms: whole-part relationship, association.

Definition

An aggregation is an association extended by the semantically non-binding comment that the classes involved do not possess an equivalent relationship but represent a whole-part hierarchy. An aggregation should describe how a whole is logically composed from its parts.

Description

Whole-part hierarchy
Aggregation means ".. consists logically of..."

Composition ⇨244

Propagation of operations

Delegation ⇨33

An aggregation can be understood as the combination of an object out of a set of individual parts, in the form of a *whole-part hierarchy*.

A distinctive feature of all aggregations is that the entirety assumes tasks in substitution of its parts. The aggregate class contains operations, for example, which do not cause a change in the aggregate itself but forward the message to its individual parts. This is known as *propagation of operations*. In contrast to the association, the involved classes do not maintain an equal-right relationship but one class (the aggregate) assumes a special role for delegation of responsibility and leadership.

In an aggregation relation between two classes, exactly one end of the relation must be the aggregate, and the other stand for the individual parts. If no aggregate was present on any of the sides, we would have a normal association; if both sides accommodated an aggregate, this would be a contradiction, with the two aggregates contending with each other for the leading role.

Aggregations are generally one-to-many relationships. One-to-one relationships usually lack the indicators for an aggregation.

Composition ⇨244

In some cases, aggregations describe relations in which the parts are existence-dependent on the whole. This means that if the aggregate (the whole) is deleted, all individual parts are deleted with it. If an individual part is deleted, the aggregate survives. This strict form is called composition and will be discussed in the next section.

N.B. placebo: association and aggregation are semantically equivalent.

It should be noted that the difference described here between an association and an aggregation is only of the nature of a comment. Strictly speaking, association and aggregation are semantically equivalent; so, for example, they will not necessarily be differentiated in the resulting program code. For example, the property of an aggregate of operating iteratively on the individual parts is very difficult to check formally and more or less represents only a declaration of intent. In his book on UML, Rumbaugh therefore speaks of a "placebo" (*see* Rumbaugh, 1999, p. 148).

In other words: if you are uncertain as to which variant is the right one, or are discussing it with colleagues, remember that strictly speaking there is no difference between them anyway. Nonetheless, aggregations can be useful in practice. An aggregation gives an important indication of the higher binding between the classes involved in the aggregation relationship, which makes class models easier to understand. In case of doubt, use the simpler variant, i.e. an association.

Notation

In the same way as an association, an aggregation is represented by a line drawn between two classes; in addition, it is marked with a small empty diamond (Fig. 5.60). This diamond is located on the side of the aggregate, that is, the entirety. It almost symbolizes the container object in which the individual parts are collected. Otherwise, all notation conventions of the association apply.

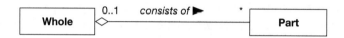

Figure 5.60　A diamond symbolizes an aggregation

The cardinality specification on the side of the aggregate is usually 1, so an omitted specification can by default be interpreted as 1. A part can belong to several aggregations at the same time.

Similarly to inheritance relations, aggregations too can be represented as tree structures, that is, on the side of the aggregate, the individual lines are combined into a common line with a common diamond.

Examples

The *Enterprise–Department–Employee* example shows that a part (*Department*) can in turn be an aggregate (Fig. 5.61).

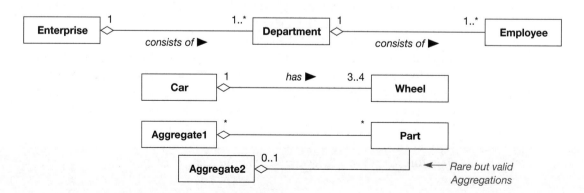

Figure 5.61　Examples of aggregations

Figure 5.62 shows an aggregation represented in the form of a tree-structure.

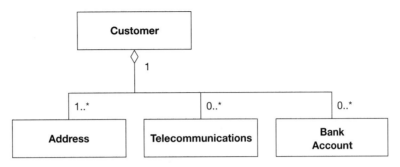

Figure 5.62 Tree-structure aggregations

5.5.4 Composition

Related terms: aggregation, association.

Definition

Existence-dependent parts

A composition is a strict form of aggregation, in which the parts are existence-dependent on the whole. It describes how a whole is composed from individual parts and how it encapsulates them.

Description

... consists of and encapsulates ...

Since a composition is a special variation of the aggregation, most of the assertions applying to the aggregation also apply to the composition. The composition too is a combination of an object from a set of individual parts. As with the aggregation, in the composition too the whole assumes tasks in representation of its parts. While one may describe aggregations as meaning "... consists logically of ...," with compositions it is a question of "... consists of and encapsulates ... ."

The following differences should be noted: the cardinality on the side of the aggregate can only be 1,[9] but each part is only part of exactly one composition object; otherwise the existence-dependency would become contradictory. The life span of the parts is subordinate to that of the whole, that is, the parts are generated together with the aggregate or subsequently, and they are destroyed before the aggregate is destroyed.

If a variable multiplicity is specified for the parts (for example *1..**), this means that they do not need to be created together with the aggregate, but can also come into being later. However, from the very moment of their creation, they belong to the whole; they are not allowed an independent existence of their own. In the same way, they can also be destroyed by the aggregate at any time; at the latest, however, together with the aggregate itself.

In C++, the differentiation between aggregation and composition leads to a corresponding implementation (*pointer* or *value*). Smalltalk and Java do not have this differentiation, because there are no such things as pointers or the like; they are principally references (sic!).

---

[9] Formally, the cardinality 0..1 on the side of the aggregate is also allowed, which is understood by some authors to mean that the part may first exist independently of the aggregate. Once, however, it has been allocated to an aggregate, it can no longer be separated from it. In view of the fact that this could also be specified more unambiguously, for example by means of a corresponding OCL expression, and that even quite ordinary associations can define existence dependencies (by noting the cardinality 1 on one side), I consider this possibility to be superfluous and confusing. In Booch et al., 1999 it is also argued that the whole is responsible for the generation of the parts, so logically it must be present before the parts.

Notation

In the same way as the aggregation, the composition is drawn as a line between two classes, equipped with a small diamond on the side of the whole. In contrast to the aggregation, however, the diamond is not empty but solid (Fig. 5.63).

See aggregation ⇨241

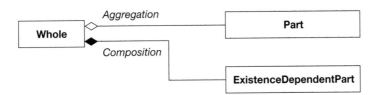

Figure 5.63 Aggregation and composition

Composition relations can be noted with a multiplicity specification, a relation name (with an optional reading direction arrow), and with role names. Several composition relations with one whole can be combined into a tree structure.

Example

A typical example of a composition is the invoice with its invoice positions. The invoice positions are existence-dependent on the invoice. As soon as the invoice is deleted, all invoice positions that it contains would also be deleted. The invoice assumes specific tasks for the whole; for example, the *Invoice* class might contain operations such as *numberOfPositions()* or *sum()*.

5.5.5 Dependency Relations

Definition

A dependency is a relation between two model elements which shows that a change in one (the independent) element requires a change in the other (the dependent) element.

Description

Dependencies may have various causes. Some examples are:

Abstraction
dependency

● A class uses a specific interface of another class. If this interface is changed, i.e. if properties are modified in the interface-providing class that are part of the interface, changes become necessary in the interface-using class as well.

Uses-dependency

● A class is dependent on another class, i.e. a change in the independent class necessitates changes in the dependent class. This occurs with indirect relationships, i.e. if an object (A) indirectly accesses its neighbor (C) via a directly neighboring object (B). In this case A is also dependent on C (Fig. 5.64).

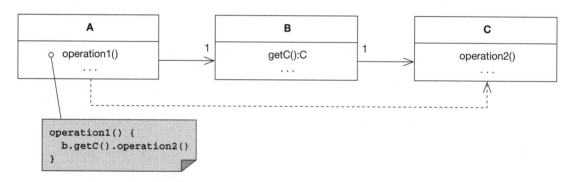

Figure 5.64 Dependencies noted graphically

● An operation is dependent on a class, that is, a change in the class potentially necessitates a change in the operation.

● A package is dependent on another package. The cause may lie in the fact that a class in one of the packages is dependent on a class in the other package.

Notation

A dependency is represented by a dashed arrow pointing from the dependent element to the independent element (Fig. 5.65).

Figure 5.65 Notation principle

Example

Figure 5.66 shows examples of dependencies between classes and interfaces, between two packages, and between an operation and a class.

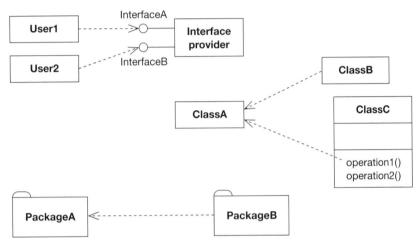

Figure 5.66 Various examples of dependency relationships

5.5.6 Refinement/Realization Relations

Definition

Refinement relations are relations between similar elements of different degrees of detail. Realization relations are relations between an interface and its implementation.

Description

Refinement relations can, for example, be used to express the following modeling situations:

Analysis/design

- a relation between the analysis version and the design version;

Clean/optimized

- a relation between a clean implementation and an optimized but potentially difficult variation;

Interface realization
⇨192

- a relation between an interface class and a class which implements this interface;

- a relation between two differently grained elements.

Refinement relations allow better documentation of specific design decisions: "The XY class was neatly designed, but we had to optimize it [...]." The result is usually an improved representation of the modeling history.

Since project budget and duration are usually limited,[10] one should not document every conceivable refinement of such relations but only those cases where the knowledge of the refinement or the previous variation appears to be of real significance.

Provided that a principal difference is made between an analysis model and a design model, refinement relations can also document the corresponding dependencies. When design decisions are made that require the analysis model to be updated, the refinement relation points to the analysis element affected.

If no explicit analysis model exists but only different versions of a continuously evolving comprehensive model, refinement relations between the analysis and design versions of an element are sensible only in exceptional cases. Refinement relations are not designed for version maintenance of model elements.

Notation

Generalization ⇨220

The refinement relation is represented as a dashed generalization arrow pointing toward the "original" variation, i.e. toward the coarser or less optimal element.

---

[10] They aren't at your place? Contact me!

Example

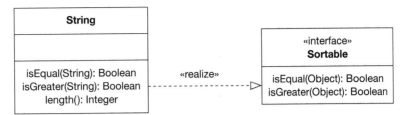

Figure 5.67   Realization relationship

Figure 5.67 shows an interface class and its implementation. In many cases, a note with an appropriate text, attached to the refinement relation, is probably of some help. Figure 5.68 shows an optimization refinement.

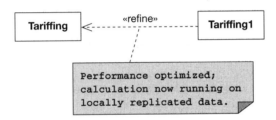

Figure 5.68   Refinement relationship

5.6 Behavioral Diagrams

This section explains in detail the individual elements of the Unified Modeling Language used for the representation of dynamic model features, each structured into definition, description, notation, and example.

5.6.1 Activity Diagrams

Related terms: object state, action state, state diagram, flow chart, object flow diagram.

Definition

Object-oriented procedure plans

Activity diagrams describe the procedural possibilities of a system with the aid of activities. An activity diagram is a special form of a state diagram, which mostly or exclusively contains activities. An activity is a state with an internal action and one (or more) outgoing transition which automatically follows the termination of the internal activity. An activity is a single step in a procedure.

Description

Activity: step in a procedure

An activity is a single step in a processing procedure. It is a state with an internal action and at least one outgoing transition. The outgoing transition implies termination of the internal action. An activity may have several outgoing transitions if these can be identified through conditions.

Activities can be part of state diagrams, but are usually employed in separate activity diagrams. Activity diagrams are similar to procedural flow charts, except that all activities are uniquely associated to objects. Activity diagrams support the description of parallel activities. For activity paths running in parallel, the order is irrelevant. They can run consecutively, simultaneously, or alternately.

Parallelism

Activities and activity diagrams are associated either to:

- a class;
- an operation; or
- a use case.

They describe the possible internal procedures for these model elements.

Compound activity

Activities can be nested hierarchically, i.e. an activity can consist of a set of detailed activities, whereby the incoming and outgoing transitions of the compound activity and of the detail model must match.

Swim lanes

Activity diagrams can be subdivided into responsibility domains, the so-called swim lanes, which allow activities to be assigned to other elements or structures. For example, the class or component to which the activities belong can be stated. If activity diagrams are employed for analysis and business process modeling, swim lanes can also be used to map organizational structures.

Another possibility for representing parallel processes are multiple transitions or triggers. If, for example, all individual positions need to be checked in a part list before the list can be closed, it is possible to model so that the individual positions are checked independently from each other, i.e. in arbitrary order and potentially also in parallel.

Multiple transitions

Activity diagrams are therefore suitable for representing the most disparate types of procedures. In contrast to sequence diagrams, they are able to describe completely the technical connections and dependencies underlying a use case. An activity diagram can even satisfy several use cases or be use-case transcendent. Business rules and decisional logics can also be represented.

Activity diagrams can be used both in a fairly fuzzy and conceptional way and for detailed specifications with a view to implementation.

Notation

An activity is shown as a shape with a straight top and bottom and with convex arcs on the two sides. The activity description, which can be a name, a freely formulated description, pseudocode, or programming language code, is placed in the symbol.

Incoming transitions trigger an activity. If several incoming transitions exist for an activity, each of these transitions can trigger the activity independently from the others. Outgoing transitions are drawn in the same way as event arrows, but without an explicit event description. Transitions are triggered implicitly by the termination of the activity (Fig. 5.69).

Conditions

Figure 5.69 Activities and transition

Conditions and branches. Outgoing transitions can be provided with conditions enclosed in square brackets. Such conditions should be Boolean expressions; alternatively, branching points may be used. Instead of binding the conditions directly to the transitions leaving the activity, an empty diamond is drawn from which the different conditions leave together with their conditions. This diamond too represents a (decisional) activity (Fig. 5.70).

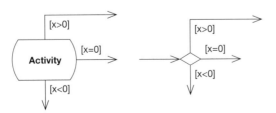

Figure 5.70 Decision/branching

AND and OR synchronization. Furthermore, transitions can be synchronized, consolidated, or divided. Consolidation is represented by a diamond with more than one incoming transition. As soon as one of the incoming transitions fires, the activity flow continues. Synchronization is represented by a bar. In this case, the activity flow continues only when all the incoming transitions are present (Fig. 5.71).

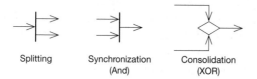

Splitting   Synchronization   Consolidation
                  (And)   (XOR)

Figure 5.71 Synchronization and splitting

Compound activities are identified by a small stylized activity diagram (Fig. 5.72).

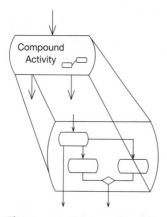

Compound
Activity

Figure 5.72 Compound activity

Loops may be represented relatively simply (Fig. 5.73). You only need a repeat or break condition and a return transition. You can place any number of activities within a loop.

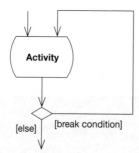

Activity

[else]   [break condition]

Figure 5.73 Repetition/loop

Optional activities can be modeled by noting a conditional branch before the optional activity and then subsequently consolidating the branches again (Fig. 5.74).

OR or AND?

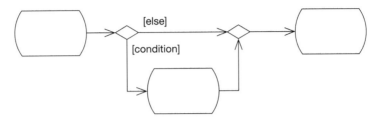

Figure 5.74 Optional activity

Sending and receiving signals. The notation elements shown in Fig. 5.75 can be used to indicate that a signal is sent to a particular object upon transition from one activity to the next, or that upon completion of an activity the next activity cannot start until a signal has been received. This allows you to synchronize concurrent processes, for example.

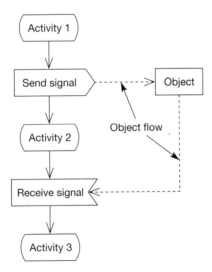

Figure 5.75 Inter-process communication

Object state. Often, activities cause changes in object states. Object states are represented as rectangles that contain the name of the object and, enclosed in square brackets, the object state.

Activities and object states are joined by dashed transition lines. If the line leads from an object state to an activity, this means that the activity presumes or requires an initial state. If the line leads from an activity to an object state, this shows the state resulting from the activity. State changes of objects need not be modeled; notation of object states is merely a way of emphasizing them when this is of particular significance (Fig. 5.76).

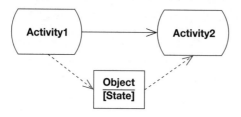

Figure 5.76 Resulting or required object states

5.6.2 Object Flow Diagrams

UML activity diagrams can also be used as object flow diagrams, which considerably increases their methodical usefulness. One diagram element that is available is the notation of resulting and required object states (*see* Fig. 5.75).

With a few extensions to the standard UML activity diagrams, they can be converted into object flow diagrams. These extensions are supported by standard modeling tools such as Rational Rose.

Since an activity can have several outgoing transitions, but specific resulting objects or object states are achieved only for specific transitions, the resulting object states must relate to concrete transitions. The following convention is sufficient to represent this with an activity diagram:

- Number the activities of a diagram or model.
- Number the outgoing transitions relating to each activity in the form *<activity number>.<transition number>*.
- With resulting objects/object states specify the transition numbers for which the result applies.

An object flow diagram can at any time be transformed into a standard activity diagram simply by not portraying the resulting objects. It is therefore very easy to generate two different views based on a model. To ensure that object flow diagrams remain easy to understand in spite of the additional notation elements (objects/states), it is a good idea to use visual stereotypes for the resulting objects/states (e.g. the entity symbol, see p. 209).

Figure 5.77 shows the principle; further examples may be found on pages 103 (Fig. 3.10) and 124 (Fig. 4.7).

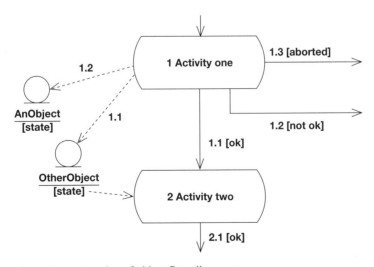

Figure 5.77 Notation of object flow diagrams

5.6.3 Collaboration Diagrams

Related terms: cooperation diagram, interaction diagram, object diagram.

Objects ⇨181

Definition

A collaboration diagram shows a set of interactions between selected objects in a specific, limited situation (context), focusing on the relations between the objects and their topography.

Description

Sequence diagram ⇨261

Basically, a collaboration diagram shows the same facts as a sequence diagram but from another perspective. The collaboration diagram emphasizes the objects and their cooperation with each other; between them, selected messages are shown. The chronological course of communication between the objects, focused upon in the sequence diagram, is marked in the collaboration diagram by numbering the messages. For two objects to communicate with each other, the sender of the message must have a reference, i.e. an association, to the receiver object.

Object relation, association ⇨225
Association ⇨225
Aggregation ⇨241

The object relation may either exist permanently, or only temporarily or locally (for example as argument of a message). Without an association having to be present, the object can always send messages to itself.

Collaboration diagrams show the chronological sequence of the messages, their names and responses, and their possible arguments. They can equally be used to represent iterations and message loops. Furthermore, they can be employed for the representation of design issues and, in a slightly more detailed form, of implementation issues.

Collaborations are always projections of the underlying complete model and are consistent with it.

Like sequence diagrams, collaboration diagrams are suited for describing individual procedural variations. They are, however, not suitable for a precise or complete definition of behavior. For this purpose, activity and state diagrams are the better choice.

Collaboration diagrams are a very good tool for explaining or documenting a specific procedural situation. They can be quickly sketched and discussed on a flip chart or a whiteboard. Employment of a CASE tool for creation of a collaboration diagram is sensible if one wishes to incorporate the diagram into the documentation for a particular description of an issue and to ensure consistency.

Notation

Notation of objects ⇨181

Between the objects, association lines are drawn on which the messages are noted. A small arrow indicates the direction of the message from sender to receiver. If arguments are passed together with the message, they are listed too. Possible responses can be shown as well; they are put in front of the actual message in the form *response:= message()* (Fig. 5.78).

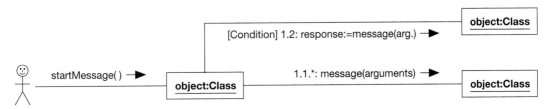

Figure 5.78 Notation of message exchange as a collaboration diagram

The chronological sequence of the messages is indicated by sequence numbers. The first message begins with number 1. The starting message – the external message that triggered the interaction – is shown without a number. This message may also start from an actor symbol.

Message descriptions are based on the following syntax:

```
PredecessorCondition SequenceExpression Response :=
MessageName (ParameterList)
```

The individual elements have the following meaning:

Predecessor

● **Predecessor condition**
This is an enumeration of the sequence numbers of other messages that need to have been sent before this message may be sent. This allows synchronization to be achieved. The sequence numbers are listed separated by commas and terminated with a slash /. The predecessor condition is optional. Example:

```
1.1, 2.3/
```

Sequences

● **Sequence expression**
To show the sequence of messages, they are numbered in ascending order. If new messages are sent within an operation which interprets a received message, they are given a new subsequence number separated by a dot. Thus messages show their depth of nesting inside other messages. Example: message 2.1.3 follows message 2.1.2. Both were sent during interpretation of message 2.1.

Instead of numbers, strings of characters can be used. The sequence expression, if specified, is terminated with a colon.

Iteration

Iterations, i.e. repeated sending of a message, are marked with an asterisk *. To describe the iteration in more detail – for example, to specify the number of iterations – an appropriate indication in pseudocode or the programming language used can be added in square brackets. Example:

```
1.2.*[i := 1..n]:
```

In the iteration, it is assumed that all messages are sent sequentially. If a parallel execution is to be indicated, the asterisk is followed by two vertical lines:

```
1.2.*||[i := 1..n]:
```

In the same way, a condition noted in pseudocode or in the actual programming language can be added, which needs to be satisfied for the message to be sent. This not only allows individual scenarios to be represented but also more general interaction structures. Example:

```
1.2.*[x > 5]:
```

● **Response**

Response

The response supplied by a message can be given a name. This name can then be used as an argument in other messages. Its scope is the same as that of local variables inside the message to be sent and may indeed be such a variable. It may also be the name of an object attribute.

● **Message name (parameter list)**

Signature,
operation ⇨186

Name of the message, usually homonymous with a corresponding operation that interprets the message. The signature of the operation is specified.

Objects that are generated within the described scenario are marked as *«new»*, objects that are destroyed are marked as *«destroyed»*, and objects that are generated and destroyed in the scenario are marked as *«transient»*.

Stereotypes ⇨209

The relation between two objects, which forms the basis for the message exchange, may have various causes which can be marked in the diagram. Where the connecting line meets the message-receiving object and the role name (attribute name) is noted, one of the following stereotypes can be indicated:

● *«association»*

The object relation is based on an association, aggregation, or composition. This is the default; the specification can therefore be omitted.

Visibility
specifications

● *«global»*

The receiving object is global.

● *«local»*

The receiving object is local in the sending operation (and thus *«new»* or *«transient»*).

● *«parameter»*

The receiving object is a parameter in the sending operation.

● *«self»*

The receiving object is the sending object.

Various arrow shapes have been defined for specifying particular synchronization conditions. They have the following meaning:

Synchronization
features

→ synchronous
→ asynchronous

● With a synchronous message, the sender waits until the receiver has accepted the message.

● Asynchronous messages end up in the waiting queue of the receiver. The sender is not interested in when the receiver accepts the message.

Example

The following example[11] (Fig. 5.79) shows the message exchange between four different objects during reservation of a mail order article. The first *reserve(o)* message contains the object *o* (the *order*) as an argument, therefore the relation with the order object bears the stereotype *«parameter»*.

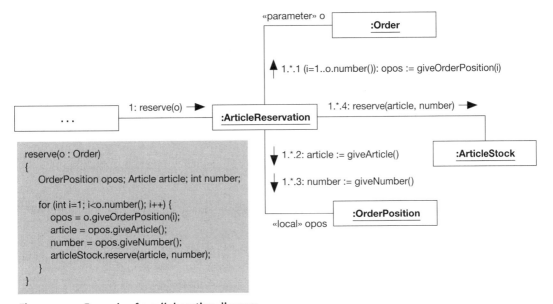

Figure 5.79 Example of a collaboration diagram

Message *1.*.1* to the order object is repeated in a loop *[i=1..*]*; as a response, an order position *opos* is returned each time. This is sent the messages *1.*.2* and *1.*.3* whose responses (*article, number*) are used as parameters in the subsequent message *1.*.4* to the *ArticleStock*.

Further examples of messages include:

● Simple message:

```
2: display(x, y)
```

---

[11] If you look closely at the design, you will notice that it is perhaps a little unwieldy and would have to be restructured. However, it does contain all the important notation elements for this diagram type.

- Nested message with response:

  ```
  2.3.4: i := count(block)
  ```

- Conditional message:

  ```
  [x > 7] 1: check()
  ```

- Synchronized and iterative message:

  ```
  2, 4.2, 4.3/ 5.1.*: notify(x)
  ```

5.6.4 Sequence Diagrams

Related terms: interaction diagram, event trace diagram, scenario, message diagram.

Definition

A sequence shows a series of messages exchanged by a selected set of objects in a temporally limited situation, with an emphasis on the chronological course of events.

Description

Collaboration diagram
⇨256

The sequence diagram basically shows the same facts as a collaboration diagram but from another perspective. In the collaboration diagram, the emphasis lies on the cooperation between objects. The chronological course of communication between objects is indicated by the numbering of messages.

Lifelines

In the sequence diagram, the emphasis is on the chronological course of messages. Objects are merely shown by vertical lifelines. This highlights the chronological sequence of the messages. Time runs from top to bottom.

Notation

Objects are represented by dashed vertical lines. On top of the line, we find the name or the object symbol. Messages are drawn as horizontal arrows between the object lines, on which the message itself is noted in the form *message(arguments)*. Similarly to the collaboration diagram, the response is shown in textual form (*response:= message()*) or as a separate but dashed arrow with an open head.

Overlapping of the dashed lifelines with broad, empty (or gray) bars symbolizes the control focus. The control focus specifies which object currently holds program control, i.e. which object is currently active. The left- or right-hand borders can be used to note freely formulated explanations, time requirements, and the like (Fig. 5.80).

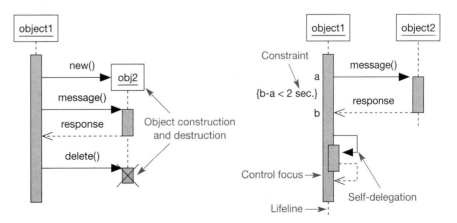

Figure 5.80 Standard notation elements of the sequence diagram

Creation and removal of objects can also be represented in sequence diagrams. The construction of a new object is indicated by a message that meets an object symbol; the destruction of an object by a cross at the end of the control focus.

Iteration

To indicate iterations, i.e. multiple sending of a message, an asterisk * is placed in front of the message (iteration mark) (Fig. 5.81).

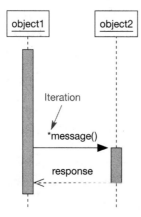

Figure 5.81   Iteration in UML

Since the UML does not provide a notation element for the subsequent synchronization point, the notation in Fig. 5.82 has become established in practice.

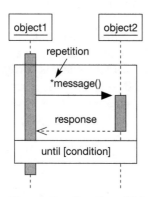

Figure 5.82   Iteration with break condition

Example

Collaboration
diagram
Example ⇨259

The following example (Fig. 5.83) shows the same situation as the example in the section on collaboration diagrams, where you will find further explanations about this example. The sequence diagram with control focus shows clearly which objects are active and when.

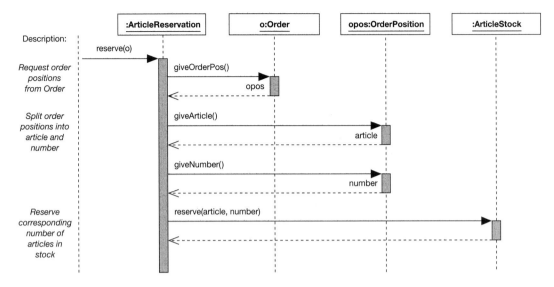

Figure 5.83 Example sequence diagram

Figure 5.84 shows a section containing indirectly recursive messages. Here, the existing control focus is overlaid with an additional one (shown slightly shifted to the right).

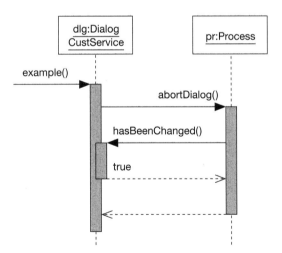

Figure 5.84 Example of an indirectly recursive call

The corresponding program instructions would look like this:

```
class DialogCustService {
    Process pr;
    boolean changed;
    public void example() {
      ...
      (pr.abortDialog(self))
      ...
    public boolean hasBeenChanged() {
      // returns true, if data has been changed
      return(changed);
    }
}
class Process {
  void abortDialog(DialogCustService dlg) {
    if (dlg.hasBeenChanged()) {
      ... // abort dialog
    }
  }
}
```

5.6.5 State Diagrams

Related terms: state machine, state transition diagram, finite automaton.

Definition and Description

A state diagram shows a sequence of states an object can assume during its lifetime, together with the stimuli that cause changes of state. A state diagram describes a hypothetical machine (finite automaton) which at any given time is found in a set of finite states. It consists of:

- a finite, non-empty set of states;
- a finite, non-empty set of events;
- state transitions;
- an initial state;
- a set of final states.

The individual elements are explained in more detail in the following sections.

Example

Further example ⇨124

The following example (Fig. 5.85) shows the state transitions for a flight reservation. Where the event names correspond to the action operations, only the operation is shown. On opening the flight, the initial state leads to the *NoReservation* state. When this state is entered, the *Reset* operation is executed.

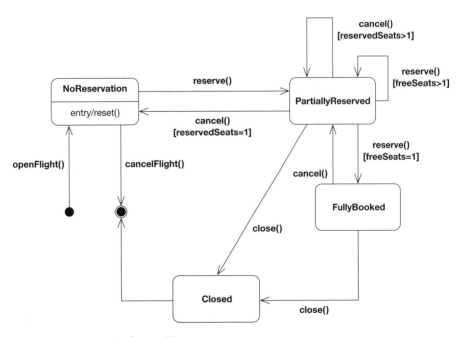

Figure 5.85 Example of state diagram

If a reservation is made for this flight, the object changes to the state *PartiallyReserved*. The *Reserve* event is associated to the homonymous Reserve action (implemented as an operation). In this operation, the actual reservation takes place, and the internal reservation counter is updated. After termination of this action, we will find the object in the *PartiallyReserved* state.

Each additional reservation leads to the same action. As long as free seats are available, the object remains in the *PartiallyReserved* state. If only one seat is left, it changes into the *FullyBooked* state. Cancellation of reserved seats is carried out in a similar way. Thus, the state diagram describes which actions are triggered by which events and under which conditions these (together with the call of the corresponding operations) are permitted.

States

Related terms: initial state, final state.

Definition

A state belongs to a single class and represents an abstraction or a combination of a set of possible attribute values that the objects of this class may assume. State diagrams describe the internal state model of an object.

Description

Not every change of an attribute value is perceived as a change of state. The abstraction consists of considering only those events that significantly affect the behavior of the object. A state can therefore also be seen as a time span between two events.

Initial state and final state

Two particular types of state are the initial and final states. No transition may lead to an initial state, and no event allows leaving the final state. States have either unique names or they are anonymous states. Anonymous states are different from each other, i.e. two unnamed states in a diagram are two different states. In all other cases, states bearing the same name are actually the same state.

State variables
Attributes ⇨183

Each state may contain a set of state variables. State variables are attributes of the class to which the state belongs. The set of state variables is therefore a subset of the class attributes. In a state, only those attributes are listed as state variables that are essential for the description or identification of the state.

Not every class needs to have states; it needs to show a significant behavior. If all operations of an object can be called in an arbitrary order independent of its internal state, state modeling is not required.

Events,
conditions,
operations

Transitions from one state to the next are triggered by events. An event consists of a name and a list of possible arguments. A state can attach conditions to an event which must be satisfied before the event can cause the transition into this state. Conditions may be formulated independently of a specific event. Events can trigger actions inside the state that are realized through appropriate operations. Three special triggers are predefined:

- entry – fires automatically when entering a state;
- exit – fires automatically when leaving a state;
- do – fires repeatedly as long as the state is active, i.e. not left.

Notation

States are represented by rounded rectangles. They may contain a name and be optionally subdivided by horizontal lines into up to three rubrics (Fig. 5.86).

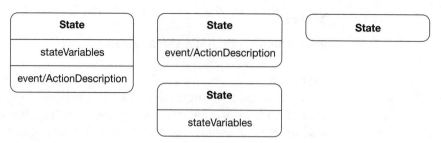

Figure 5.86   Notation variants for states

The top rubric contains the name of the state. It may be omitted; in that case, the state is an anonymous state (Fig. 5.87). For clearer visual structuring of diagram layouts, states may occur more than once in the same diagram.

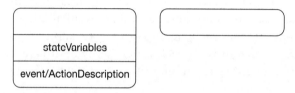

Figure 5.87   Anonymous states

Attributes ⇨183   In a second rubric, existing state variables may be listed. Since state variables are attributes of the class, they are noted in exactly the same way:

```
variable : Class = InitialValue {Feature} {Constraint}
```

The third available rubric of the state symbol contains a list of possible internal events, conditions, and operations resulting from them. They are noted in the following format:

```
event / ActionDescription
```

The action description can be the name of an operation, or it can be formulated freely. It may contain state variables, attributes of the class, or parameters of the incoming transitions.

Initial states are drawn as small solid circles, final states as empty circles surrounding smaller solid circles (Fig. 5.88).

● Initial state   ◉ Final state

Figure 5.88   Initial state and final state

Example

Figure 5.89 shows a state of the class *Contract*. Once a customer has been assigned and the state left, selected customer data are to be automatically inserted into the contract form.

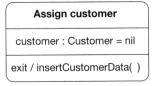

Figure 5.89 State with action description

Substates

ADVANCED UML

States can be nested into further, either sequential or parallel substates. In simultaneous, concurrent substates, the state symbol is subdivided into additional rubrics with the aid of dashed lines.

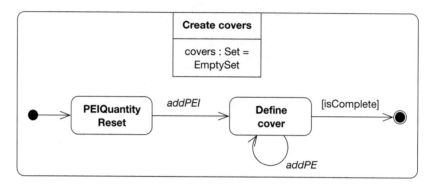

Figure 5.90   Nested states

Figure 5.90 shows a sequential nesting. When an insurance contract is stipulated, a product is selected (for example, home contents), which consists of several product elements (*PEI*), such as theft of bicycle, breakage of glass, and so on. For each product element, a cover must be created. The illustration shows the *Create covers* state of this context.

Figure 5.91 shows the notation of parallel substates.

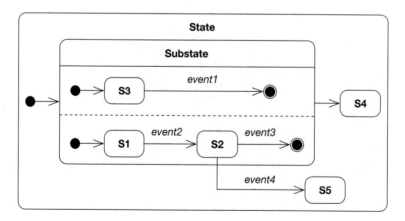

Figure 5.91   Parallel substates

Events and Transitions
Related terms: state transition.

Event
Transition

Definition
An event is an occurrence which has a particular significance in a given context, can be localized in space and time, and needs to be taken into account because it triggers a state transition.

Description
An event may have the following causes:

- a condition (defined for a transition) is satisfied;
- the object receives a message.

States and events can be used to draw up state diagrams which describe when an object is allowed to receive specific events, and which consequences this has for the status of the object. Specific events can only be processed sensibly if the object is in a suitable state for doing so. It may also be stated that an event may lead to different actions, depending on the state the object is in, and on the conditions attached to the event.

State transitions are usually triggered by events which are noted on the arrows that connect the states. Transitions without event specifications are triggered automatically as soon as the actions belonging to a state are terminated.

Condition

Events may be provided with conditions. The conditions attached to an event must be satisfied for the state transition to occur. Conditions may be formulated independently from the events. Upon transition from one state to the other, an event may furthermore be sent to another object (target object). In this way the state machines of different classes may be linked with one another.

Event and action

Notation
Events are represented by arrows leading from one state to the next (Fig. 5.92). An arrow may also point back to the state it started from. On the arrows, the transition descriptions are noted in the following form:

```
event(arguments)
[condition]
/operation(arguments)
^targetObjects.sentEvent(arguments)
```

Figure 5.92   **Transition**

5.7 Implementation Diagrams

This section describes in detail the elements of the Unified Modeling Language used for the representation of implementation issues.

5.7.1 Component Diagrams

Related terms: component, subsystem, module, package.

Definition

A component is an executable piece of software with its own identity and well-defined interfaces. A distinction should be made between component definitions (e.g. "person") and component instances (e.g. "Gabby Goldsmith").

Component diagrams show the interrelations between components.

Description

Interfaces ⇨192
Packages ⇨218

In practice, UML components are very similar to packages: they define boundaries, and group and structure a set of individual elements. Components may have interfaces. Components or component diagrams may under certain conditions also be needed to protocol compiler and run-time dependencies.

Dependencies ⇨246

The files that are to contain the program code for the individual classes must be defined at the latest at implementation start, depending on the programming language used. In Smalltalk, where no module concept is needed, this problem is different from C++, where the appropriate *.cpp and *.h files need to be created.

I generally use UML components for description of larger sets of technically related classes, such as all classes that have to do with partner management. The Partner component could, for example, contain the classes *Person, LegalEntity, NaturalPerson, PartnerRole, PremiumPayer, PolicyHolder, MailRecipient, Mediator, InsuredParty, Address, BankAccount, PhoneNumber*, and so on – just anything that technically has to do with Partner and has no better place to go.

Interfaces

However, the combination of a set of elements to a bigger unit is only one aspect. Another one is providing one or more common interfaces. Thus, while all elements contained in a component know each other well (practically completely in fact), only a section is made externally available. The properties a component exports are defined by its explicit interfaces.

Packages versus components

Packages and components can be used for very similar purposes. While packages represent a more logical view, components emphasize the physical perspective.

5.7.2   Deployment Diagrams

Related terms: node, node diagram, configuration diagram.

Description

A node is an object which is physically present at runtime and has computing power or memory, such as computers (processors), devices, and the like.

Deployment diagrams show which components and objects run on which node (processes, computers) – how they are configured and which communication relations exist between them.

Notation and Example

Components ⇨272
Interfaces ⇨192
Dependency ⇨246

Components are represented by bricks. Nodes that communicate with each other, i.e. have the appropriate relations, are connected with one another by association lines. Optionally, components or runtime objects (processes) may be placed inside the bricks. Interfaces and dependency relations between these elements are also allowed.

Nodes are identified either by their name alone or by a name followed by a specification of the node type:

NodeName
Name:NodeType

This kind of diagram is often created with the aid of conventional drawing programs. Instead of ordinary bricks, more colorful clip-art is used (pictures of printers, computers, and the like) (Fig 5.93).

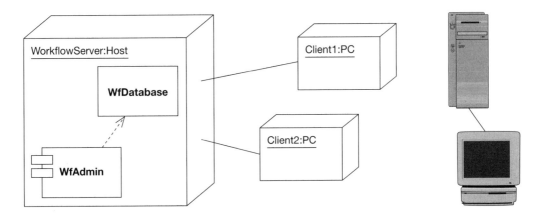

Figure 5.93   Deployment diagram

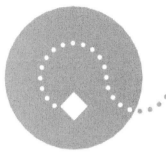

Appendices

Appendix A Glossary 277

Appendix B References 289

Glossary

This glossary defines the most important terms of object-orientation and UML.

Abstract class No object instances of an abstract class are ever generated; it is intentionally incomplete, thus forming a basis for further subclasses that can have instances. C++: virtual class.

Abstract data type (ADT) The concept of abstract data type is similar to that of class. An abstract data type is the combination of data and operations that can be performed with this data.

Abstract operation ⇨operation An operation for which only a ⇨signature is defined, but no sequence of instructions; that is, the operation is defined but not yet implemented. It is implemented in a derived class. C++: virtual operation.

Abstraction A method in which the essential features of an object or a concept are singled out under a specific point of view.

Action state (activity) A state with an internal action and one or more outgoing transitions which automatically follow termination of the internal action. An activity is a single step in a process. It may have several outgoing transitions provided that these can be distinguished through conditions.

Active class ⇨active object A class whose instances are executed in parallel and have their own thread.

Active object ⇨active class Instance of an active class.

Activity diagram A special form of state diagram which pre-eminently or exclusively contains ⇨action states (activities).

Actor An entity located outside the system which is involved in an interaction with the system described in a use case. An actor may be a person, e.g. a user, but may also be another technical system, e.g. SAP, the operating system, etc.

Aggregation ⇨association, ⇨composition A special form of association in which the involved classes do not have an equivalent relation with each other but represent an entirety-part hierarchy. An aggregation describes how an entirety is composed of its parts.

Analysis (Object-oriented) analysis is the name for all activities in the framework of a software development process that serve determination, clarification, and description of the requirements towards the system (that is, clarification of *what* the system is supposed to perform).

Annotation ⇨notes

Application component ⇨component Technical ⇨subsystem.

Architecture Specification of the fundamental structure of a system.

Argument Concrete value of a ⇨parameter.

Assertion ⇨constraints Boolean expressions that should never become untrue and, if they do, indicate errors. Typically, assertions are activated only during the development phase.

Association ⇨directed associations, ⇨bidirectional associations Describes a relation between classes, i.e. the common semantics and structure of a set of ⇨object relations. We differentiate between ⇨directed associations (directly navigable only in one way) and ⇨bidirectional associations (directly navigable in both directions). The two ends of an association are ⇨association roles.

Association class ⇨attributed association, ⇨resolved association, ⇨implicit association class A model element that disposes of the properties of both a class and an association. It may be seen as an association with additional class properties (attributed association) or as a class with additional association properties (association class).

Association role The role a type or a class plays in an ⇨association. This means that a role represents a class in an association. The distinction is important because a class may also have an association relation with itself and in this case, the two association ends can only be distinguished by means of their role specifications.

Attribute A named property of a type. An attribute is a data element equally contained in each object of a class and represented by each object with an individual value. In contrast to objects, attributes have no own identity outside the object of which they are a part. Attributes are completely under the control of the objects of which they are parts.

Attributed association ⇨association, ⇨association class An association that has its own attributes.

Base class ⇨superclass

Bidirectional association ⇨association An association directly navigable both ways, that is, an association in which it is possible to navigate directly from each of the involved ⇨association roles to the opposite one.

Binding ⇨dynamic binding

Bound element ⇨parameterized class

Business class ⇨class ⇨instantiation ⇨business objects.

Business event (process) A (business) object (for example a concrete contract), triggered by an event (for example receipt of application form), which is processed by means of the activities described in a business process.

Business model (business class model) ⇨domain class model Class model which pre-eminently or exclusively contains ⇨business classes (domain-specific elementary terms in form of classes).

Business object ⇨object Represents an object, a concept, a place, or a person out of real business life in a technically rough degree of detail, that is, in an elementary concept or term (contract, invoice, and so on). For practical realization, business objects are aggregations of fundamental domain objects (⇨domain classes: invoice positions, address, and so on) reduced to technically motivated properties, to which everything else is delegated. Typically, they define interfaces and are a kind of façade.

Business process ⇨workflow A combination of organizationally potentially distributed but technically related activities needed to process a business event (for example a concrete application form) in a result-oriented fashion. The activities of a business process are usually chronologically and logically related to each other. A business event is usually triggered by an event (for example receipt of an application form).

Cardinality ⇨multiplicity Number of elements.

Class The definition of attributes, operations, and semantics of a set of objects. All objects of a class correspond to that definition.

Class attribute, class variable ⇨attribute Class attributes do not belong to an individual object but are attributes of a class (for example in Smalltalk).

Class card ⇨CRC card

Class diagram Shows a set of static model elements, in particular classes, and their relations.

Class library A collection of classes.

Class operation, class method ⇨operation Operations which do not operate on an object but on a class (for example in Smalltalk).

Class template ⇨parameterized class

Collaboration ⇨collaboration diagram The context of a set of interactions.

Collaboration diagram Shows a set of interactions between a set of selected objects in a specific limited situation (context) with an emphasis on the relations between the objects and their topography. Similar to the ⇨sequence diagram.

Collections Objects that reference a set of other objects and provide the operations needed to access those objects.

Component An executable and interchangeable software unit with well-defined interfaces and its own identity. A distinction should be made between component definitions (e.g. "person") and component instances (e.g. "Gabby Goldsmith").

Component diagram Shows organization and dependencies of ⇨components.

Composite ⇨aggregation A strict form of aggregation in which the parts are existence-dependent on the whole. It describes how something whole is composed of individual parts which it encapsulates.

Concrete class A ⇨class that can instantiate ⇨objects. See ⇨abstract class.

Concretization ⇨specialization

Concurrency Two or more activities are performed simultaneously (in parallel).

Configuration diagram ⇨deployment diagram

Consistency constraint ⇨constraint A constraint between several associations which represent partly redundant facts. The constraint specifies the consistency condition.

Constraint An expression which restricts possible contents or states, or the semantics of a model element, and which must always be satisfied. The expression may be a ⇨stereotype or ⇨property values, a free formulation (⇨note), or a ⇨dependency relation. Constraints in the form of pure Boolean expressions are also called ⇨assertions.

Container class ⇨collection

CRC cards (class card) Filing cards on which the name of the class, its responsibilities, and its collaborations are described.

Data abstraction The principle of making only the operations applicable to an object externally visible. The actual internal realization of the operations and the internal structure of the object are hidden. This means an abstract view of the semantics without considering the actual implementation.

Default implementation Concrete implementation of an actual abstract operation for providing subclasses with a default behavior.

Delegation A mechanism by which an object does not (completely) interpret a message itself but forwards it to another object.

Dependency A relation between two model elements which shows that a change in one (the independent) element requires a change in the other (the dependent) element.

Deployment diagram A diagram which shows the configuration of the ⇨nodes and their ⇨components, processes, and objects present (employed) at runtime.

Derived association ⇨association, ⇨derived element An association whose concrete object relations can at any time be derived (calculated) from the values of other object relations and objects.

Derived attribute ⇨attribute, ⇨derived element Calculated from the values of other attributes, derived attributes cannot be modified directly and are implemented or set by means of a calculation operation.

Derived element A model element which can at any time be calculated from another element and is shown only for clarity, or added for design purposes, without, however, adding any semantic information.

Design (Object-oriented) design is the name for all activities in the framework of the software development process in which a model is logically and physically structured, and which serve to describe *how* the system fulfills the requirements described in the ⇨analysis.

Design pattern Generalized solution ideas for repeatedly occurring design problems. They are not ready-coded solutions but merely describe the solution approach.

Directed association ⇨association, ⇨navigation An association in which it is possible to navigate directly from one of the involved ⇨association roles to the other, but not vice versa.

Discriminator Differentiation feature for structuring of the model semantics into ⇨generalization or specialization relations.

Domain Application or problem area inside which the technical modeling takes place. Usually, the part of the entire model is viewed as an application area model (domain model) that relates to the actual subject-specific problems. Implementational, cross-sectional, and other aspects are not part of it. In the context of application architecture, it usually refers to the domain class model (that is, without framework, GUI, controller, and other classes).

Domain class ⇨class Usually technically motivated class that represents a concept of the problem domain. Used in contrast to ⇨business classes.

Domain model A class model pre-eminently or exclusively containing domain classes.

Dynamic binding, late binding This term denotes that a ⇨message is assigned only at runtime to a concrete ⇨operation which then interprets it.

Dynamic classification An object is consecutively an instance of different classes of a subtype structure, that is, it can change its class membership during the course of its lifetime.

Event An occurrence which, in a given context, has a meaning and which can be localized in space and time.

Framework Set of cooperating classes which under specification of a process (*"Don't call the framework, the framework will call you"*) provides a generic solution for a number of similar problems or tasks.

Fundamental class ⇨domain class

Generalization ⇨specialization/concretization

Generic class ⇨parameterized class

Generic design Use of templates and macros for design (in CASE tools).

Generic programming Use of templates, ⇨parameterized classes, and the like in programming.

GUI Graphical User Interface.

Identity ⇨object identity

Implicit association class The (nameless) ⇨association class of an ⇨attributed association.

Information hiding Deliberate hiding of implementation details. Externally, an interface is provided, but the internals (for example of a class) are not visible. Thus, the way in which the interface is served remains invisible.

Inheritance ⇨simple inheritance, ⇨multiple inheritance, ⇨multiple classification, ⇨dynamic classification Inheritance is a programming language concept for the implementation of a relation between a superclass and a subclass in which subclasses can share properties of their superclasses. Inheritance usually implements ⇨generalization and specialization relations. Alternatives: ⇨delegation, ⇨aggregation, ⇨generic programming, ⇨generic design.

Instance ⇨object For domestic use, instance and object can be regarded as synonyms. In UML 1.0, however, there are some inconsistent accentuations.

Instantiation Creation of an object of a class.

Interaction diagram Collective term for ⇨sequence diagram, ⇨collaboration diagram, ⇨activity diagram.

Interface ⇨interface classes Interfaces describe a selected part of the externally visible behavior of model elements (mainly of classes and components), that is, a set of signatures.

Interface classes Interface classes are ⇨abstract classes (more precisely: types) which exclusively define ⇨abstract operations. Interface classes are classes marked with the ⇨stereotype *«interface»*. They are specifications of the externally visible behavior of classes and contain a set of ⇨signatures for operations which classes desiring to implement this interface must provide.

LIVERPOOL
JOHN MOORES UNIVERSITY
AVRIL ROBARTS LRC
TEL ...

Interface inheritance Inside a ⇨specialization relation, only an ⇨interface is inherited.

Invariant A property or an expression which needs to be satisfied across the entire lifetime of an element, for example an object.

Link A concrete relation between two objects, that is, the instance of an ⇨association. An object has a link to another object when it has a reference to it. Such references are usually implemented as ⇨attributes, which, however, does not matter to the modeling.

Message ⇨operation, ⇨method Mechanism by means of which objects can communicate with each other. A message conveys object information on the activity the object is expected to carry out, i.e. a message prompts an object for execution of an operation. A message consists of a selector (a name) and a list of arguments, and is addressed to exactly one receiver. The sender of the message can have a response object returned. Through ⇨polymorphism, a message can lead to the call of several homonymous ⇨operations.

Metaclass A class whose instances are in turn classes. This concept exists only in some object-oriented languages (for example in Smalltalk).

Metamodel A model which defines a language that can be used to define a model.

Method ⇨operation In Smalltalk, operations are called methods. In UML, a method is defined as the implementation of an operation. In practice, the use of method and operation as synonyms is not critical.

Multiple classification An object is an instance of several classes at the same time (not possible in C++, Java, and Smalltalk).

Multiple inheritance A class has several direct superclasses (not possible in Java and Smalltalk).

Multiplicity Range of allowed ⇨cardinalities.

N-ary association An ⇨association in which more than two ⇨association roles are involved.

Navigation, navigability ⇨navigation specifications Navigation refers to the possible ways of accessing objects (and their attributes and operations) in a network of objects. Access routes consisting of a single relationship are called *directly navigable*.

Navigation specifications Description of access paths and access restrictions and their results (for example, by means of ⇨OCL).

Node A physical runtime object that uses a computer resource (processor, memory). Runtime objects and components can reside on nodes.

Non-directed association ⇨bidirectional association

Notes Comments or annotations to a diagram or one or more arbitrary model element/s without semantic effect.

Object ⇨instance An actual existing and acting unit with its own identity and defined boundaries which encapsulates state and behavior. The state is represented by ⇨attributes and ⇨relations, the behavior by ⇨operations or ⇨methods. Each object is an instance of a class. The defined behavior equally applies to all objects of a class, as does the structure of their attributes. The values of the attributes, however, are individual for each object. Each object has its own identity, unchangeable and independent from its attributes and the like.

Object-based A programming language or a database is called object-based if it supports the concept of data abstraction but partly or entirely lacks more advanced concepts such as class, inheritance, polymorphism, and so on.

Object diagram A diagram that shows objects and their relations at a given point in time. Usually a ⇨collaboration diagram or a special variation of the ⇨class diagram.

Object identity Property which distinguishes an object from any other object, although it can have the same attribute values.

Object-oriented programming language Object-oriented programming languages satisfy the following basic concepts:

- objects are abstract units;
- objects are instances of a class, that is, they are derived from a class;
- classes inherit properties, thus forming an inheritance hierarchy;
- objects are referenced dynamically, that is, binding is dynamic, thus allowing polymorphism.

OCL, Object Constraint Language OCL defines a language for description of ⇨constraints, ⇨invariants, ⇨pre- and postconditions, and ⇨navigation inside UML models.

OO Abbreviation for object-orientation.

Operation ⇨method, ⇨message Operations are services, which may be requested of an object by means of a ⇨message, intended to cause a specific behavior. They are implemented by means of ⇨methods. In practice, operation and message are often used as synonyms.

OR constraint ⇨constraint A constraint between associations which all lead from a common class to other different classes. This constraint specifies that the objects of the common class support ⇨object relations (or, more precisely, ⇨association roles) with only one of the other classes (exclusive OR).

Ordered association ⇨association Association in which the object relations are ordered in some specific manner.

Ordering constraint ⇨constraint A constraint of an association which specifies that its elements (⇨object relations) are ordered in some specific manner.

Package Collections of arbitrary model elements used to structure the entire model into smaller, clearly visible units. A package defines a namespace, that is, inside a package the names of the elements contained must be unique. Each model element can be referenced in other packages but belongs to exactly one (home) package. Packages may in turn contain packages. The topmost package contains the entire system.

Parameter Parameters are specifications of variables which pass operations, messages, or events, and are modified or returned by them. A parameter may consist of a name, a type (class), and a passing direction (in, out, inout).

Parameter list Enumeration of the names of arguments and, where needed, their types, initial values, and the like.

Parameterized class Template equipped with generic formal parameters used for generation of normal (non-generic) classes. The generic parameters serve as placeholders for the actual parameters which represent classes or simple data types.

Partition ⇨discriminator Entirety of subclasses based on the same discriminator.

Pattern ⇨design pattern

Persistent object Object whose lifespan exceeds the running time of a program session. For this purpose, such objects are stored on non-volatile media (for example in databases).

Polymorphism Polymorphism means that homonymous messages to compatible objects of different classes may trigger a different behavior. In dynamic polymorphism, a message is assigned to a concrete operation not at compile time but at reception during program runtime. The precondition for this is ⇨dynamic binding.

Postcondition A condition which describes a state that must be given after termination of an operation or the like.

Powertype Type (class) whose instances are subtypes (subclasses) of another type (class).

Precondition A condition which describes a state that must be given before the start of an operation or the like.

Propagation ⇨delegation Extension of the properties of a class through use of operations of other classes.

Property, tagged value Properties are user-defined, language- and tool-specific keyword/value pairs (*tagged values*) which extend the semantics of individual model elements with special characteristic features. The difference to the ⇨stereotype is that a stereotype extends the metamodel with a new element. Property values, in contrast, allow individual instances of existing model elements (for example, a specific operation) to be extended with specific features.

Protocol A set of signatures.

Qualified association ⇨association, ⇨qualifier Association in which the referenced set of objects is subdivided into partitions with the aid of qualifying attributes, and where, viewed from the initial object, each partition may only occur once.

Qualifier ⇨qualified association The attribute via which, in an association, the opposite side is accessed. The qualifier is defined as a part of the association; however, this attribute must be defined in the class it is used to access.

Referential integrity Rule which describes the integrity of object relations, in particular if one of the objects involved or the object relation itself is to be deleted.

Refinement Relation between similar elements of different degree of detail or specification. Refinement relations are stereotypes of ⇨dependency relations.

Relationship Connection between model elements with semantic contents. Generic term for ⇨association, ⇨aggregation, ⇨composition, ⇨generalization, and ⇨specialization.

Requirement Statement on the performance to be supplied. Requirements describe the scope of the functions and performance of a product, for example the software that is to be developed.

Resolved association ⇨association, ⇨association class An ⇨attributed association in which the attributes have been converted into a common class, and the attributed association has been transformed into two common associations including the newly created class.

Responsibility Includes the attributes and the interpretable messages of an object.

Role ⇨association role

Scenario A specific sequence of actions. For example, a concrete process path in a use case (so to say, an instance of the use case). *See* ⇨sequence diagram.

Self *self* (Smalltalk) and *this* (Java, C++) are predefined programming language keywords. With *this* or *self*, an object can send a message to itself, i.e. it calls another of its own methods. Messages that an object sends to itself with *this* or *self* are treated in exactly the same way as external messages. It can also access the attributes of its own class.

Self-delegation For the execution of an operation, a partial task is delegated to another operation of the same class (that is, an object sends a message to itself).

Sequence diagram Shows a set of interactions between a set of selected objects in a specific limited situation (context) with the emphasis on chronological sequence. Similar to the ⇨collaboration diagram. Sequence diagrams may exist in generic form (description of all possible scenarios), or in instance form (description of exactly one specific ⇨scenario).

Signature The signature of an operation is composed of the name of the operation, its parameter list, and the specification of a potential return type.

Simple inheritance ⇨inheritance In simple inheritance, a subclass inherits only from a direct superclass.

Specialization, generalization ⇨inheritance Generalization (or specialization) are taxonomic relations between a general and a special element (or vice versa), where the more special element adds further properties, extends the semantics, and behaves in a compatible way with the general element. Generalization and specialization are abstraction principles for hierarchic structuring of the model semantics under a discriminating aspect (⇨discriminator).

State Abstraction of the possible attribute values of an object. A state belongs to exactly one class and represents an abstraction or combination of a set of possible attribute values that the objects of this class may assume. In UML, a state is a condition or situation in the life of an object during which a specific condition is satisfied, activities are carried out, or an event is expected.

State diagram, state machine Shows a sequence of states an object can assume during its lifetime, and the stimuli that make state changes happen. A state diagram describes a hypothetical machine (finite automaton) which at any point in time is found in a set of finite states. It consists of:

- a finite, non-empty set of states;
- a finite, non-empty set of input symbols (events);
- functions which describe the transition from one state to the next;
- an initial state;
- a set of final states.

Static classification An object is and remains an instance of exactly one class, i.e. it cannot change class membership during its lifetime. *See* ⇨dynamic classification.

Stereotype Project-, enterprise-, or method-specific extensions of existing model elements of the UML metamodel. According to the semantics defined with the extension, the modeling element to which a stereotype is applied is semantically directly affected. In practice, stereotypes indicate in particular the possible usage conditions of a class, a relation, or a package. Other extension mechanisms in UML are ⇨properties and ⇨constraints.

Subclass A specialization of a superclass which inherits all properties of the superclass.

Subset constraint ⇨constraint A constraint/dependency between two associations. The elements (⇨object relations) of one association must be part of the elements of the other association.

Subsystem ⇨component A very large component or a component composed of a large quantity of individual components. Helpful for structuring of very large systems.

Super *super* (Smalltalk, Java) is a programming language keyword. It ensures that the message always goes to the next higher class that disposes of the specified operation.

Superclass ⇨generalization A generalization of selected properties of its ⇨subclass(es).

Superstate ⇨state Contains other states or substates.

Swimlane Areas separated by lines in ⇨activity diagrams, which describe the responsibilities of the elements contained in the diagram.

Tagged value ⇨property

Template ⇨parameterized class

Ternary association ⇨n-ary association An association in which three association roles are involved.

This ⇨self

Transition Passage from one ⇨state to another, often triggered by an ⇨event.

Type Definition of a set of operations and attributes. Other elements are type-conformant if they dispose of the properties defined by the type. In practice, often used as an equivalent to description of ⇨interfaces.

Unidirectional association ⇨directed association

Use case Describes a set of activities of a system that leads to a tangible result for the actors from the point of view of these actors. A use case is always initiated by an actor. Otherwise, a use case is a complete, indivisible description.

Use case diagram A diagram which shows the relations between ⇨actors and ⇨use cases.

Use case model A model which describes the functional requirements to a system in the form of use cases.

Utility Utility classes are collections of global variables and functions which are combined into a class and defined there as class attributes and operations. Thus, utility classes are not proper classes. A class is marked as a utility by means of the ⇨stereotype *«utility»*.

Virtual class ⇨abstract class

Virtual operation ⇨abstract operation

Visibility marks   Restrict accessibility of attributes and operations (*private*, *protected*, *public*, etc.).

Workflow ⇨business process   Computer-aided automation and support of a business process or a part of it.

Workflow engine   Software which controls workflows. Creates, activates, suspends, and terminates workflow instances (i.e. computer-aided manifestations of a business event).

Workflow instance   Computer-aided manifestations of a business event; controlled by a workflow engine.

Appendix B

References

Alexander, C. *et al.* (1977) *A Pattern Language*, Oxford University Press, New York.

Alexander, C. *et al.* (1979) *The Timeless Way of Building*, Oxford University Press, New York.

Alexandrescu, A. (2001) *Modern C++ Design: Generic Programming and Design Patterns Applied*, Addison-Wesley, Boston.

Beck, K. Foreword by E. Gamma (1999) *extreme Programming explained*, Addison-Wesley Longman.

Beck, K. (1997) *Smalltalk best practice patterns*, Prentice Hall, Upper Saddle River.

Beck, K., Cunningham, H. (1989) *A laboratory for teaching object-oriented thinking*. Proceedings of OOPSLA ´89, SIGPLAN notices (ACM) Vol. 24, New Orleans, 10/89.

Beyer, M. (1993) *BrainLand: Mind Mapping in Aktion,* Junfermannsche Verlagsbuchhandlung, Paderborn.

Bittner, U., Hesse, W., Schnath, J. (1995) *Praxis der Software-Entwicklung, Methoden, Werkzeuge, Projektmanagement – eine Bestandsaufnahme*, Oldenbourg, Munich.

Booch, G. (1986) *Software Engineering with Ada*, Benjamin/Cummings, Redwood City.

Booch, G. (1991) *Object-oriented design with applications*, Benjamin/Cummings, Redwood City.

Booch, G. (1994) *Object-oriented analysis and design with applications*, 2nd ed., Benjamin/Cummings, Redwood City.

Booch, G. (1996) *Properties and Stereotypes*, ROAD, Feb, p. 2ff.

Booch, G., Rumbaugh, J., Jacobson, I. (1999) *Unified Modeling Language User Guide,* Addison Wesley Longman.

Brooks, F.P. (1975) *The Mythical Man-Month*, Addison Wesley, Massachusetts.

Buschmann, F., Meunier, R., Rohnert, H., Sommerlad, P., Stal, M. (1996) *Pattern-Oriented Software Architecture: A System of Patterns*, Wiley, New York.

Chen, P. (1976) *The Entity-Relationship Model, Toward a Unified View of Data*, ACM Transactions on Database Systems, Vol. 1.

Chotjewitz, D. (1994) *Das Abenteuer des Denkens*, Alibaba Verlag, Frankfurt am Main.

Coad,P., Yourdon, E. (1991a) *Object-Oriented Analysis* (2nd ed.), Prentice Hall, Englewood Cliffs.

Coad, P., Yourdon, E. (1991b) *Object-Oriented Design*, Prentice Hall, Englewood Cliffs.

Cockburn, A. (1998) *Surviving Object-Oriented Projects, A Manager's Guide*, Addison Wesley Longman.

Constantine, L., Lockwood, L. (1999) *Software for Use, A Practical Guide to the Models and Methods of Usage-Centered Design*, Addison Wesley Longman.

Cook, S., Daniels, J. (1994) *Designing Object Systems: Object-Oriented Modeling with Syntropy*, Prentice Hall.

Dahl, O.-J., Nygaard, K. (1996) *Simula, an Algol-based simulation language*, Communications of the ACM, 9(9).

DeMarco, T., Lister, T. (1999) *Peopleware*, Dorset House, New York.

DeMarco, T. (1997) *The Deadline*, Dorset House, New York.

Döbele-Martin, C., Martin, P. *Ergonomie-Prüfer, Handlungshilfen zur ergono- mischen Arbeits- und Technikgestaltung*, Technologieberatungsstelle beim DGB Landesbezirk NRW, Reihe Technik und Gesellschaft, Vol. 14, p. 93ff.

Dörner, D. (1989) *Die Logik des Mißlingens. Strategisches Denken in komplexen Situationen*, Rowohlt Verlag, Reinbek.

Douglass, B. (1999) *Doing Hard Time, Developing Real-Time Systems with UML, Object, Framework and Patterns*, Addison Wesley Longman

Fayad, M., Laitinen, M. (1998) *Transition to Object-Oriented Software Development*, John Wiley & Sons.

http://www.martinfowler.com/isa

Fowler, M., Scott, K. (1997) *UML Distilled, Applying the Standard Object Modeling Language*, Addison Wesley.

Fowler, M. *et al.* (1999) *Refactoring, Improving the Design of Existing Code*, Addison Wesley Longman.

Gamma, E., Helm, R., Johnson, R., Vlissides, J. (1995) *Design Patterns: Elements of Reusable Object-Oriented Software*, Addison Wesley, Reading.

Goldberg, A., Robson, D. (1993) *Smalltalk-80: The Language and its Implementation*, Addison Wesley, Reading.

Goldberg, A., Rubin, K.S. (1995) *Succeeding with Objects, Design Frameworks for Project Management*, Addison Wesley, Reading.

Graham, I., Bischof, J., Henderson-Sellers, B. (1997a) *Associations considered a bad thing*, in JOOP 2/97, p. 41ff.

Graham, I., Henderson-Sellers, B., Younessi, H. (1997) *The OPEN Process Specification*, Addison Wesley (ACM Press), Harlow.

The GUI-Guide, Microsoft.

Habermas, J. (1988) *The Theory of Communicative Action*, vol. 2, Polity Press, Cambridge.

Harel, D. (1987) *Statecharts: A Visual Formalism for Complex Systems*, in Science of Computer Programming 8, p. 231ff.

Heisenberg, W. (1989) *Ordnung der Wirklichkeit (1942)*, Piper.

Henderson-Sellers, B., Graham, I.G., Firesmith, D.G. (1997) *Methods unification: The OPEN methodology*, JOOP, May 1997, p. 41ff.

Irion, A.M. (1995) *Regelwerk und Qualitätscheckliste zur Bildung von Fachbegriffen bei der Entwicklung und Administration einer normierten Unternehmensfachsprache*, dissertation, University of Konstanz.

Jacobson, I., Christerson, M., Jonsson, P., Övergaard, G. (1992) *Object-Oriented Software Engineering, A Use Case Driven Approach*, Addison Wesley, Workingham.

Jacobson, I., Booch, G., Rumbaugh, J. (1999) *The Unified Software Development Process*, Addison Wesley Longman.

Joos, S., Berner, S., Glinz, M., Arnold, M., Galli, S. (1997) *Stereotypen in objektorientierten Methoden – Einsatzgebiete und Risiken*. Vortrag im GROOM-UML-Workshop, Mannheim, 10 October.

JUnit, Beck, K., Gamma, E. http://www.junit.org

Kruchten, P. (1998) *The Rational Unified Process, An Introduction*, Addison Wesley, Longman.

Larman, C. (1997) *Applying UML and Patterns, An Introduction to Object-Oriented Analysis and Design*, Prentice Hall, New Jersey.

Leffingwell, D., Widrig, D. (2000) *Managing Software Requirements, A Unified Approach*, Addison Wesley, Reading, Massachusetts.

Martin, J., Odell, J. (1992) *Object-Oriented Analysis & Design*, Prentice Hall, Englewood Cliffs.

McMenamin, S.M., Palmer, J.F. (1984) *Essential System Analysis*, Prentice Hall, Englewood Cliffs.

Meyer, B. (1988) *Object-Oriented Software Construction*, Prentice Hall, Englewood Cliffs.

Miller, G. *The Magical Number Seven, Plus Minus Two: Some Limits on Our Capacity for Processing Information*, The Psychological Review, Vol. 63.

Miller, G. (1975) *The Magical Number Seven after Fifteen Years*, Wiley, New York.

Oestereich, B. (ed.) *et al.* (2001) *Erfolgreich mit Objektorientierung, Vorgehensmodelle und Managementpraktiken für die objektorientierte Softwareentwicklung*, 2nd ed, Oldenbourg Verlag, Munich.

Oestereich, B. (1999) *Developing Software with UML, Object-Oriented Analysis and Design in Practice*, Addison Wesley Longman.

Oestereich, B. (1998) *Objektorientierte Geschäftsprozeßmodellierung mit der UML*, in Objekt-Spektrum, 2/98, p. 48.

Oestereich, B. (2000) *Die Macht des Rhythmus: das OEP-Timepacing-Verfahren*. in Objekt-Spektrum, 2/2000, p. 57.

Railton, A., *Der Käfer – Der ungewöhnliche Weg eines ungewöhnlichen Automobils*, eurotax.

Robertson, S., Robertson, J. (1999) *Mastering the Requirements Process*, Addison Wesley, Harlow.

Royce, W. (1998) *Software Project Management, A Unified Framework*, Addison Wesley, Reading, Massachusetts.

Rumbaugh, J., Blaha, M., Premerlani, W., Eddy, F., Lorenson, W. (1991) *Object-Oriented Modelling and Design*, Prentice Hall, Englewood Cliffs.

Rumbaugh, J., Blaha, M., Premerlani, W., Eddy, F., Lorenson, W. (1993) *Objektorientiertes Modellieren und Entwerfen*, Hanser, Munich.

Rumbaugh, J. (1996a) *A state of mind: Modeling behavior*, in JOOP July, p. 6ff.

Rumbaugh, J. (1996b) *A search for values: Attributes and associations*, in JOOP June, p. 6ff.

Rumbaugh, J. (1996c) J. *A matter of intent: How to define subclasses*, in JOOP Sept., p. 5ff.

Rumbaugh, J., Booch, G. (1995) *Unified Method for Object-Oriented Development, Documentation Set 0.8*, Rational Software Corporation, Santa Clara.

Rumbaugh, J., Jacobson, I., Booch, G. (1996) *The Unified Modeling Language for Object-Oriented Development, Documentation Set 0.9 Addendum*, Rational Software Corporation, Santa Clara.

Rumbaugh, J., Jacobson, I., Booch, G. (1997) *The Unified Modeling Language, Documentation Set 1.0*, Rational Software Corporation, Santa Clara.

Rumbaugh, J., Jacobson, I., Booch, G. (1997) *The Unified Modeling Language, Documentation Set 1.1a6*, Rational Software Corporation, Santa Clara.

Rumbaugh, J. (1996) *Packaging a system: Showing architectural dependencies*, in JOOP Nov., p. 11ff.

Rumbaugh, J. Jacobson, I., Booch, G. (1996) *The Unified Modeling Language Reference Manual*, Addison Wesley Longman.

Rumbaugh, J. (1997) *OO Myths: Assumptions from a language view*, in JOOP, Feb., p. 5ff.

Rumbaugh, J. (1997) *Modeling through the development process*, in JOOP May, p. 5ff.

Rupp, C. *et al.* (2001) *Requirements Engineering*, Hanser, Munich.

Scheer, A.-W. (1994) *Business Process Engineering – Reference Models for Industrial Enterprise-Modeling*, Springer, Berlin.

Scheer, A.-W., Nüttgens, M., Zimmermann, V. (1997) *Objektorientierte Ereignisgesteuerte Prozeßkette (oEPK) – Methode und Anwendung,* Veröffentlichungen des Instituts für Wirtschaftsinformatik, Vol. 141, Saarbrücken.

Kelly, R., Roubaud, J., Schuldt (1995) *Abziehbilder, heimgeholt. Essay 27.* Literaturverlag Droschl, Graz.

Shlaer, S., Mellor S.J. (1991) *Object Lifecycles – Modelling the World in States*, Prentice Hall, Englewood Cliffs.

Sims, O. (1994) *Business Objects: Delivering Cooperative Objects for Client-Server.* McGraw-Hill, New York.

Skubliks, S., Klimas, E. Thomas, D. (1996) *Smalltalk with style*, Prentice Hall, Upper Saddle River.

Summerville, I., Sayer, P. (1997) *Requirements Engineering, A good practice guide*, Wiley, Chichester.

UML 1.2
OMG UML Revision Task Force: *OMG UML 1.2*, 1998.

UML 1.3
OMG Unified Modeling Language, 1999, http://www.omg.org/uml

UML1.4
OMG Unified Modeling Language, 2000, http://www.omg.org/uml

Wallrabe, A., Oestereich, B. (1997) *Smalltalk für Ein- und Umsteiger*, Oldenbourg, Munich.

Warmer, J., Kleppe, A. (1999) *The Object Constraint Language, Precise Modeling with UML*, Addison Wesley Longman, Reading, Massachusetts.

Wirfs-Brock, R., Wilkerson, B., Wiener, L. (1990) *Designing Object-Oriented Software*, Prentice Hall, Englewood Cliffs.

Wirfs-Brock, R., Johnson, R. E. (1990) *Surveying current research in Object-Oriented Design*, in Commun. ACM 33, No. 9.

Yourdon, E. (1989) *Structured Walkthroughs*, Prentice Hall, Englewood Cliffs.

Index

abstract classes 178–9, 186, 192
abstract classes principle 34–5
abstract operations 186
abstract tagged values 207
abstraction 3, 15
abstraction dependencies 246
action states 250
active objects 47
activity diagrams 68–70, 99–102, 142–3, 160,
    250–4
actor-role patterns 151–2
actors 67–9, 72–6, 119, 130–1, 160–71
adapters 57
advantages 2–3, 7, 15–16
agents 115–18
aggregations 35–8, 50, 225, 241–4
analysis 63–111
annotation 212
anonymous states 267
application architecture 114–18, 127
application domains 87–9
application modules 217
applications 8–11
architecture
    application 114–18, 127
    client-server 114–56
    patterns 56
arguments 186
arrays 42
assertions 197
associations 35–8, 50, 225–45, 241, 244
    attributes 228–30
    calculated 235
    classes 228–9
    constraints 231–2
    derived 235
    directed 237–8
    generalized 239
    inheritance 239
    n-ary 236
    partitioned 233
    qualified 233–4

recursive 225
specialized 239–40
sub 239
super 239
ternary 236
unidirectional 237
associative arrays 233
associative collections 42
attributed associations 228–30
attributes 20–2, 138–42, 172–3, 183–5
    association 228–30
    class 175, 184
    derived 184
    redundancy 31
automated test cases 132–8

base classes 25–34
basic concepts 1–42, 157–274
behavior-driven design 141
behavioral diagrams 160, 166, 250–71
benefits 2–3, 7, 15–16
bind stereotypes 177
binding 45
bound elements 176
boundaries 53
branches 251
bridges 57
business
    cases 72–6
    classes 92–4
    essence 76–82
    events 161, 163
    processes 68–70, 161, 163
    use cases 72–6

C++
    access possibilities 184, 187
    aggregations 244
    attributes 183
    classes 175–6, 180
    compositions 244
    messages 40

C++ (Continued)
  polymorphism 45
  program files 272
  static 175
caching 184
calculated associations 235
cardinalities 36
categories 214–15
characteristics 207
class-object relationships 182
classes 19–22, 24–37, 172–80, 217
  abstract 178–9, 186, 192
  association 228, 228–9
  attributes 175, 184
  base 25–34
  business 92–4
  classification 50–6
  collections 42–4
  control 51–2
  controller 117
  diagrams 26, 28, 92–3, 160, 172–249
  entity 51, 117
  generic 176
  interface 52–3, 192–6
  meta 175
  modeling 140
  operations 175
  parameterized 176–7
  polymorphism 44–7
  primitive 54–5
  sub 25–34, 220–4
  super 25–34, 178, 220–4
  tests 135–8
  utility 180
  virtual 178
client-server architecture 114–56
coherence principle 24–5, 122
collaboration diagrams 40–1, 129–32, 160,
    256–60
collaborations 213
collecting materials 87–9
collections 42–4
comments 212
commercial essence 76–82
commercial value 74, 163
communication 39–42, 58–61, 115–18, 225–45
complexity 2–3
component-specific class models 120–3
components 58–61, 214–15, 217–18, 272
  dependencies 125–7
  diagrams 160, 272
  dialog 144

domain 117–20
external system 119
instances 59, 272
interfaces 60–1, 121, 127–9
models 120
tests 132–5
use case controller 118
workflow 118
composite patterns 57–8
compositions 36–8, 149–50, 152–5, 225, 244–5
compound activities 252
concepts 1–42, 157–274
concretization 26, 220
conditions 197, 271
configuration diagrams 273
consistency constraints 200
consolidation 252
constraint-responsibility principle 31–4
constraints 20–2, 149–50, 197–207, 209
  association 225–6, 231–2
  attribute 183
  class 172–3
  consistency 200
  dialog 144
  enumeration 203–4
  formula 202
  interface 193
  named 198–9
  operation 186
  order 202
  ordered 232
  subset 199–200
  value 201–2
contact partners 65–8
container classes 42–4
container objects 233
context 198
contravariance principle 221
control classes 51–2
controller classes 117
controllers 114–18
cooperation diagrams 256

data elements 183
data interfaces 105–8
data structures 56
data transfer objects 116, 128–9
data-driven design 141
databases 47–50
decorative stereotypes 209
decorator patterns 57
delegation 33–4, 224

dependencies
  abstraction 246
  component 125–7
  use- 246
dependency relationships 195, 246–7
deployment diagrams 160, 273
derived associations 235
derived attributes 184
derived elements 235
descriptions
  essence 78–82
  interface 104–8
  use case 166–9
descriptive stereotypes 209
design 113–56
design patterns 56–8, 151–5, 213
design rules 146–55
diagrams
  activity 68–70, 99–102, 142–3, 160, 250–4
  behavioral 160, 166, 250–71
  class 26, 28, 92–3, 160, 172–249
  collaboration 40–1, 129–32, 160, 256–60
  component 160, 272
  configuration 273
  cooperation 256
  deployment 160, 273
  event trace 261
  implementation 160, 272–3
  interaction 256, 261
  message 261
  node 273
  object flow 102–3, 125–6, 160, 250, 255
  sequence 40–1, 160, 261–4
  state 160, 250, 265
  use case 68–70, 75, 160–71
dialog
  agents 116
  components 144
  contexts 142
  controllers 115–16
  elements 143–4
  interfaces 105–8
  specification 143–4
dictionaries 42, 94–9, 233
differential programming 27
directed associations 237–8
discriminators 25–6, 220–2
domain components 117–20, 128–9
domain experts 67
domains, application 87–9
dynamic classification 181
dynamic polymorphism 44–7

early binding 45
Eiffel 176
encapsulation 244
encapsulation principle 20–2
entity classes 51, 117
entity relationship modeling (ERM) 11, 15
enumeration 55–6, 139–40, 203–4
ERM *see* entity relationship modeling
essence descriptions 78–82
essential use cases 76–82, 163
event trace diagrams 261
events 271
exceptions 193
excluded use cases 74
explorative interface prototyping 108–11
extend relationships 170
extend stereotypes 192
external system components 119
Extreme Programming (XP) 75

façades 53, 57, 154–5
factory services 217
features 207
final states 267
finite automata 265
flowcharts 68, 250
formula constraints 202
frameworks 117
function collections 180
functional interfaces 105–8
functional requirements 89–92, 190
functions 186
fundamentals 157–274

generalization 220–4
generalization/specialization principle 25–34
generalization/specialization relationships 170
generalized associations 239
generic classes 176
generic operators 45
generic relationships 15

has-a relationships 15, 35–8
history 3–7
holistic thinking 11–16
Hollywood principle 117

idioms 56
implementation diagrams 160, 272–3
implementation stereotypes 221
implicit association classes 229

include relationships 170
inheritance 45, 150–2, 220–4
   implementation 221
   multiple 27, 147–50, 224
   principle 25–34
   specification 221
initial states 267
instance relationships 19
instance variables 183
instances 19–20, 181–2
   component 59, 272
instantiation relationships 175, 182
integrity rule 197
interaction diagrams 256, 261
interfaces
   classes 52–3, 192–6
   component 60–1, 121, 127–9
   data 105–8
   descriptions 104–8
   dialog 105–8
   domain component 128–9
   functional 105–8
   objects 53
   prototyping 108–11
   stereotypes 192–4, 210
   system 104–8
   use case controller 127–8
invariants 136, 192–3, 197
is-a inheritance 221
is-a relationships 15
is-a semantics 26
iterations 257–8, 262

Java
   classes 14, 22, 29–31, 37–9
   constraints 203
   messages 40

keys 22–3, 42
keywords 207–8

language consolidation 97–9
late binding 45
legacy hunting 27
legacy systems 119
lifelines 261
links 225
lollipops 194–5
loops 252

matching operations 40
materials 87–9
mechanisms 213

members 183
memento patterns 57
message diagrams 261
message exchange principle 39–42
messages 186, 258
metaclasses 175
metaphors 110–11
methodologies 9–16
methods *see* operations
mind maps 88–9
models 18, 110–11
   class 120–3
   collaboration 129–32
   component 120
   entity relationship 11
   process 99–104
   state 123–5
modules 217, 272
multiple classification 181
multiple inheritance 27, 147–50, 224
multiple transitions 251
multiplicity 225–7, 229–30, 244
multiplicity indication 35

n-ary associations 236
named constraints 198–9
naming conventions 145
navigability 237
networks 11
nodes 273
non-functional requirements 190
normal use cases 163
notation 4, 19–42
   abstract classes 178–9
   activity diagrams 251–4
   actors 165
   aggregations 242
   associations 226–7
   attributed associations 228
   attributes 172–3, 182, 185
   classes 172–3
   collaboration diagrams 256–9
   components 217–18
   compositions 245
   constraints 197
   dependency relationships 195, 246–7
   deployment diagrams 273
   derived associations 235
   design patterns 213
   directed associations 237
   events 271
   inheritance 221–2

interfaces 194–5
notes 212
object flow diagrams 255
objects 181–2
operations 173, 187
packages 216
parameterized classes 177
qualified associations 233
realization relations 248
refinement relations 248
responsibilities 189
sequence diagrams 261–2
specialized associations 239
state diagrams 265
states 267–9
stereotypes 210
subsystems 214
tagged values 187, 208
transitions 271
use case descriptions 166–8
use case diagrams 162
utility classes 180
notes 212

Object Constraint Language (OCL) 197–206
Object Management Group (OMG) 4, 158
object-class relationships 19
object-oriented programming languages 3–7
object-responsibility principle 27–31
object/class principle 19–20
objectives 64–5
objects 19–20, 87–9, 172, 181–2
active 47
connections 225
data transfer 116, 128–9
diagrams 250
factories 172
flow diagrams 102–4, 125–6, 160, 250, 255
identity principle 22–3
interface 53
passive 47
properties 20–2
services 217
states 102–4, 250, 253–4
obligations 90
observer mechanisms 60
observer patterns 57
observer services 217

OCL see Object Constraint Language
OMG see Object Management Group
operations 20–2, 136–8, 173, 186–8
class 175
matching 40
propagation 37, 241
operators, generic 45
optional activities 253
OR constraints 200–1
order constraints 202
ordered constraints 232
overloading 44–7

packages 214–17, 272
parallelism 250–1
parameterized classes 176–7
parameters 21
part/whole relationships 15, 35–8, 241–3
partitions 220–1, 233
passive objects 47
patterns 56–8, 151–5, 213
performance requirements 89–92
persistence 47–50
polymorphism principle 44–7
postconditions 76–86, 136, 193
practical applications 8–11
pragmatic use cases 163
preconditions 76–86, 136, 193
predecessor conditions 257
primitive classes 54–5
primitives 139
principles
abstract classes 34–5
coherence 24–5, 122
constraint-responsibility 31–4
contravariance 221
encapsulation 20–2
generalization/specialization 25–34
Hollywood 117
inheritance 25–34
message exchange 39–42
object identity 22–3
object-responsibility 27–31
object/class 19–20
polymorphism 44–7
substitution 25–34, 221
procedures 186
process controllers 117
process models 99–104

process-oriented component tests 132–5
processes
    business 68–70, 161, 163
    social 3
propagation of operations 37, 241
properties 19–22, 151
property strings 207
protocols 19
prototype classes 19
prototyping 108–11
purposes 189

qualified associations 233–4
query stereotypes 186

realization relationships 192, 248–9
recursive associations 225
redefining stereotypes 210
redundancy 31, 149
refinement relationships 248–9
relationships 11–12, 20–2, 146–56, 161, 225
    class-object 182
    extend 170
    generalization/specialization 170
    generic 15
    has-a 35–8
    include 170
    instance 19
    instantiation 175, 182
    object-class 19
    realization 192
    refinement 248–9
    use case 170–1
reliability requirements 89–92
requirements 76–8, 89–92, 190–1
responses 258
responsibilities 24–5, 121–2, 189
responsibility domains 250–1
responsibility zones 125–6
restrictions 197
restrictive stereotypes 210
restructuring classes 140–1
results 73–5, 163
roles 151, 164–5, 225–7
routines 186

scenarios 40–1, 75, 163, 261
secondary use cases 163
selectors 186
self 198
semantics 136

sequence diagrams 40–1, 160, 261–4
sequence expressions 257
sequential collections 42
services see operations
signaling 253
signatures 136, 186
singletons 53, 57
Smalltalk
    actor-role pattern 151
    attributes 183
    binding 45
    class operations 187–8
    messages 40
    new 175
    program files 272
social processes 3
software complexity 2–3
software problems 9–10
specialization 220–4
specialization/generalization relationships 170
specialized associations 239–40
specification inheritance 221
splitting 252
stable requirements 76–8
stakeholders 65–8
stakeholders interests 70–1
state diagrams 160, 250, 265–6
state machines 265
state models 123–5
state transitions 265, 267, 271
state-dependent messages 123
states 121–2, 265–9
    object 102–4, 253–4
    sub 270
static polymorphism 44–5
stereotypes 165, 171–2, 197, 211, 226
    bind 177
    decorative 209
    descriptive 209
    enumeration 140
    extend 192
    implementation 221
    interface 192–4, 210
    query 186
    realize 192
    redefining 210
    restrictive 210
    temporary 225
    utility 180
    workflow 68
stories 75

structured analysis and design 11, 15
structures 56
studying materials 87–9
sub use cases 170
subassociations 239
subclasses 25–34, 220–4
subset constraints 199–200
substates 270
substitution principle 25–34, 221
subsystems 214–15, 217, 272
super use cases 170
superassociations 239
superclasses 25–34, 178, 220–4
supportability requirements 89–92
swim lanes 125–6, 250–1
synchronization 252
system ideas 64–5
system interfaces 104–8
system performance 89–92
system theory 11
system use cases 82–6

tagged values 172, 183, 186, 187, 197, 207–9
tasks 189
technical dictionaries 94–9
templates 176–7
temporary stereotypes 225
ternary associations 236
test cases 102, 132–8
transitions 267, 271
triggers 73–5, 163, 251, 267
types *see* classes
typical software problems 9–10

unidirectional associations 237
usability requirements 89–92
usage contexts 209
use case controllers 116

components 118
interface 127–8
use case descriptions 166–9
use case diagrams 68–70, 75, 160–71
use case process models 99–104
use case relationships 170–1
use cases 4, 91, 160–71
business 72–6
essential 76–82, 163
excluded 74
normal 163
pragmatic 163
secondary 163
sub 170
super 170
system 82–6
uses-dependencies 246
utility classes 180
utility stereotypes 180

value constraints 201–2
variable requirements 76–8
variables 183
view agents 116
virtual classes 178
visibility 184
visibility marks 226
visibility specifications 258–9
visitor patterns 57

whole-part hierarchies 35–8, 241–3
whole-part relationships 15, 241
workflow components 118
workflow controllers 116–17
workflow stereotypes 68

XP *see* Extreme Programming

Also in the Object Technology Series

UML and the Unified Process
Jim Arlow and Ila Neustadt

This book provides an indispensable guide to the complex process of object-oriented analysis and design using the Unified Modeling Language (UML). It describes how the process of OO analysis and design fits into the software development lifecycle, as defined by the Unified Process (UP).

UML and the Unified Process contains a wealth of practical and useful techniques that can be applied immediately. You will learn OO analysis and design techniques, UML syntax and relevant aspects of the UP as you progress through the text. It also provides an accessible, accurate and succinct summary of both UML *and* UP from the point of view of the OO analyst and designer.

This book provides:

- Chapter roadmaps, detailed diagrams and margin notes allowing a rapid overview, enabling you to focus on your needs
- Outline summaries for each chapter making it ideal for revision and a comprehensive index, so the book can be used as a reference

The accompanying website (**www.umlandtheunifiedprocess.com**) *provides:*

- A complete worked example of a simple e-commerce system
- Useful links to Open Source and proprietary software

ISBN 0 201 77060 1

Visit us on the world wide web at
www.it-minds.com
www.aw.com/cseng

Find more information about the **Object Technology Series** at
www.aw.com/cseng/otseries

Also in the Component Software Series

Component-Based Development
Principles and Planning for Business Systems
Katharine Whitehead

This book introduces the key principles of component-based development (CBD) that need to be understood in order to adopt a component-based model of software development, and explains the benefits of adopting such an approach for an organization. It guides the reader through the program-planning process, and outlines the need-to-know issues in designing and assembling components.

Software developers, architects and IT project managers will learn how to spring-board over to using a component-based approach, and discover the organizational issues affecting its adoption.

Key features of the book include

- Insights into component characteristics, and how they are defined and scoped
- Consideration of the software architecture and infrastructure within which components can operate effectively
- Practical advice on building and assembling components
- A case study showing the highs and lows experienced by a finance company which is evolving its software development to a component-based approach, using CORBA, to introduce call centers and internet-based systems.

ISBN 0 201 67528 5

Visit us on the world wide web at
www.it-minds.com
www.aw.com/cseng

Find more information about the **Component Software Series** at
www.aw.com/cseng/catalog/series/0,3841,1,00.html

From the Component Software Series

Realizing eBusiness with Components
Paul Allen

Unfortunately, there is a great deal of hype and over-expectation surrounding e-business. Many organizations are jumping on the e-business bandwagon without understanding what they are getting into. Lack of planning and analysis, resulting in inflexible solutions that are unable to integrate with existing systems, are all too common. At the same time, e-business calls for a closer relationship between those involved in business development and those required to support these initiatives within the company's information technology infrastructure.

This book is designed to provide practical advice for planning, analysis and design of e-business systems using component-based development (CBD). Just as e-business is more than a series of web pages, so CBD is not just an approach to problem-solving using software building blocks. It includes architectures, processes, modeling techniques, economic models and organizational guidelines, all of which are well placed to ease migration of large organizations to e-business.

The author defines the key concepts relating to CBD, and introduces component standards, component frameworks, middleware and all the relevant internet technologies. The book also deals with issues such as the business case for adopting CBD, pragmatic approaches to modeling business requirements, putting CBD to work using the Catalysis process, migrating to CBD from legacy systems, and the issues associated with sourcing components from off-the-shelf purchasing to bespoke design.

This book shows you:

- how to obtain commitment for a CBD strategy at board level
- how to deploy catalysis modeling techniques and other commercial approaches
- how to use component modeling techniques to create innovative eBusiness solutions
- how to gain competitive advantage with TNBT and Collaborative Commerce

The core of the book is an extensive example that tracks the experiences of a typical company, with a traditional set of business processes and supporting software systems, through various stages along the road to e-business.

ISBN 0 201 67520 X

Visit us on the world wide web at
www.it-minds.com
www.aw.com/cseng

Find more information about the **Component Software Series** at
http://cseng.aw.com/catalog/series/0,3841,1,00.html

For where to go, who to read and what to know in the world of IT.

If you're looking for books on IT then visit: **www.it-minds.com**, the place where you can find books from the IT industry's leading IT publishers.

Infinite choices for the IT Minded

[Choice of publishers]

IT-Minds is home to some of the world's leading computer book publishers such as Sams, Que, Addison-Wesley, Prentice Hall, Adobe Press, Peachpit Press, Cisco Press and Macromedia Press.

[Choice of ways to learn]

We publish for those who are completely new to a computer through to the most cutting-edge technologies for the IT professional and our products offer a variety of ways to learn. IT-Minds offers you tutorials, handy pocket guides, comprehensive references, exam guides, CD based training materials and Executive Briefings.

[Choice of subjects]

We also cover the A-Z of computer subjects: From ASP, Bluetooth, C++, Database, E-Mail, Flash, Graphics, HTML … to Windows XP, XML, Yahoo and Zope.

As an IT mind you also have access to:

- News from the IT industry
- Articles written by our featured authors
- Free weekly newsletters
- Competitions to win prizes
- Testing and assessment products
- Online IT training products

[Custom Solutions]

If you found this book useful, then so might your colleagues or customers. If you would like to explore corporate purchases or custom editions personalised with your brand or message, then just get in touch at **www.it-minds.com/corporate.asp**

Visit our website at:

[www.it-minds.com]

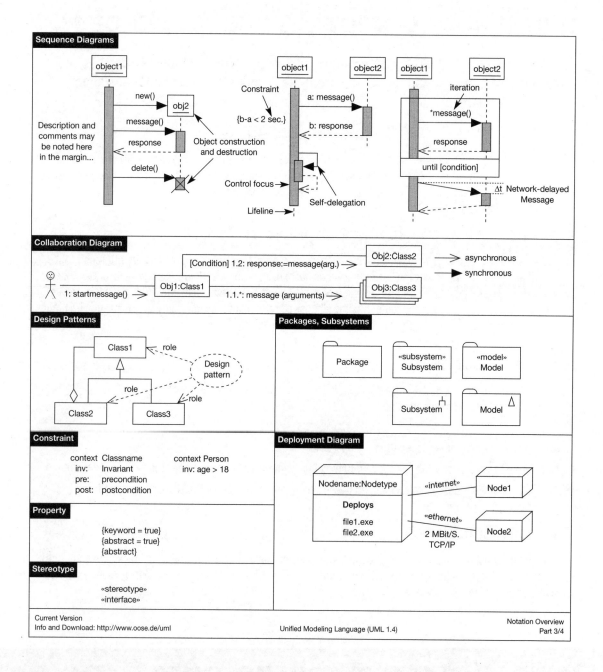

Sequence Diagrams

object1

new() → obj2

message()

response

delete()

Description and comments may be noted here in the margin...

Object construction and destruction

Control focus

Lifeline

Self-delegation

Constraint

{b-a < 2 sec.}

object1   object2

a: message()

b: response

object1   object2

iteration

*message()

response

until [condition]

Δt Network-delayed Message

Collaboration Diagram

[Condition] 1.2: response:=message(arg.) →   Obj2:Class2

1: startmessage() →   Obj1:Class1

1.1.*: message (arguments) →   Obj3:Class3

→ asynchronous

▶ synchronous

Design Patterns

Class1   role

Design pattern

role

Class2   Class3

role

Packages, Subsystems

Package

«subsystem» Subsystem

«model» Model

Subsystem

Model

Constraint

context Classname
inv: Invariant
pre: precondition
post: postcondition

context Person
inv: age > 18

Property

{keyword = true}
{abstract = true}
{abstract}

Deployment Diagram

Nodename:Nodetype

Deploys

file1.exe
file2.exe

«internet»   Node1

«ethernet»
2 MBit/S.
TCP/IP   Node2

Stereotype

«stereotype»
«interface»